SECOND   EDITION

VOICE and DICTION

JON EISENSON

A N D   A U D I O L O G Y ,   S T A N F O R D   U N I V E R S I T Y

tdkgfvθðszʃʒtʃdʒmnŋlrjhwʍ

C O L L I E R — M A C M I L L A N   L I M I T E D ,   L O N D O N

THE MACMILLAN COMPANY, NEW YORK
COLLIER-MACMILLAN CANADA, LTD., TORONTO, ONTARIO

Printed in the United States of America

TO FREDA, ELINORE, AND ARTHUR

PREFACE TO THE FIRST EDITION

It is probable that two kinds of students will use this book. The first group will include those with a strong interest in speech and in speaking. Because of their attitudes and aspirations, these students see an importance in learning to speak really well. Many of them are already confident and adequate speakers, but they are not satisfied with just passing competence. The student who is preparing to enter a profession such as law, the ministry, teaching, medicine, psychology, or politics—to name but a few—realizes that he can enhance his professional effectiveness by becoming skillful in speech. Speech will be a principal tool and medium in his profession. Knowledge that cannot be applied and transmitted does not translate itself into skill, and professional success demands skill as well as knowledge. When a profession requires ability to communicate, those who do not have this ability must acquire it, or be satisfied with lesser positions than they might otherwise attain. In many instances, they may have to change to other professions or vocations demanding less communicative skill in general and less effective voice and diction in particular.

The second group of students to use this text probably will include persons who were not self-motivated to study and improve their voice and diction. Someone—a teacher, counselor, or friend—may have suggested, directed, or required that the student's speech be improved. Possibly the student may have had some awareness that his speech was not "just right." He may have intended to do something about the matter at some vague and indefinite time. He may even have tried to improve his voice, his diction, or both and may have succeeded to some degree. But now a decision has been made, by him or for him, that further improvement is necessary if he is to have adequate and effective speech. We hope that even if the motivation is external the student will not resist the instruction and the opportunity for training that will be his in a course in the improvement of voice and diction.

All of us have acquaintances or friends who do not speak as well as they might. On every campus there are students to whose speech we must "tune in" repeatedly over a period of time if we are to understand it. Most of these are native speakers; a few may be foreign born. There are also some students who have few friends because of real or imagined limitations associated with their speech. Our initial relationships are established through oral language. If oral language is inadequate in manner or in content, personal relationships may suffer. Fortunately, there are very few instances in which inadequate voice and diction need remain so. With proper motivation, and with knowledge and materials for the direction and application of such motivation, adequate voice and diction are possible for almost all of us and better than adequate voice and diction for many of us. We hope that the student is ready and willing (we have no doubt that he is capable) to work toward this objective.

In the development of this book, the author continues with a basic assumption made in other of his writings. The assumption is that intelligent human beings want to have some body of information about skills they are expected to acquire. Intelligent persons tend to have curiosity; they want to know something of the *what* as well as the *how* of activities they are expected to undertake. We hope that in the body of the text we have supplied enough of this kind of information about voice and diction to satisfy normal curiosity. Greater curiosity may be satisfied by an investigation of the references in the footnotes and in some of the suggested projects.

Where the student will begin in the study of this book and how he will proceed will depend upon the organization and objectives of his course. For students who are in a course devoted primarily to voice and secondarily to diction, the first part will be studied before the second. For students in a class with primary interest in diction, the first two chapters are likely to be followed by the material on speech sounds in the second part of the book. For students in a course in which voice and diction are given equal consideration, the order of study will be determined by the instructor's choice of approach. This, of course, need not be predetermined. The approach may well be decided by the particular needs of the students in a particular class and may vary accordingly.

We enjoyed writing the book. Some of the selections used as exercise material are borrowed or adapted. We are grateful to the individuals and to the sources that made this possible. A few of the selections are from our own collection of "writings that could be verse." We hope that the reader will find these acceptable.

JON EISENSON

PREFACE TO THE SECOND EDITION

The objectives and the organization of materials for the second edition of *The Improvement of Voice and Diction* remain essentially unchanged from those indicated in the preface of the first edition. Our fund of information about human communication, however, is ever increasing. We have tried to incorporate some of the information from the fields of phonetics, linguistics, and speech science into our discussions of the aspects of voice and diction treated in this text. We selected the additional materials so that the student can make ready application of his knowledge in the improvement of his own voice and speech. With our continued assumption that an intelligent student of any subject, including one that may be considered a "skill subject," wants to know the *why* and the *what* as well as the *how* for the skills he is interested in acquiring, we have expanded some discussions and added a new background chapter, "Our Changing Speech Patterns." We believe that the changes, the expansions and additions, make for a well-rounded book that maintains a balance between theoretic information and practical approaches for the improvement of skills in voice and diction. In revising the practice materials, we have added exercises and selections for the sounds that are most troublesome in American-English speech. Though many exercises are new, we have retained some of the older materials that we consider to be "tried and true" and too useful to be dropped even for a revised second edition. Though we have made many changes in the text, we avoided making them merely for the sake of change.

The glossary and appendixes should, we think, enhance the value of the book for the student. Once again, we enjoyed writing the book. We hope that some of the enjoyment will be shared by the student readers.

JON EISENSON

CONTENTS

VOICE

CHAPTER 1

Basic Considerations

Part One has several objectives. The first is to create awareness of what constitutes an effective voice; the second is to indicate how voice can be produced and controlled so that common faults are overcome or avoided; and the third is to suggest how voice can be improved as an instrument of communication.

EFFECTIVE VOCALIZATION

Responsiveness

Beyond anything else, an effective voice is responsive to the intentions of the speaker. By expressing responsiveness, voice helps to communicate the speaker's feelings and thoughts so that he is readily able to let his listener know how he thinks and how he feels as well as how he feels about what he thinks.

Appropriateness of Attributes

An effective voice is so intimately associated with what the speaker is saying that it attracts no attention to itself and therefore

3

does not distract attention from what the speaker is trying to communicate. Distraction may result from either the characteristics of the voice or the manner in which the voice is produced. If the duration, quality, pitch, loudness, or any combination of these is faulty or in some way not consistent with the contents of the speech, an element of distraction is introduced. For example, matters of importance are usually spoken slowly rather than hurriedly. Unless secretiveness is to be suggested, they are uttered more loudly than items of lesser importance. Solemn utterances are usually associated with a relatively low pitch and lighter remarks with relatively higher pitches. A reversal of these pitch-contents relationships is likely to be either distracting or misleading. Excessive nasality, huskiness, or any other vocal characteristic which is striking may serve as a distraction. In a somewhat more fortunate way, a very fine voice may also be temporarily distracting if it directs the listener's attention to its unusual qualities. Most listeners, however, soon accept the fine voice and respond to the contents of the speech. On the other hand, a voice which includes a constant element of irritation may continue to distract and so impair the speaker's ability to communicate.

Manner of Production

A voice may have acceptable characteristics but still be ineffective if the speaker's manner of producing his voice attracts attention. If he is obviously straining to be heard, if his external throat muscles appear tense or his jaw tight, the listener may be distracted by what he observes. If the listener must force himself to maintain attention, the effort may be unpleasant, and the listener may also become tense as a result of what he sees. On the other hand, the overrelaxed speaker, who seems almost too tired to vocalize and articulate, may fatigue his listener-observer.

Sex, Age, and Physique

Another area of appropriateness is related to the sex, age, and physical build of the speaker. We expect men's voices to be different from women's. We expect mature persons' voices to sound different from children's. We expect persons who are big to have "big" voices.

A high-pitched, "thin" voice may be acceptable from a small, delicate girl or a little boy, but it is not likely to be acceptable from either a man, a physically mature-looking woman, or a large boy.

Listener's Criteria

From the viewpoint of the listener, an effective voice is one which can be heard without conscious effort or strain. It is consonant with the speaker's message and helps make the message readily audible and intelligible. An effective voice is pleasant to hear, but the pleasure should be unconscious and should not dominate the listener's reactions as it might if he were listening to a good singer. To be effective, voice should be as loud as the specific speaking situation demands. If the speaker is talking to a group, his voice should be heard with ease by every listener, but none should be disturbed because of its loudness. In a conversational situation, the listener with normal hearing and normal power of concentration should not have to ask the speaker to repeat because of a failure to hear, nor should he wish to move away to avoid discomfort from overloudness. In summary, the listener, if he were inclined to be analytic, should be able to conclude that the speaker's voice, as well as his actions, suits the words, the over-all situation, and the speaker as an individual.

Objective Self-listening

Although it is not always easy to see ourselves as others see us, the mechanics for hearing ourselves as others hear us are available to most of us. Tape or disc recordings of reasonable fidelity can be made at low cost at record shops, speech clinics, or agencies specializing in recording equipment. Most academic speech departments have adequate equipment for recording and playing back samples of speech. Although the most useful recording is one made when the speaker is not aware that he is being recorded and so is most himself, "candid" recordings are not always possible. If the recording is staged rather than candid, we recommend that it include conversational speaking as well as material read in a conversational voice and material spoken as if for a small audience. If the speaker frequently makes public addresses, he should also include some material spoken as if he were making a public address. Equipped with such a recording, the speaker about to be a self-listener should then hear himself on an instrument with playback fidelity at least equal to that of the recording instrument. So set, the speaker should ask himself these questions:

1. Is my voice pleasant to hear?
2. Does my voice have any characteristics I would consider undesirable in another speaker?
3. Does my voice reflect what I intended to convey in thought and in feeling?
4. Were the changes in pitch, loudness, duration, and quality consonant with the varying contents of my utterances?
5. Would I listen to this voice if I were not the speaker?
6. Does the voice reflect me as a personality?

If the speaker-listener is completely satisfied with all of his answers, then he is one of the fortunate persons making the most of the gift of a good voice. If he is not entirely satisfied, then we assume he recognizes the need for improvement and is both ready and willing to do whatever is necessary to bring it about.

It is important to indicate at this point that what an individual hears when he listens to himself talking is different from what another person hears when listening to him. As Black and Moore point out:

> *The two listeners—the one who is only listening and the one who is listening to himself while talking—do not have the same experience. The speaker who is monitoring his own voice hears a sound that no other listener hears. This is dramatically demonstrated as a person listens to a high-fidelity recording of his own voice. He is now an outside listener. The recordings of all his acquaintances' voices sound right, but the same apparatus when turned upon his own voice gives completely erroneous results!*[1]

Because we are so close to the source of our voices we cannot hear how they sound as can a listener who is separated from us by physical distance. We hear ourselves through the tissues of our bodies, especially the bones of the head, as they directly conduct the sounds we produce to our hearing mechanism. We also hear

[1] J. W. Black and W. E. Moore, *Speech* (New York: McGraw-Hill, 1955), p. 57.

ourselves through the initially external stimulation of the sound waves produced when we talk at the same instant that the sounds are conducted to our hearing mechanism. You can appreciate some of the difference between the two avenues of auditory stimulation if you stop up your ears while talking. You would then be hearing more nearly through bone conduction than you would with your ears "open." Your voice sounds different and somewhat strange. You may contrast this immediately by repeating what you have said with your ears unstopped. You should, if at all possible, contrast this immediately by listening to a high-fidelity voice recording. Only then, making due allowance for subjective reactions, would you be able to hear yourself as others hear you. Among the important differences resulting from our multiple-conduction feedback system of listening to ourselves is that ". . . we misjudge our own pitch, loudness, and quality, and probably our rate."[2] Because we cannot hear ourselves as others hear us, it behooves us to accept the evaluation of others, especially if the others are objective and professionally trained voice teachers or therapists. Fortunately, despite the limitations of our self-monitoring system, there is considerable evidence to show that learning to listen is helpful in the improvement of both voice and diction.

Listening to Others

Before turning the mirror on ourselves it might help to do some directed listening to the voices that are part of our everyday living. We may find that some of our acceptances and rejections of individuals are related to their voices. Following are a few projects that should be useful.

Exercises for Listening to Others

1.   Tune in to a daytime television "soap opera" and with eyes closed listen to the voices of the performers. Can you identify the hero or heroine through the medium of voice alone? Can you detect the villain? How about the family friend? What are the specific vocal attributes of each that influenced your decisions?

2.   Compare the newscaster you habitually turn on with one you

[2]*Op. cit.*, p. 58.

seldom hear. Do the vocal characteristics of the newscasters have anything to do with your choice? List the vocal characteristics you like and dislike for each. Which of the two has a more favorable balance?

3. Listen critically to two or three of your friends. Are there any characteristics of their voices you particularly like? Are there any you would like to have modified?

4. Listen critically to some persons you do not particularly like. Do you hear any vocal characteristics that might account for your reaction to them?

5. Recall a teacher, present or past, whom you consider especially effective. Is the voice of the teacher an important factor in your judgment? Describe his vocal attributes. Contrast this teacher with one you consider ineffective. Describe the voice of this teacher and determine whether it was a factor in your evaluation.

6. Tune in to a radio or television round-table discussion on a controversial topic. Do you find yourselves inclined to the point of view of any of the speakers because of the way he sounds? Do you find yourself disinclined to any for the same reason? List as specifically as you can the attributes and their effects on you. How would the following terms suit the individual speakers: agreeable, irritable, pompous, antagonistic, aggressive, soft-spoken, firm, tired, energetic, pedantic, indecisive, weak, complaining, congenial, authoritative, warm, cultured, charming?

7. Listen to a radio or television network program in which there is a professional moderator and two or more participants. Compare the vocal tones of the moderator with those of the participants. Observe whether the moderator reveals any partiality or personal prejudices through his voice.

8. Listen to a group of friends or acquaintances engaged in a conversation or discussion on a controversial topic. Do the participants reveal their personalities as well as their viewpoints through their voices? What terms listed in project (6) or terms of your own choosing would you apply to them?

9. Do you know any public figures who have had voice training? (Many public figures have had such training and some prepare specifically for each important address.) Can you recall any changes resulting from this training? Are there any who might benefit from voice training? What vocal characteristics would you like to have improved?

Physical Health

For most speakers who are not especially aware of their speech and who are not trained self-listeners, voice is likely to reflect changes in both physical and mental health. In the absence of any specific and chronic condition affecting either aspect of health, vocal efforts will be adversely affected by such conditions as fatigue, involvements of the respiratory tract, and conditions which produce either hypertense or hypotense musculature.

Perhaps the single cause which most frequently affects our voices is the common cold. The cold, because it directly involves the nose and throat, impairs normal vocal reinforcement. In addition, if the larynx is involved, the vibrators (vocal bands) may be thickened and so may produce tones which are not adequately reinforced. If there is a significant amount of inflammation, we tend to avoid laryngeal pain by keeping our vocal bands apart, and as a result we produce breathy and husky tones.

Akin to the effects of the common cold are those produced by allergies which involve the respiratory tract. These may include nasal congestion, irritation of the throat and larynx, and coughing. If the coughing is persistent and severe, the vocal bands may become involved. We may begin to appreciate the effects of persistent coughing from the following:

When you cough you force air through the windpipe at a speed approaching or exceeding that of sound, which is 723 miles an hour at sea level. . . . By the time the air reaches the level of the Adam's apple, its speed has dwindled to hurricane velocity of about 100 miles per hour. When it blows out of the mouth the air is moving at fifteen miles per hour, a mere zephyr.[3]

Most of us may be able to vocalize effectively despite the possible abuse to which our vocal bands are subjected when occasionally air

[3]"Science Notes," New York *Times*, April 17, 1955. This note is presumably based on the experimental findings of B. B. Ross, R. Gramiak, and R. Hahn, "Physical Dynamics of the Cough Mechanism," *Journal of Applied Physiology*, 1955, 8:264–268. They found that, depending upon various external pressures and the size of the opening of the trachea, the velocity of air during a cough may range from a speed equivalent to a 15-mile per hour wind to that of a 100-mile per hour hurricane. "If . . . the tracheal lumen is compressed to one-sixth its normal cross section area, the linear velocity thus generated is 28,000 cm/sec., nearly 85% of the speed of sound."

is propelled at speeds which may be supersonic. It should be no surprise, however, that many of us cannot be chronic coughers and effective vocalizers, especially if the coughing is violent and hacking.

Good vocal hygiene calls for either avoiding the conditions which are conducive to poor vocalization or reducing vocal efforts when such conditions cannot be avoided. In regard to matters of physical health, persons who must speak often have an obligation to practice good vocal hygiene. Dr. Brodnitz is succinct in his advice on how to maintain a healthy voice. He says "... keep your body in good shape to withstand the rigors of wind and weather; dress sensibly but do not undermine your resistance by pampering yourself; plan your meals in accordance with nutritional requirements; get as much rest and sleep as possible; exercise moderately."[4]

Mental Health

A mentally healthy person is one who is aware of what is going on about him and responds, without violence to his own integrity, to the demands of his environment. Mental health and the healthy, well-adjusting personality are attained through continuous effort. Speech and voice are both the tools and the results of the process of adjustment.

The young infant responds to his environment and expresses himself almost entirely through his voice. If a baby cries much of his waking time, he may be colicky. If he whines and is almost always on the verge of crying, he is an unhappy baby. If he coos to amuse himself but does little crying except for evident biological reasons, he is a happy or at least a satisfied baby. If he cries occasionally and coos sufficiently to amuse others as well as himself, he is a normal baby. Whatever his condition, whether it is temporary or chronic, he expresses it through his voice. And at each successive stage of his development, from babyhood to maturity, his voice continues to express—to reveal or to betray—his personality and his mental health.

Earlier in this chapter we suggested that the speaker become an objective self-listener and answer the question of whether the voice he heard reflected him as a personality. Another question to be answered was whether the voice had any characteristic which would

[4]F. S. Brodnitz, *Keep Your Voice Healthy* (New York: Harper & Row, 1953), p. 105.

be considered undesirable in another speaker. Here are some further questions we hope the listener, if he is a well-adjusted person, can answer in the negative. Does your voice suggest a whine when no whine is intended? Do you sound as if you are complaining about something when you intend to state a fact? Do you sound defeated? Do you sound aggressive rather than poised and secure? Do you sound chronically tired, bored, annoyed, or just too, too sophisticated for this mundane world in general and your associates in particular? If the answer is "yes" to any of these questions and there is no intention to suggest the trait which is expressed, insight and recognition should be of help in motivating a change.

Among the more frequent vocal problems associated with maturation is the failure of the voice to drop in pitch during physiological adolescence. Occasionally we meet chronological adolescents and postadolescents who still speak in their childhood pitch range. Sometimes we even find the habitual pitch level raised above that of preadolescence. Although in rare instances this vocal problem may be related to disturbances in motor control or in the glands, more often the cause is emotional. The chronological adolescent, whether boy or girl, who wants to continue to be mother's or daddy's child, or who is apprehensive for other reasons about growing up and assuming grown-up responsibilities, may be announcing the wish or the fear through an infantile voice.

Another adolescent problem frequently associated with vocal disturbance may arise from strong identification with an older person. As a result of this identification, an adolescent girl may imitate the pitch and other vocal characteristics of an idolized adult. Unfortunately, the voice of the adult may be the product of a vocal mechanism unlike that of the imitator. The woman teacher on whom the high school girl possibly has a "crush" may properly be a contralto with a pitch range too low for the larynx of the imitator. The effect may be a strained, husky voice. The problem for the boy in high school may be even more acute if he is intended by nature to be a tenor and his hero-figure is a person with a bass voice.

The author has had several male students who might have had good tenor voices, and possibly even been effective speakers within the upper part of their baritone range, but who wanted very much to speak like bassos. Within the bass range, unfortunately, they were constantly hoarse and could not be heard beyond the first two or three rows of a classroom. Psychological investigation strongly suggested that the young men were overanxious to be recognized as men—and fearful that they might not be so regarded. The author has also had several middle-aged male voice patients with much the same problems of voice and associated psychodynamics. He has also had a number of women voice patients who were referred to him by laryngologists because of thickened vocal bands resulting from habitual vocalization in too low a pitch range. In several instances the women were working in professional areas which until recently had been considered the province of males. The suspicion of "masculine protest" was supported by the psychodiagnostic evaluation.

Sometimes, to the misfortune of the speaker, habits of voice may persist and so reveal the maladjustments, personality, and mental health of a past period. Voice production is a motor act, and motor acts which are repeated tend to become habitual. Thus, the once dependent person may still sound dependent, and the once aggressive "chip-on-the-shoulder" individual may still sound as if he were obviously hostile. With conscious effort, vocal habits can be modified so that we reveal ourselves as we are when we speak rather than as we were during a period of past adjustment difficulties. If, however, adjustment difficulties continue to be present, effective voice is not likely to be achieved unless therapy includes the problems for which the voice is a symptom.

The Effective Vocalizer

If we examine our reactions to individuals who have effective voices, we are likely to conclude that by and large they are also effective as persons. Voice, or any other attribute of human behavior, is not a free-floating essence or a blithe, disembodied spirit. It is, on the contrary, an essential product and aspect of human behavior. It may sometimes be possible for a mentally or physically sick individual who has had considerable professional training to produce voice effectively for a specific purpose and for a limited time, as actors and some public speakers may be required to do. Even professional performers, however, cannot continue to vocalize effectively, act effectively, or in general pretend effectively for an indefinite period. In our discussion in subsequent chapters we shall assume that we are addressing ourselves to essentially healthy persons. This assumption permits leeway for the expression of a little bit of neuroticism which is or should be the privilege of all. It also allows for occasional physical ailments—even those which may be classified as psychosomatic because the body does protest what the mind sometimes must accept.

If the reader is at any time in doubt as to whether his lack of effective voice may be associated with either a temporary or a chronic state of subpar physical or mental well-being, proper medical consultation is in order. Certainly no person who has suffered from chronic hoarseness, or who has had any disturbance centered in the larynx, should undertake voice training without examination and clearance from his physician. If possible, the physician should be a specialist in diseases of the throat. Although voice training can improve most persons' vocal efforts, such training should not be undertaken when a physician prescribes vocal rest. We would also urge that no person become his own physician or use as a substitute for a physician a friend who has had what may appear to be similar voice symptoms. There is danger in using a friend's prescription. The individual who would be an effective vocalizer should have a personal examination by his own physician.

CHAPTER 2

The Mechanism for Speech

Early in life, normal human beings develop the ability to produce meaningful wave patterns in light and air. These patterns are known as speech symbols. The mechanisms by which the symbols are produced serve the biological functions of breathing and eating. Under voluntary control, however, these mechanisms can be modified in their functioning to serve the purposes of vocalization and articulation and thus the production of symbols used in speaking.

In this chapter we shall discuss the mechanisms through which human beings achieve speech, are able to communicate their thoughts and feelings, or, when it suits their needs, are able to conceal rather than reveal their thoughts and feelings. We shall first consider how speech noise (voice) is produced and then how noise and breath are modified to produce articulated sound in a manner unique to human beings.

The human vocal mechanism deserves understanding and respect for what it is—a sensitive instrument capable of permitting us to produce a type of sound of distinct quality called *voice*. Direct comparisons with mechanical instruments tend to minimize the attributes and potential of the vocal mechanism and its product. There are, however, several parallels between the human vocal mechanism and some musical wind instruments that may help to give us at least an intellectual appreciation of how each functions.

VOICE PRODUCTION

In most wind instruments, sound is produced when air is blown over a reed or through vibrating lips as in the case of a trumpet and a trumpeter. The reed or the reed substitute (lips) is usually near the blowing end of an elongated tube. The quality of the sound produced with a wind instrument is determined partly by the size, shape, and nature of the material, partly by the length, thickness, and type of reed, and partly by the ability of the person doing the blowing. The human voice-producing mechanism permits even the average speaker to be a virtuoso. Without conscious practice, most of us become skilled in making our voice mechanisms respond to our wishes. We play our vocal apparatus through ranges of pitch, loudness, and quality not possible by any known combination of wind instruments. The extreme flexibility of the vocal mechanism is the basis for its superiority over musical wind instruments.

Requisites for Sound Production

In order to produce sound, whether it be music, noise, or voice, three essential conditions must prevail: (1) There must be a body capable of being set into vibration; (2) there must be an available force which may be applied to the body to set it into vibration; and (3) there must be a medium for transmitting the results of the vibration to individuals capable of awareness and response. The first two requisites are found in the normal human mechanisms for breathing and will be discussed subsequently. The third requisite is air.

With modifications which are brought about by recognition of need, a normal human being is readily able to make his breathing mechanisms serve for voice production while the function of respiration is sustained. We shall be able to understand how voice production is accomplished through a study of the nature and structure of the vocal mechanism. In our discussion an overall view of the voice-producing mechanism rather than a detailed consideration of its component parts will be our objective.

The Vocal Bands

The vocal bands or vocal folds (lips) are bodies capable of vibration, thus meeting the first requirement for sound production. Biologically, the potential vibrators function as part of a valve mechanism to prevent foreign matter from entering the windpipe

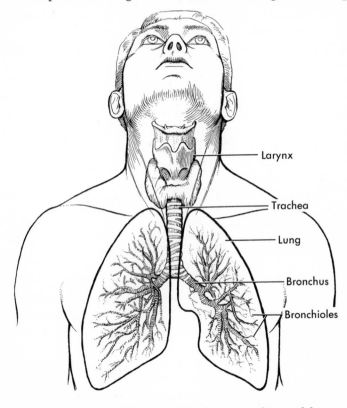

FIGURE 2–1.   Front upright view of the larynx, trachea, and lungs.

The larynx is a structure of cartilage, muscles, and membranous tissue at the top of the trachea. The largest cartilage of the larynx is the *thyroid*, consisting of two fused shieldlike parts. The vocal bands are attached to the inner curved walls of the thyroid cartilage laterally, and in front to the angle of the two fused parts of the thyroid. At the back, the vocal bands are attached to the arytenoid cartilages.

The trachea divides into two *bronchi*. Each *bronchus* divides into tubes of decreasing size known as *bronchioles*.

(*trachea*) and involving the lungs. The vocal bands are two small, tough folds of connective or ligamentous tissue situated in the larynx or voice box at the top of the trachea (see Figures 2–1 and 2–2). The bands are continuous with folds of muscle tissue and are connected to cartilages of the larynx.

The *trachea* is a tube or a "pipe" about four inches in length and an inch in diameter that is continuous between the pharynx and the lungs. In construction, the trachea is a series of incomplete rings of cartilage and membranous tissue (see Figures 2–1 and 2–2). This construction provides form and elasticity so that there is no danger

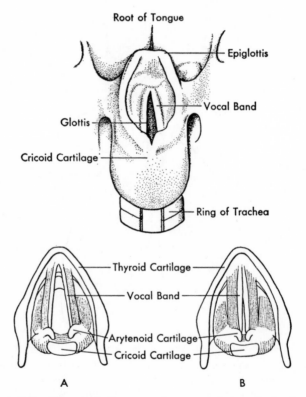

FIGURE 2–2. View and diagrammatic representation of the larynx and vocal bands showing attachments to cartilages and larynx.

Upper Diagram: The larynx viewed from above and behind (posterior aspect).

Lower Diagrams: (*A*) Vocal bands shown in position for quiet breathing. (*B*) Vocal bands in position for vocalization.

of tube constriction or collapse when air is drawn into the lungs. The elastic nature of the trachea also permits movement in swallowing and in speaking. These movements may be felt by finger contact and observed in a mirror. In swallowing, we may note that the top of the trachea moves upward and slightly forward toward the chin. The movements are usually more apparent in men than in women, especially in those men who have a conspicuous Adam's apple.

The trachea subdivides into two tubes known as *bronchi*. Each *bronchus* further divides and subdivides into smaller tubes within the lungs. These smaller-sized tubes are known as *bronchioles*.

If we could view the vocal bands from above, as in Figure 2–2, they would appear as flat folds of muscle which have inner edges of connective tissue. The vocal bands are attached to the inner curved walls of the thyroid cartilage at either side. At the midline, the bands are attached to the angle formed by the fusion of the two shields of the thyroid cartilage. At the back of the larynx, each band is attached to a pyramidal-shaped cartilage called the arytenoid.

Because of their shape and muscular connections, the arytenoid cartilages can move in several directions. In doing so, they directly influence the position and state of tension of the vocal bands. The arytenoid cartilages can pivot or rotate and tilt backward and sidewise. As a result of these movements, the vocal bands can be brought into a straight line along the midline position so that there is only a narrow opening between them (*B* in Figure 2–2), or they can be separated for quiet breathing (*A* of Figure 2–2). If the bands are brought together in a narrow V, as in the upper part of Figures 2–2, noisy whispering or possibly breathy voice would be produced if an effort were made to vocalize.

The small, tough vocal bands, ranging in length from seven-eighths inch to one and one-fourth inches in adult males and from less than one-half inch to seven-eighths inch in adult females, are directly responsible for the sound called voice produced by human beings.

The *frequency of vibration* of the vocal bands is determined by their length, thickness, and degree of tension when they begin to vibrate. Pitch is our subjective reaction to frequency changes or differences.[1] We think of pitch as being high, medium, or low or

---

[1]Technically, pitch may be considered as that attribute of auditory sensation in terms of which sounds may be ordered on a scale extending from low to high, such as a musical scale. (*American Standard Acoustical Terminology*, 1951, New York, American Standards Association.)

we use such terms as soprano, alto, tenor, baritone, or bass to designate ranges of vocal pitch.

Although the term *vibration* is used to designate the action of the vocal bands, a more accurate term might be *flutter*. When the column of breath is forced through the narrowed opening between the approximated vocal bands, they are literally blown apart and then come together in a flutterlike manner. If the breath stream is steady and controlled, the result will be a sequence of rhythmical flutters which produce in turn a rhythmical sequence of air puffs. The vocal tone is a product of the number of flutters, or vibrations, per unit of time and the vigor with which the bands are blown apart. The greater the number of flutters or vibrations, the higher the pitch. The greater the vigor with which the vocal bands are blown apart, the louder the tone. When the vocal bands flutter or vibrate with evenness and regularity, "smooth" or "pure" tone is produced. Irregularity of vibration, caused either by inadequate control of the breath stream (poor motive control) or from an unfavorable condition of the vocal bands, will result in the production of uneven or "noisy" vocal tones.

Frequency of vibration varies directly (increases) according to the tension and inversely (decreases) according to the mass and length of the vibrating bodies. Because most men have longer and thicker vocal bands than most women, male voices are on the average lower in pitch than female voices. The average fundamental frequency for male voices is 128 cycles (waves) per second; it is 256 cycles per second for female voices.

Variation from our fundamental frequencies is, for the most part, a result of the changes in tension of our vocal bands. We have considerable control over their state of tension. Such control becomes evident each time we sing the musical scale or a song or raise or lower the pitch level of a sound or a word when talking. Variation also occurs as a result of involuntary changes in the vocal bands associated with over-all states of bodily tension. The tensions of the vocal bands vary as other muscles voluntarily or involuntarily become tense or relaxed. If you are habitually a tense individual, you are likely to vocalize at a higher pitch level than if you are habitually a relaxed person. Immediate responses to situations are productive of over-all changes in bodily tension which are likely to be associated with tension changes in the vocal bands and therefore in their frequency of vibration. These changes become apparent in situations conducive to excitement and elation at one extreme and sadness or depression at the other. (This will be considered in some detail in Chapter 7, "Pitch and Voice Improvement.")

The Motive Force

The second requisite for sound production, the force which vibrates the vocal bands, is the column of air or expired breath stream. In ordinary breathing, the vocal bands are open in a wide-shaped V so that the stream of breath meets no resistance as it is exhaled. For purposes of vocalization, we recall, the vocal bands are brought together so that there is a narrow, relatively straight opening rather than a V-shaped one. The result is that the exhaled air meets resistance. In order for the air to be expired, the air column must be more energetically exhaled than it is in ordinary breathing. The energetic exhalation vibrates the vocal bands and voice is produced.

As indicated, vocalization for speech requires control. Control,

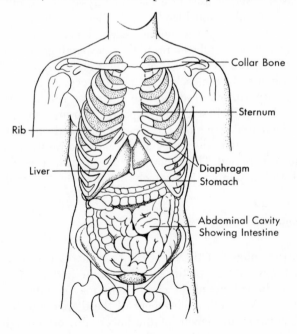

FIGURE 2–3.   The chest (thoracic) and abdominal cavities.

which normally takes place without conscious effort on our part, is achieved usually by the action of the muscles of the abdominal walls and the muscles of the chest cavity.

The *chest cavity* (thoracic) consists of a framework of bones and cartilages which include the collarbone, the shoulder blades, the ribs, the breastbone, and the backbone. At the floor of the chest cavity, and separating it from the abdominal cavity immediately below, is the diaphragm. We can locate the large, double-dome-shaped muscle called the diaphragm by placing our fingers just below the sternum or breastplate and moving them around the front, sides, and back of the thoracic cavity to the spinal column. In breathing, the diaphragm rises toward the chest cavity during exhalation and descends toward the abdominal cavity during inhalation. In breathing for purposes of speech, both the normal respiratory rhythm and the extent of the upward and downward excursions may be modified according to the speaker's immediate needs.

The *lungs* function as air reservoirs. The lungs, which contain much elastic tissue, consist of a mass of tiny air sacs supplied by a multiple of air tubes and blood vessels. Because the lungs contain no muscle tissue, they can neither expand nor contract directly. They play a passive role in respiration, expanding or contracting because of differences in pressure brought about by the activity of the abdominal and rib muscles that serve to expand and control the thoracic cavity. Air is forced into the lungs as a result of outside air pressure when the chest cavity, expanded through muscle action, provides increased space for the air. Air is forced out of the lungs when the chest cavity decreases in size and the pressure of the enclosed air is increased. This is normally accomplished through action in which the diaphragm is passively but importantly involved.

Diaphragmatic Action

When the volume of the chest cavity is increased, air is inhaled into the lungs by way of the mouth or nose and the trachea. An increase in the volume of the chest cavity may be effected through a downward, contracting movement of the diaphragm, through an upward, outward movement of the lower ribs, or through a combination of both activities. During inhalation, the diaphragm is active in contracting, thereby lowering the floor of the thoracic cavity. When inhalation is completed, the diaphragm becomes passive and relaxes. The abdominal organs then exert an upward pressure and so the diaphragm is returned to its former position. When it becomes necessary to control exhalation for purposes of vocalization and speech, the muscles of the front and sides of the abdominal

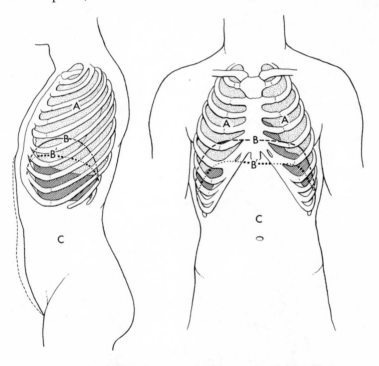

FIGURE 2–4. Diaphragmatic and abdominal activity in breathing.

A. The thorax or chest cavity.

B. The diaphragm passive and "relaxed" as at the completion of exhalation.

B'. The diaphragm contracted as in deep inhalation.

C. The abdominal cavity. Note the forward movement of the abdominal wall which accompanies the downward movement of the diaphragm during inhalation.

(The crosshatched portion of the lung represents the additional volume of the expanded lung as in deep inhalation.)

wall contract and press inward on the liver, stomach, and intestines. These abdominal organs exert an upward pressure on the under-surface of the diaphragm. This pressure, combined with the down-ward-inward movement of the ribs, increases the pressure within the thorax, causing the air to be expelled from the lungs. Throughout the breathing cycle, the diaphragm is roughly dome-shaped. The height of the dome is greater after exhalation than after inhala-tion.

It is important to understand that the diaphragm, though passive in exhalation, does not relax all at once. If it did, breath would be expelled suddenly and in a manner which would make sustained vocalization impossible. Fortunately, the diaphragm maintains some degree of muscle tension at all times. When the diaphragm relaxes because of the pressure of the abdominal organs, it does so slowly and gradually as the air is expired. Thus a steady stream rather than a sudden rush of breath is provided for the purposes of speech.

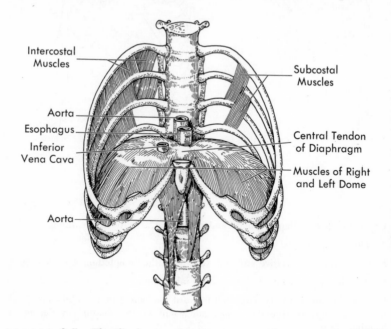

F I G U R E 2–5. The diaphragm, showing upper, or thoracic, surface; dome, or central tendon; and attachments to the lower ribs and the vertebrae. (After V. A. Anderson, *Training the Speaking Voice*, New York, Oxford University Press, 1961, p. 29. By permission.)

Breathing for Speech

In breathing for ordinary life processes, the periods for inhalation and exhalation are approximately equal. Breathing for speech, however, usually requires that this regular rhythmic respiratory cycle be modified so that the period of exhalation exceeds that of inhalation. Normally, for speech, we inhale quickly between units of utterance and exhale slowly while speaking. This modification necessitates a degree of voluntary control not required for automatic breathing. Such control is usually achieved by abdominal activity.[2] This point will be considered in greater detail in our discussion on voice improvement.

In normal nonspeech breathing, an average of about a pint of air (500 cc.) is interchanged in each respiratory cycle. Conversational speech may require little or no more air; vigorous speaking may require more air. Seldom, however, do we use more than 10 to 20 per cent of the total amount of air our lungs are capable of holding. Control of breath and the appropriate use of our resonators for reinforcement of vocal tones rather than amount of breath are essential to adequate voice production.

Reinforcement of Sound Through Resonance

The requisites of sound production are satisfied when a force is applied to a body capable of vibration and is transmitted or conducted through a medium to a receiver. From a strictly physical point of view, a receiver is not necessary. Psychologically, however, there can be no report or corroboration of the occurrence of a sound unless the sound is received. The receiver must be capable of auditory sensitivity within the pitch range of the vibrating body. Furthermore, the receiver's auditory sensitivity or threshhold for hearing must be low enough for the intensity level of the sound. If a receiver is at a distance from the source of a sound (the initiating vibrating body), considerable energy would have to be applied to set the body

[2]Stetson demonstrated that in the normal speaking act, short, individual breath pulses that correspond to the successive oral syllables result from the action of the rib-connecting (intercostal) muscles. (See R. H. Stetson, *Motor Phonetics*, 2nd ed., Oberlin College, Oberlin, Ohio, 1951, and R. H. Stetson and C. V. Hudgins, "Functions of the Breathing Movements in the Mechanism of Speech," *Arch. Neer. Phon. Exper.*, 1930, 5:1–30.)

into vibration with a resultant amplitude to produce a sound of sufficient intensity to be heard. At least, this would be the situation if a body were to be set into vibration in an "open field," by which we mean under conditions in which the sound is not reinforced through resonating bodies. We are assuming, also, that the sound is not amplified through mechanical devices such as an electrical sound system. Fortunately, the human voice does have the immediate benefit of reinforcement through resonating bodies. Later we shall consider how reinforcement through resonance is accomplished in the human voice mechanism. For the present, we shall discuss as briefly and as simply as possible the nature of two kinds of resonance-reinforcement that may take place for any sound.

Forced Resonance. Forced resonance or forced vibration takes place when a body that is set into vibration has a contact with another body which has the capability of the same frequency of vibration. The result of this contact is to set the second body into vibration. In effect, a sound has been directly transmitted from one body to a second, and so the sound is reinforced. This is partly what happens when the sounding body of a piano vibrates, and when a vibrating string of a violin transmits sound by way of the bridge to the body of the violin. It is also partly what happens when a tuning fork is set on a box or a board or a table top. The effect is the production of a sound we perceive as louder than would be the case if there were no forced vibration or forced resonance.

Cavity Resonance. A second form of reinforcement that is common for musical instruments, and for sound enhancement in general, takes place as a result of cavity resonance. By cavity we mean a partially enclosed body. Examples would be the shell or conventional stage for an orchestra, the tubular arrangement of a wind instrument, a tumbler or drinking glass, the "cavities" of the mouth, pharynx, and larynx of the human body. Each cavity, depending upon its size, shape, and opening has a natural frequency range for the sounds it will reinforce with *optimum efficiency*—for the sound range with which *the cavity is in tune*. Even a limited knowledge of musical instruments should lead us to generalize that the larger the cavity body, the lower its natural frequency range (the more efficiently the resonating cavity will reinforce low-pitched sounds). Conversely, the smaller the cavity body, the higher its natural frequency range. Thus, a bass violin, with its large cavity, is tuned for the reinforcement of low-pitched ranges of sound and a violin (fiddle), which has a smaller body, is tuned for the reinforcement of high-pitched ranges of sound. These ranges, of course, are relative to the family of string instruments. Comparable correlations between the size and pitch range hold for wind instruments. Thus we account for the differences in the range of sound for woodwind instruments which are similar in shape but different in size.

Reinforcement and Coloring of Vocal Tones

If we depended only on the energetic use of controlled breathing to make ourselves heard, we would have little "broadcast" ability without the help of mechanical (electrical) amplification. Fortunately, our vocal mechanisms are constructed so that a building up of laryngeal tones takes place through the reinforcement capacities of the resonators of our vocal apparatus. Before considering the contribution of each of our principal resonators—the cavities of the larynx, throat (pharynx), and mouth (oral cavity)—we shall briefly discuss the overall reinforcement of laryngeal tones.

The tones which are initiated in the larynx are modified and reinforced or "built up" in the structures beneath and above the vocal bands. The result of what takes place in these subglottal and supraglottal structures is the production of voice that emphasizes or brings out the potentialities of some vocal characteristics and minimizes or damps out others.

The chest or thoracic structure reinforces and modifies the laryngeal tone through a combination of forced (bone) and cavity resonance. When the vocal bands are set into action, with a resultant vocal tone, the tone is transmitted to bones of the chest. We can feel this effect by placing a hand on the upper part of the chest while vocalizing an *ah*. We should also be able to note that there is considerably more bone vibration felt with the vocalization of an *ah* than an *ee*. We may then appropriately conclude that our lower laryngeal tones are given considerably more reinforcement through the forced (bone) resonance than are the higher-pitched laryngeal tones. Except to avoid cramped postures, there is nothing we can do to enhance this type of vocal reinforcement. There is, however, much that we can do in regard to cavity reinforcement, which we shall now consider.

As already indicated, the principal human vocal resonators are the cavities of the larynx, pharynx, mouth, and the nasal passages. To a significant degree, also, the tracheal area just below the larynx as well as the bronchi reinforce laryngeal tones.

Each of the principal resonators by virtue of its size, shape, and tissue texture has special properties that enable it to make a unique contribution to the modification and reinforcement of the initial laryngeal tone and the production of the final or "finished" voice that the listener hears. We should be mindful, however, that at all times the vocal tones that emerge are the products of the contributions resulting from combined characteristics of all the resonators as well as the bony structures of the chest and head. Though some tones may have primary or predominant coloring resulting from the properties of one of the principal resonators, the others contribute to the finished voice. The discussion which follows considers the features of each of the principal resonators and the contribution each makes to our vocal efforts.

The Larynx as a Resonator

Vocal tones, as soon as they are initiated, are reinforced in the larynx. If the larynx is free from organic pathology and not under strain and if the speaker initiates and maintains vocalization without abnormal tension, there is little he can or need consciously do about obtaining good laryngeal resonance. If the speaker has laryngitis, however, normal laryngeal reinforcement is not possible. If you suffer from laryngitis, it is best to reduce your talking to a minimum, and if possible, do no talking. If the condition is recurrent, or persistent, a visit to a physician is in order.

Tension of the extrinsic muscles of the larynx, as indicated, interferes with the reinforcing function of the larynx. Such tension is also likely to interfere with the free action of the vocal bands for good tone production. The extrinsic muscles of the larynx are those which connect it to the jaw and other bones and cartilages so that it will maintain its normal position when at rest and be lifted upward and forward for swallowing. Tension is necessary in the act of swallowing. You can feel the tension of the extrinsic muscles by placing your hand on your throat as you swallow. Such muscular tension should, however, be avoided in most speech efforts. We approximate such tension for the vowels of *see* and *sue* but should avoid it for speech efforts in general. The suggestions given for easy initiation of tone may be reviewed here as practice to avoid unnecessary laryngeal tension (see pages 60–64.)

The Pharynx

The pharynx, or throat cavity, has the necessary attributes for optimum sound reinforcement. How a cavity resonates (reinforces) a given tone or range of tones is determined by several factors. These include the size, shape, and nature (material, tension, etc.) of the cavity walls and the size of its opening as related to the source of sound (vibrating body) and/or other connecting cavities. The pharynx, because of its size and the control we can exercise over it to modify shape and tension, is much more important as a vocal reinforcer than is the larynx. We modify the length of the cavity each time we swallow or each time the soft palate is raised or relaxed. We change the quality of vocal tones through changes in the tension of the pharyngeal walls. Growths, such as enlarged adenoids or tonsils, may damp vocal tones and modify loudness as well as sound quality. When, because of infection or emotional tension, the pharynx is abnormally tense, the voice quality tends to become strident and metallic. Higher-pitched tones are reinforced at the expense of low tones. The result sometimes is an unpleasant voice that lacks adequate loudness and carrying power. When the pharyngeal tensions are normal, the voice is likely to be rich and mellow—at least as rich and mellow as the individual throat permits.

Our understanding of the action of the pharynx as a resonator can be enhanced by a brief review of its structure. If we examine Figure 2–6 we will note that the pharynx begins just above the larynx and extends up to the entrance to the nasal cavity. The portion near the larynx—the *laryngopharynx*—is capable of considerable modification. The diameter can be changed for the reinforcement of fundamental tones and overtones produced in the larynx. The tones we identify as the vowels of our language are in part produced as a result of action of the laryngopharynx.

The *oropharynx* is the area just above the laryngopharynx. The oropharynx can pair with either the area below (the laryngopharynx), or above (the nasopharynx), or with the oral cavity (mouth), or with all three together to modify vocal tones. As a result, the oropharynx can act subtly or grossly to reinforce tones and to produce sounds of different qualities.

The *nasopharynx* is the uppermost part of the pharyngeal cavity. This area can in effect be separated from the mouth cavity and

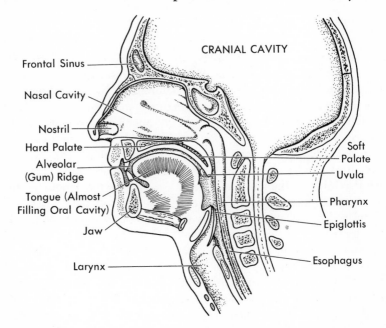

FIGURE 2–6. Section of head showing principal resonators and organs of articulation.

connected with the nasal cavity through the act of elevating the soft palate. When the soft palate is lowered, the nasopharynx can be paired with the lower part of the pharynx or with the oral cavity. The nasopharynx is directly involved in the reinforcement of the nasal consonants *n, m,* and *ng.*

The Oral Cavity

The mouth, or oral cavity, is the most modifiable of all the resonators of importance for speech. Except for that part of the roof of the mouth which constitutes the hard palate, all the parts which together form or are included in the oral cavity are capable of considerable movement. The lower jaw can move to create an oral cavity limited only by the extent of the jaw's action. The tongue, though attached to the floor of the mouth, can be elevated, flattened, extended out of the mouth, drawn up and curled within the mouth, or can almost fill the closed mouth. The lips can close tight along a straight line, open centrally or laterally to various-sized apertures, or open wide as the lower jaw drops to permit a view of the back of the throat. The soft palate and uvula can be elevated to increase the size of the back of the mouth or relaxed to make the back of the mouth continuous with the throat. Through these many modifications, the oral cavity and the organs within it not only produce the various sounds of our language but reinforce them as well.

The Nasal Cavity

Except when the nasopharynx is coupled with the nasal cavity, we have little direct control over the latter. Unfortunately, the linings of the nasal cavity and the cavity itself are considerably affected not only by physical illnesses involving the upper respiratory tract, but by emotional disturbances as well. The condition of the nose, it appears, is often an excellent indicator of what is happening to us physically and emotionally. It fills up when we have a cold, when we are allergic, when we are very happy, and when we are acutely sad. When, for any of numerous reasons, the nasal cavity is not free, adequate reinforcement of nasal sounds in particular and nonnasal sounds in general is difficult if not impossible.

The Sinuses

The role of the sinuses as resonators has not been clearly established. We have four pairs of sinuses which drain into the nasal cavity. Most of us become aware of our sinuses when they are infected and drain the products of their infection into our respiratory tract. Short of trying to keep well so that we can avoid the unpleasant condition called sinusitis, there is little we can do about the sinuses to influence voice. Unlike most of the other cavities associated with the respiratory tract, we cannot control or modify the size, shape, or surface tension of the sinuses to affect the reinforcement of vocal tones.

Flexibility of the Vocal Mechanism

Earlier in the chapter we compared the voice mechanism with a wind instrument. In our comparison, the point was made that the vocal mechanism was considerably more flexible and therefore superior to any wind instrument as a producer of sound. The reeds of a wind instrument are fixed in size and degree of tension. Human vocal bands, however, can be changed in length and tension so that a comparatively wide range of pitch is possible. Through muscular contraction our resonating cavities can be modified so that the sound produced by the vocal bands can be variably reinforced. Normally, we can direct our voice through a combination of resonators so that sound emerges either orally or nasally. The manner in which we open and shape our mouths permits us to produce a variety of sounds that are most readily exemplified in the vowels of our language. When the lips, the tongue, and the palate become more actively involved in the modification of sound, articulation, an aspect of sound production peculiar to human beings, becomes possible. This aspect of sound will be considered after our discussion of the attributes of voice and some factors that are related to vocal changes.

CHARACTERISTICS OF SOUND—AND VOICE

All sounds, including those which are vocal, have four fundamental characteristics or attributes. These are *loudness, pitch, duration,* and *quality.* When we respond to a given sound, whether it be the barely audible sound of a dropped pin or a clap of thunder, we are responding to a combination of attributes. The results of our experiences enable us to recognize certain sounds as belonging to the things which make them. So, also, we are usually able to associate voices with the persons who produce them. Tom's voice is a complex of his particular vocal attributes, as are the voices of Harry and Dick. If we know Tom, Dick, and Harry well, and have fair sensitivity to voice, we are likely to identify each by his voice. If we lack sensitivity to vocal differences, or if the sum of Tom's vocal attributes is much like Dick's or Harry's, we may occasionally make mistakes in our identification. Usually, however, one attribute of voice is likely to be different enough so that the sum produces a voice sufficiently individualized to permit reliable identification.

The human voice as a sound producer is not limited to one given pitch, loudness, duration, or even quality. The human mechanism with its subtle and complex neuromuscular controls is capable of a range of variation for each of the sound attributes. A baritone vocalizer may produce sounds that overlap the upper range of the bass and the lower range of the tenor. A female contralto may be able to overlap the high tenor and much of the soprano ranges. No speaker produces tones at a single loudness level. As we speak, we vary the intensity of our sounds from syllable to syllable, word to word, sentence to sentence, and, of course, from occasion to occasion. We vary the duration or time given to utterance as well as the pitch and loudness. We are able to speak rapidly, slowly, or at a moderate rate according to need as well as habit. Although our vocal qualities are relatively limited by the size and shape of our resonating cavities, these attributes can be modified. Some of us are even able to control vocal quality well enough to imitate other speakers. Most of us who do not habitually speak nasally or harshly can do so at will. All things and sound attributes considered, the normal human being can do considerably more with his sound-making apparatus than expert musicians can do with their musical instruments.

The Individuality of the Human Voice

Although some persons achieve reputations as vocal mimics because of their ability to simulate the vocal production of popular or well-known personages, each of us has a voice with individual features that are almost as distinctive as our fingerprints. Our ability to hear these distinctive features may not be as keen as our ability to see differences in fingerprints, but vocal differences are able to be discerned when they are transformed from audible into visible forms. A device which transforms the vocal features of voice to visible patterns has been developed by the Bell Telephone Laboratories. Voice-prints, such as those in Figures 2–7 and 2–8, bring out differences that reveal the individuality of the voice. The recording technique, developed by Dr. Lawrence Kersta of Bell Laboratories, indicates loudness, resonance, and pitch. In combination, these are presumably never the same for **any two people.**

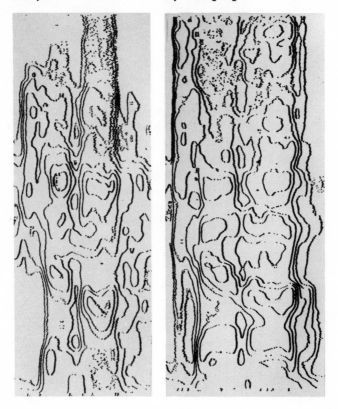

FIGURE 2–7 (Left).   John F. Kennedy's voice-print, made during a talk he gave in the White House, shows Bostonian delivery in compressed dark lines at top. (LIFE Magazine © 1963 Time Inc. All Rights Reserved.)

FIGURE 2–8 (Right).   Elliott Reid uses the same text and intonations as President Kennedy, but the graph his voice makes is radically different. (LIFE Magazine © 1963 Time Inc. All Rights Reserved.)

CORRELATES OF VOCAL CHANGES

Unless we consciously try to conceal our feelings as we talk, we are likely to reveal them by the way we sound. Voice, when not intentionally controlled, is a barometer of our affective states, our feelings and our moods. This is so essentially because voice is a product of muscular activity which in turn is intimately related to the emotional state of the organism. In a state of heightened emotion, as in anger or fear, we experience muscular tension. The muscles involved in voice production share in the increased total body tension. Thus when vocalization takes place it is on a higher pitch level than normal. Another involuntary change which accompanies heightened emotion is the addition of sugar to the blood stream. This enables us to engage in energetic activity which is sometimes an aspect of heightened emotion. The effect on a voice is to increase its loudness. The overall effect of heightened feeling on utterance is that the voice becomes high pitched, loud, and rapid.

In contrast, depressed or let-down states are associated with vocal tones which are low in pitch level and relatively weak in loudness. This is so because the muscles of the body as a whole, and the vocal bands in particular, become overrelaxed or hypotonic, and energetic activity is reduced. The overall effect on utterance is to make it relatively low in pitch and volume and slow in rate.

Voice that is dominated by intellect rather than emotion tends to be moderate in pitch as well as in loudness. This does not imply that intellectual efforts are devoid of feeling. It does imply that intellectual efforts accompanied by vocalization are normally not characterized by the exaggerated range and intensity of feeling which characterize emotional behavior. Under intellectual control, we are able to simulate emotion, to suggest how we would sound if angry, afraid, ecstatically happy, or depressed. When these pretenses are not necessary, we are ourselves. If we are our normal selves, we are usually moderate not only in our behavior in general but in the intensity of our feelings and in the manner in which our voices reveal (or sometimes betray) how we feel and think.

ARTICULATED SOUND

When breath which is set into vibration by the action of the vocal bands reaches the mouth as part of a speech effort, the breath stream is further modified by the action of the tongue, lips, palate, and/or cheeks to produce voiced articulated sound. If the breath stream is not set into vibration, then voiceless articulated sound may be produced. The organs of articulation serve essentially as interrupters, filters, or modifiers of the breath stream. Some sounds—vowels and diphthongs—are produced only by an adjustment of the size and shape of oral and adjacent cavities. These adjustments modify but do not impede or interrupt the laryngeal or vocal tone. Other sounds are produced by a stoppage or diversion of the breath or the vocal tone. Thus we have consonants resulting from sudden interruptions, little explosions, or hissings because air is forced through narrow openings. The manner and place of interruption result in the production of articulated speech sounds. Each sound has its own characteristics or phonetic attributes. Oral speech consists of combinations of articulated sounds. When these sounds, produced according to the conventions of our language, are appropriately grouped and readily audible, we speak intelligibly.

The Articulators

Most of the articulated sounds of American-English speech are produced as a result of the activity of the lips and parts of the tongue. These mobile articulators assume positions or make contact with fixed or relatively fixed parts of the upper jaw and the roof of the mouth (see Figure 2–9).

The lips and teeth enclose the oral cavity. The tongue lies within and almost completely fills the oral cavity. From the point of view of articulatory action the tongue may be divided into the following parts: the anterior portion or tongue tip, the blade, the mid-tongue, and the back. The roof of the mouth may be divided into the gum ridge or alveolar process (directly behind the upper teeth), the hard palate, the soft palate (velum), and the uvula.

The larynx also serves an articulatory function because the presence or absence of vocalization distinguishes many pairs of sounds such as *b* and *p* and *z* and *s*. The sound *h* is produced as a result of a degree of contraction within the larynx sufficient to produce audible friction.

Details as to the manner in which the articulators function to produce the different sounds of our language will be considered in Chapter 11. At the present time let us consider briefly the controlling mechanism through which man is enabled to make vocal noises, to modify these noises into distinguishable sounds and intelligible words, to use these words to express his feelings, his wishes, and

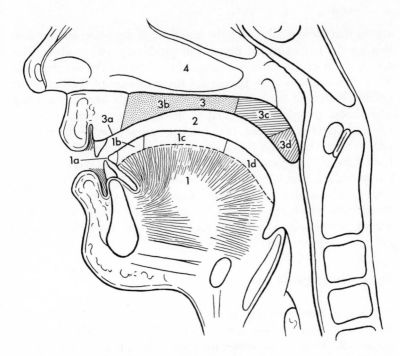

FIGURE 2–9.   The oral cavity and its articulators.

1. Tongue. *1a.* Tongue tip. *1b.* Blade of tongue. *1c.* Front of tongue.
1d. Back of tongue.

2. Mouth (oral) cavity.

3. Palate.   *3a.* Gum, or alveolar, ridge.   *3b.* Hard palate.   *3c.* Soft palate.
3d. Uvula.

4. Nasal cavity.

his needs, and to become a member of a symbol-producing and
symbol-responding culture.

THE NERVOUS SYSTEM

The Cerebrum

Many animals produce vocal noises, but only man can make
sounds that make sense. We speak because we are able to integrate

organs that biologically serve the functions of digestion and respiration for the nonbiological purpose of producing oral symbols. The achievement of speech is neurologically related to the development of the cerebrum in man. Except for the cerebrum of the brain, the nervous system of the human being is surprisingly like that of a dog and almost completely like that of an ape. The cerebrum is significantly different in man. It is larger in proportion to the nervous system as a whole than it is in animals, and it includes a bulgelike frontal area of greater size than that found in animals with otherwise comparable nervous systems. The brain is a coordinator and integrator of activity. In the brain, impulses set up by sounds and movements which are received by the ear, the eye, or other sense organs, are translated into images or into words which have significance and meaning.

The Cerebral Cortex

The gray outer covering of the brain is especially involved in the function of speech. The cortex contains ten to twelve billion or more nerve cells. Parts of the cortex have specialized functions which are involved in the peculiarly human ability to produce and understand oral (speech) or written symbols. These areas are indicated in Figure 2–10. The marked areas include those for *hearing, seeing,* and *speech movement.* These areas are significant because of their evident capacity to evaluate specialized experiences *for the brain as a whole.* For example, the auditory area in the lower middle part of the brain evaluates sounds, so that noises may be interpreted as *barks, wind in the trees,* or *words.* Similarly, the area in the back part of the brain (the occipital lobe) interprets impulses coming from the eye. Through this area we are able to recognize and identify objects we see and to read and so to make sense out of markings called letters and words.

The Central Nervous System as a Whole

In addition to the cerebrum, there are other parts of the central nervous system which are essentially involved in the production of speech. The parts are represented in Figure 2–11. Briefly stated, the

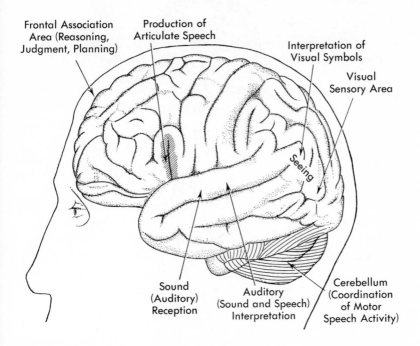

Frontal Association Area (Reasoning, Judgment, Planning)

Production of Articulate Speech

Interpretation of Visual Symbols

Visual Sensory Area

Seeing

Sound (Auditory) Reception

Auditory (Sound and Speech) Interpretation

Cerebellum (Coordination of Motor Speech Activity)

FIGURE 2–10. The cerebral cortex and cerebellum and some "specialized" areas related to speech.

other parts serve the following functions in the integrated speech act.

The *cerebellum*, or little brain, receives impulses from higher brain centers. The impulses are sorted, arranged, and correlated so that the coordinated and precise muscular activity needed for speech becomes possible. Damage to the cerebellum may seriously impair the flow and control of coordinated speech activity. Damage of this sort is found in many cases of cerebral palsy.

The *medulla* contains the center essential for respiration, and damage to it may impair normal breathing. Bulbar polio involves such damage, and consequently the need for a mechanical respirator in cases of this disease should be clear.

The *bulb*, the *spinal cord*, and the nerves emanating from them control the muscles involved in the coordinated act of speaking. The *phrenic* nerve which emerges from the spinal cord in the region of the neck extends to the diaphragm. The phrenic nerve supplies

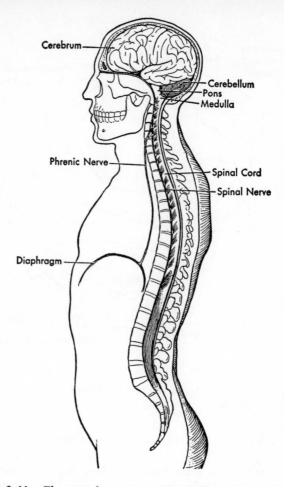

FIGURE 2–11.   The central nervous system in relation to speech.

The *cerebrum* performs the integrative activity upon which normal, meaningful speech is dependent.

The *cerebellum* "sorts and arranges" muscular impulses that come to it from higher brain centers. Impulses are here correlated so that precise muscular activity such as is needed for speech becomes possible.

The *pons* is a bridge of nerve fibers between the cerebral cortex and the medulla.

The *medulla* contains the respiratory and other vital reflex centers.

The *spinal cord* and its nerves control the respiratory muscles.

The *phrenic nerve* emerges from the spinal cord in the neck region and extends to the diaphragm. It supplies the impulses which cause the diaphragm to contract in breathing.

40

the impulse which causes the diaphragm to contract and so brings about inalation in breathing.

Other nerves which initiate movements involved in speech are the trigeminal (face and jaw muscles), the glossopharyngeal (tongue and pharynx), the recurrent laryngeal (larynx), and the glossal (tongue).

In the absence of pathology, the central nervous system, dominated by the cerebral cortex, controls the impulses involved in the act of speaking. Through this system, we are able to be articulate about our impressions, to reveal what we think and how we feel. Sometimes, if it suits our purpose, we conceal rather than reveal either our feelings, our thoughts, or both. The degree of expertness with which we use our speech apparatus varies considerably from person to person. All of us, however, with unimpaired physical mechanisms and with normal personalities should be capable of speaking adequately. How to make the most of our mechanisms so that we fully utilize our capabilities to vocalize and articulate with ease and intelligibility will be considered in the chapters that follow.

CHAPTER 3

Breathing for
Effective Vocalization

Physicians specializing in the treatment of the throat, and those few who treat vocal disorders as well as diseases of the throat, recognize that most vocal disorders are a result of the use of *inappropriate force, wrong pitch, incorrect breathing, or a combination of them*.[1]

Although our experience does not show that most speakers necessarily breath incorrectly, use force inappropriately, or pitch their voices at wrong levels, a knowledge of what can be done to improve voice may be helpful to all of us. Certainly the speaker who wants a better than ordinary voice or who aspires or needs to use voice as an instrument for his vocation or profession has an obligation to himself as well as to his listeners to know what students in the field of voice recommend as to the use of force, pitch, and breathing. We shall begin with a consideration of breathing.

[1] For a discussion of this viewpoint by a physician, see F. S. Brodnitz, *Keep Your Voice Healthy* (New York: Harper & Row, 1953), Chap. XII.

The basic physiology of respiraion is succinctly and clearly considered in T. E. Rogers' *Elementary Human Physiology* (New York: John Wiley, 1961) Chap. VIII.

BREATHING FOR SPEECH (VOICE AND ARTICULATION)

Earlier, in our discussion of the mechanism for speech, we pointed out that breathing for speech calls for a modification of the normal respiratory cycle so that (1) the inspiration-expiration ratio is changed to provide a much longer period of exhalation than of inspiration and (2) a steady stream of air is initiated and controlled by the speaker to insure good tone. These modifications, we have found, are usually achieved most easily by the type of breathing which emphasizes abdominal activity.

At the outset, we would like to point out that good breathing for speech production is by no means synonymous with deep breathing. Many good speakers use no more breath for vigorous speaking, or public speaking, than they do for conversational speech. Seldom is it necessary for any person to employ more than one fifth of his breath capacity for any vocal effort.

Breathing for speech should meet the following objectives:

1. It should afford the speaker an adequate and comfortable supply of breath with the least awareness and expenditure of effort.

2. The respiratory cycle—inhalation and exhalation—should be accomplished easily, quickly, and without interference with the flow of utterance.

3. The second objective implies ease of control over the outgoing breath so that breathing and phrasing—the grouping of ideas—can be correlated functions.

If these are not established and are not habitual accomplishments, they can be most readily achieved, we believe, through establishing abdominal control of breathing.

Abdominal Breathing

If we observe the breathing of a person or an animal who is sleeping on his back or side, we should be able to note that during inhalation the abdominal area moves upward or forward while during exhalation the abdominal area recedes. Figure 2–4 visualizes what we can see in the way of abdominal activity as well as what we cannot see in the way of diaphragmatic activity for breathing which emphasizes abdominal control. (See page 23.)

The essential point for us to appreciate is that in breathing that is characterized by action of the abdominal muscles, the muscles of the abdomen relax in inhalation and contract in exhalation. When we learn how to contract or pull in the abdominal walls consciously, and how much and how fast to control such contraction, breathing for speech becomes *voluntary if needed.* If the reader is now exercising such control unconsciously, the suggested exercises which follow are not particularly important for him. If he is not, or if he finds that he cannot easily sustain a hum or a gentle whisper for from twenty to thirty seconds, then the exercises should be followed. These exercises are designed to create awareness and conscious control of abdominal action in breathing.

Exercises for Control of Abdominal Action in Breathing

1. Lie on a couch or bed with a firm mattress. Spread your hands on the abdominal area immediately below the ribs so that the thumbs point to the rear and the fingers point forward. Inhale for normal, nonspeech breathing. Your hands should rise during inhalation and fall with the abdomen during exhalation. If the action is reversed, then the breathing is incorrect and should be changed to bring about the suggested activity. Repeat until the suggested action is accomplished easily. Be sure that you are not wearing a tight belt or a confining article of clothing while doing this and the following exercises.

2. Sit in a relaxed position in a comfortable chair with a firm seat. Your feet should be flat on the floor. Place your hands as in exercise (1). Now the abdominal walls should push forward on inhalation and pull in on exhalation.

3. Repeat as in exercise (2). Then inhale gently for about five seconds and exhale slowly, sustaining the exhalation for ten seconds. If you find yourself out of breath before the end of the ten-second period, then you have probably exhaled too quickly. Try the exercise again, intentionally slowing down the exhalation.

4. Inhale fully and then breathe out slowly and completely. Your hands should still be following the movement of the abdominal walls. Repeat, but this time press gently but firmly with your hands to force the expulsion of air from your lungs. Repeat, counting to yourself while exhaling. At this point you should be able to count for about thirty seconds before becoming uncomfortable.

5.   Repeat, but this time vocalize a clear *ah* while exhaling. *Start your vocalization the moment you begin to exhale.* Stop before becoming uncomfortable. Repeat, vocalizing a sustained *hum* while exhaling. The *ah* and *hum* should be sustained longer than a nonvocalized exhalation.

6.   Inhale deeply and then count out evenly and slowly until you feel the need for a second breath. Maintain even pitch and loudness levels. Repeat, but this time keep your hands at your sides and concentrate on a gradual pulling in of the abdominal wall during the counting. You should be able to count to at least twenty on a sustained exhalation. In any event, continue to practice until a count of at least fifteen is attained. With continued practice, a count of twenty to thirty (at the rate of two numbers per second) should become possible after a normal inhalation and a full thirty-second count after a deep inhalation.

7.   With hands at your sides, repeat the above exercise on two successive breaths. Be certain that you do not exhale to a point of discomfort. Nor should you inhale so deeply that some air has to be exhaled for the sake of comfort.

8.   Repeat, reciting the alphabet instead of counting. Avoid wasting breath between utterance of the letters. Note how far you are able to go on a single normal breath and on a single deep breath.

9.   Repeat, whispering the alphabet. Note the letter you reached before requiring a second breath. Depending upon the degree of whisper, this might be only a third or a half of the number of letters of your vocalized effort. This is normal. A whisper is wasteful of breath.

10.   Count, with vocalization, in groups of three. Avoid exhalation during pauses. Did you come close to the number you reached in counting without grouping? If you did not, then you probably exhaled between groups of numbers. Try it again until the two counts are about even.

11.   Repeat exercise (10), using the alphabet instead of counting.

12.   Recite the months of the year with pauses after March, June, and September. You should have no difficulty reciting all twelve months even with "seasonal" pauses.

13.   Try to say each of the following sentences on a single breath.

    a.   Let all who enter here beware!
    b.   The road is long that has no turning.

    c.   Alone, alone, all, all alone.
    d.   The day was warmed by a gentle breeze.
    e.   All aboard who are going aboard.

14.   If you had no difficulty with the single sentences, then try uttering these longer sentences and complete each on a single, sustained breath. Do not, however, force the expulsion of air beyond a point of comfort.

    a.   He's a fool that makes his doctor his heir.

—BENJAMIN FRANKLIN

    b.   Plato held that rhetoric was the art of ruling the minds of men.

    c.   Her blue eyes sought the west afar,
         For lovers love the western star.

—SIR WALTER SCOTT, The Lay of the Last Minstrel

    d.   For he who fights and runs away
         May live to fight another day;

—OLIVER GOLDSMITH, The Art of Poetry

    e.   Upon what meat doth this our Caesar feed,
         That he is grown so great?

—WILLIAM SHAKESPEARE, Julius Caesar

    f.   The day is cold, and dark, and dreary;
        It rains, and the wind is never weary;

—HENRY WADSWORTH LONGFELLOW, The Rainy Day

The following exercises involve the use of speech sounds which have an aspirate quality. They are normally more wasteful of breath than most of the previous exercises. They are, however, important in establishing breath control because much of what we say includes nonvocalized (voiceless) sounds as well as those which have a definite whispered or fricative quality.

Exercises for Establishing Breath Control

1.   Inhale normally and then release the breath while producing the sound *s*. Be sure the sound is evenly maintained. Try to sustain the *s* for ten seconds. Repeat with the sound *sh*, then *th* as in *think*, and *f* as in *fall*.

2.   Inhale deeply, but avoid discomfort. Repeat exercise (1). Compare these efforts with the length of time for a sustained *m* or *ah*. You are not likely to sustain any of these breathy sounds as long as *m* or *ah*, but you should come fairly close.

3.   Try saying each of the following sentences on a single breath. If you do not succeed the first time, try a deeper inhalation on successive trials. Do not intentionally whisper.

a.   Whenever he thought about it, Harry thought of himself as a hero.

b.   His faithful dog Fido shared Harry's beliefs.

c.   Heaven is said to help those who help themselves.

d.   The sun sank slowly and was followed by darkness and cold.

e.   What is held as truth by most of us is not the truth for all of us.

f.   When I was five, I thought my father was the smartest person alive.

g.   The crisp and crackly leaves fell from the tree.

h.   If you listen in respectful silence, you may appear to be very wise.

i.   The rushing stream washed the soil along with it.

j.   Some critics hold that several of the plays attributed to Shakespeare were written by Marlowe.

k.   Other cynical critics hold that many of Shakespeare's plays were written by another author with the same name.

4.   If you have been successful with all of the sentences, then try these couplets, each on a single breath. If you pause at the end of the line, try not to exhale at the pause.

a.   Of all the tyrannies on human kind
   The worst is that which persecutes the mind.

   —JOHN DRYDEN, *The Hind and the Panther*

b.   Words are like leaves; and where they most abound,
   Much fruit of sense beneath is rarely found.

   —ALEXANDER POPE, *An Essay on Criticism*

c.   The drying up a single tear has more
   Of honest fame than shedding seas of gore.

   —LORD BYRON, *Don Juan*

d. Go put your creed into your deed,
    Nor speak with double tongue.

—RALPH WALDO EMERSON, *Ode, Concord*

e. My life is like a stroll upon the beach,
    As near the ocean's edge as I can go.

—HENRY DAVID THOREAU, *The Fisher's Boy*

Clavicular Breathing

Older readers, or readers who have had older teachers, may have been exposed to a type of breathing which emphasized movement of the upper part of the rib cage and the clavicles. It is difficult now to understand the rationale of this type of breathing for speech. If there was a rationale, it was somehow based on the belief that by expanding the least expandable part of the thoracic cavity, more space for air and, with deep breathing, more air could be brought into the lungs. With the additional hard-to-get quantity of air, better physical hygiene in general and better voice in particular were then supposed to be readily achieved. Now, with our understanding that it is not the amount of breath but the control of the breath stream that is important, any technique that emphasizes quantity of air is not held in high regard. Even if quantity of air were important, it could be more easily increased through deep breathing with abdominal and lower rib-cage activity than with clavicular breathing which, at best, merely elevates the chest as a whole. In fact, clavicular breathing tends to be shallow rather than deep and requires more frequent inhalation than does abdominal breathing. Beyond this, clavicular breathing has definite disadvantages in that it has been found to be associated with a marked tendency of the muscles of the larynx and throat to become too tense for proper vocalization and reinforcement of tone.

To check on any tendency toward clavicular breathing, stand before a full-length mirror and breathe in deeply. Relax, then exhale fully. Repeat twice. Note, and correct, any tendency of the shoulders to be appreciably elevated or of the chest as a whole to be raised. Abdominal breathing, which we recommend, would call for little or no movement of the shoulders or upper chest. Movement, if it is to be discerned, would be of the lower chest and abdominal areas. Usually this will require a profile rather than a full-front view.

An added check, as well as an exercise to correct the tendency toward clavicular breathing, is the following: Place your hands on your chest with your fingers spread and the thumbs pointing toward the collarbone. Take a deep breath, then say the days of the week. Observe, and, if necessary, use the pressure of your hands to prevent any appreciable upward movement of the upper chest and shoulders. For variety, the exercise might be done with counting from one through ten or reciting the alphabet in sequences from *a* through *l* and *m* through *z*. If upper chest movement is inhibited, the normal compensatory action will bring about the desired movement of the abdominal and the lower chest muscles. Be certain that the movement is forward during inhalation and inward during exhalation.

Breathing and Phrasing

In the exercises to establish abdominal breathing and the awareness of breath control, our emphasis was on sustaining a sound, a series of words, or a sentence on a single breath. For ordinary conversational speech, and for most public speaking purposes, length of uninterrupted utterance is not as important as the interruption of a unit of thought because of the need for additional breath. The occasions are infrequent when a speaker will need to utter more than twelve to fifteen syllables on a single breath. The speaker must learn to anticipate inhalation and to stop at an appropriate point to inhale. If he learns this, he will avoid having to stop at an inappropriate point because he cannot continue speaking without another breath. The appropriate or natural stopping places are at the ends of units of thought, *between phrases or sentences.* Unless the speaker is reading or reciting verse with regular meter, the units of thought are likely to be of varying lengths. Breathing must therefore be adjusted to anticipated needs. For example, if the speaker cannot comfortably quote Emerson on a single breath to the effect that "His heart was as great as the world, but there was no room in it to hold the memory of a wrong," he has a choice of at least two stopping places. He may, without doing violence to the thought, stop at the places indicated by the vertical lines: "His heart was as great as the world ‖ but there was no room in it ‖ to hold the memory of a wrong." We might note, incidentally, that some but not all units of thought are marked off for us by punctuation. Some units of thought have no punctuation marks. The reader must, on the basis of meaning, decide where and whether to phrase. The good vocal phraser uses punctuation as a guide but is not a slave to it.

A speaker with a fair breath capacity and good breath control might easily go as far as the second vertical line before stopping for a breath. Unless he feels that he is equal to the entire sentence, however, he should not try to go beyond the second vertical line because to do so would mean interrupting a unit of thought in order to inhale.

In exercises (1)–(5) immediately following, possible stops for inhalation are indicated by vertical lines. In terms of your own breath capacity, mark off the places at which you plan to inhale. Inhale briefly at these places so that there is no suggestion of awkward pausing. Try to inhale as infrequently as possible so that the reading does not become jerky. Maintain abdominal control of breathing. If necessary, place your hands on the abdominal wall to feel the pushing away at the inhalations and the pulling in at the exhalations while reading aloud.

Exercises for Abdominal Breathing and Phrasing

1. Breathe in as you would for inhalation during casual conversation, then count at the rate of two numbers per second, pausing, and if necessary inhaling, at the marked places.

1-2-3-4-5-6-7-8-9-10-11 || 12-13-14-15-16-17-18-19-20-21

The first grouping should have been produced easily on a single breath; the second would be somewhat more difficult because of the additional syllables.

2. Repeat as above, but this time pause and renew your breath supply after fourteen; then count from fifteen through twenty-one.

3. Count as long as you can on a single deep breath, but avoid becoming uncomfortable either because of too deep an inhalation or too exhaustive an exhalation. Note the point at which you pause for breath. Then count again, but this time intentionally pause and inhale two numbers earlier in the sequence than you had to pause the first time. Count again to the same number.

4. Recite the alphabet, pausing, and inhaling if necessary, only at the marked places. Be sure to pause if you do not need to inhale.

a-b-c-d-e-f-g-h || i-j-k-l-m-n-o-p-q || r-s-t-u-v-w-x-y-z

Were you able to go beyond the first group? With practice, the entire alphabet should be recited easily after a single, moderate inhalation.

5.   Read the following sentences aloud, pausing, and breathing if necessary, at the marked places. In addition to the initial breath, it should not be necessary to inhale more than once for each sentence.

  a.   Sheridan advised to believe that story false || that ought not to be true.

  b.   A classic is something that everybody wants to have read || and nobody wants to read.

  —SAMUEL CLEMENS, *The Disappearance of Literature*

  c.   The more things a man is ashamed of || the more respectable he is.

  —GEORGE BERNARD SHAW, *Man and Superman*

  d.   Fear cannot be without hope || nor hope without fear.

  —BENEDICT SPINOZA, *Ethics*

6.   In the following exercises, read the material aloud to determine where you need to stop for breath. Pause to indicate phrasing, but inhale only when you cannot go on comfortably to the next phrase on the remaining breath.

  a.   Lord Chesterfield recommended: "Never hold any one by the button or the hand in order to be heard out; for if people are unwilling to hear you, you had better hold your tongue than them."

  b.   "What a blessed thing it is," said Holmes, "that nature, when she invented, manufactured and patented her authors, contrived to make critics out of the chips that were left.

  c.   Oscar Wilde, who helped to make cynicism an English fashion, held that though education was an admirable thing it was well to remember from time to time that nothing that was worth knowing could really be taught. Perhaps what Wilde really meant was that what is worth knowing is what is left after the specifics we have been taught have been forgotten.

Avoiding Waste of Breath

If while executing the exercises earlier in the chapter the reader had difficulty in counting up to fifteen on a single breath, it may have been that too much breath was wasted in the vocal effort. The most likely cause of wasted breath is a failure to bring the vocal bands close enough together to prevent leakage of air during vocalized speech efforts. Whispered or semiwhispered speech is necessarily wasteful of breath because then the vocal bands are kept fully or partially open. This may be noted in an examination of Figure 3–1, which shows the positions of the voice bands in quiet breathing, whispering, and vocalized speaking. In order to overcome breathiness, it will help first to become aware of a speech effort which, by nature of the sounds employed, is necessarily breathy. The following sentences contain a number of voiceless fricative and plosive sounds which are normally and appropriately characterized by a breathy quality. Hold your palm turned inward, about six inches in front of your mouth, as you say:

1. The humid air made the day sultry and uncomfortable.
2. Peter and Paul enjoyed playing outside.
3. The gray mist settled over the city and rested for the night.
4. Sharon and Pam liked to window shop.

In contrast with the above sentences, those that follow contain only voiced sounds and few which have a plosive quality. Say the following, again holding your hand in front of your mouth to feel the difference in breathiness.

1. Dan will do all a man may do.
2. Will was never ill.
3. The boys ran around the bend.
4. None knew the old man.

The following sentences contain a few sounds which are normally breathy. Try to say them with as little waste of breath as possible. Shorten all *f*, *v*, *th*, *s*, *z*, and *sh* sounds to reduce the length of these fricative-breath consonants. With good breath control, each sentence should be said on a single inhalation.

1. The meaning of "no news is good news" is not always clear.
2. Sam and Lillian walked hand in hand along the lake.

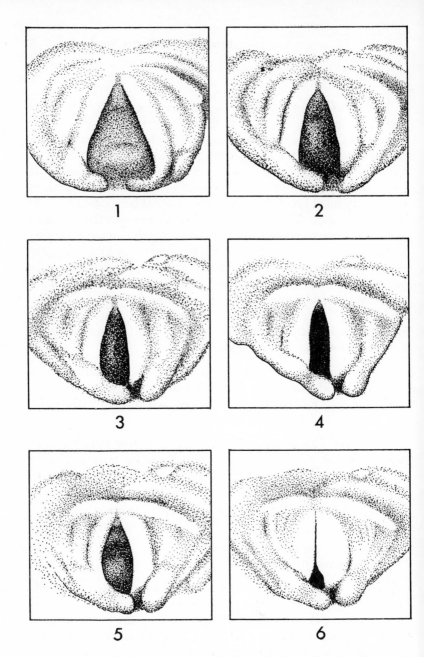

FIGURE 3–1. Diagrams based on high-speed photos showing changes in positions of vocal bands from quiet breathing (1, 2) to whispering (3, 4, 5) to vocalization (6).

3. The siren warned that a house was on fire.
4. The ship set out to sea despite the storm.
5. Goethe thought the man happy and wise who is able to appreciate the difference between his wishes and his powers.

Excessive breathiness may be a result of carrying over the aspirate quality of a sound to the succeeding vowel. This effect may be avoided, or reduced, by taking care not to prolong the aspirate sounds and to emphasize the full vocalization of the vowels and diphthongs. Special caution is necessary when the initial sound is an *h* as it is a particularly breath-consuming sound. With these thoughts in mind, try to say the following pairs of words so that there is no more aspiration on the vowel or diphthong of the second word of the pair than there is on the first. There should, of course, be no aspirate quality in the first word of each pair.

I	sigh	arm	farm
ale	pale	out	shout
oar	core	arc	park
air	fair	eel	wheel
ear	tear	old	hold
at	fat	end	send
am	ham	ark	shark
awe	saw	aid	shade

In each of the following sentences, emphasize the production of the vowel or diphthong sounds. Despite the temptation provided by initial aspirate sounds, avoid excessive carry-over of breathiness to the succeeding sounds.

1. Harry wished his friends health and happiness.
2. Hoping against hope is hoping still.
3. Paul hiked four miles through the forest.
4. People need not be poets to be impressed with the coming of spring.
5. George Eliot wrote that because a woman's hopes are woven of sunbeams, a shadow can quickly disperse them.
6. Goldsmith pointed out that people seldom improve when they simulate themselves.
7. Schlegel considers the historian to be a prophet who looks backwards.

8.   Cicero held that it is fortune, not wisdom, that controls man's life.

9.   Chesterfield wrote that style is the dress of thought.

10.   Ben Franklin observed that pride that dines on vanity sups on contempt.

Affected or Imitative Breathiness

Many persons vocalize with a breathy quality out of choice. The choice is not always a conscious one. Frequently it has its beginning in imitation born of admiration of a popular figure. Often the figure is a performer, a star of radio, screen, and television. So called "sultry-voiced" singers influence the vocal efforts of many high school and college adolescents who want to be sultry-voiced whether or not they can sing. Many young children have husky and breathy voices because of unconscious imitation of their mothers, and a few, perhaps, of their fathers. Unfortunately, excessive breathiness frequently has an adverse affect on the laryngeal mechanism as well as on the ability of the speaker to maintain as long a series of phrases or sentences as the nonbreathy speaker. The overall result is a vocal habit which loses its attractiveness in the postadolescent period. The breathy vocalizer then finds himself or more frequently, herself, a fatigued speaker, and occasionally one with thickened vocal bands. If this becomes the case, then considerable vocal reeducation is in order. Good voice production is achieved with good breath control. With such control, clear rather than breathy quality should be established throughout the normal pitch range. Clear tones are produced with a minimum use of air for a maximum vocal effort. Clear tones are economical of spent energy.

The following exercises are intended as a general review opportunity for the practice of breath control. In doing them, make certain (1) that there is no evidence of clavicular breathing; (2) that abdominal activity and lower chest activity characterize the breathing for vocalizations; (3) that inhalations are correlated with units of meaning; and (4) that there is no waste of breath at pauses for phrasing when there is no need for inhalation, or because of excessive aspiration on specific speech sounds, or as a characteristic of the vocal effort as a whole.

Exercises for Practice of Breath Control

1. But words are things, and a small drop of ink,
   Falling like dew upon a thought, produces
   That which makes thousands, perhaps millions, think.

   —LORD BYRON, *Don Juan*

2. Kings are not born; they are made by universal hallucination.

   —GEORGE BERNARD SHAW, *The Revolutionist's Handbook*

3. Laughter is not at all a bad beginning for a friendship, and it is far the best ending for one.

   —OSCAR WILDE, *The Picture of Dorian Gray*

4. A man's real life is that accorded to him in the thoughts of other men by reason of respect or natural love.

   —JOSEPH CONRAD, *Under Western Eyes*

5. Horace Mann considered that the telling of truth was a serious responsibility. He advised, "You need not tell all the truth, unless to those who have a right to know it all. But let all you tell be truth."

6. Were we deprived of the power to choose,
   We should in fact our very being lose;
   Machines we would be by the Almighty wrought,
   Curious automatons endowed with thought.

   —VOLTAIRE, *On Liberty*

CHAPTER 4

Production of Clear Tones

Voice, we now realize, is a product of integrated muscular activity. The combination of tendinous tissue and muscles which constitute the vocal bands is set into vibration as a result of integrated activity of the muscles of respiration and those controlling laryngeal action. When the integration is right and the approximated vocal bands are brought together closely enough so that there is sufficient resistance to the column of air being forced up from the lungs, voice is produced. When the vocal bands are not approximated so that there is adequate resistance to the column of air, then the result is either a semivocalized effort or unvocalized breathing, depending upon the degree of approximation (see Figure 3–1). Our immediate concern will be to establish the concept and technique for the initiation of good, clear tones.

Good tones are free from the effects of tension or strain. Good tones are initiated with ease, appropriately reinforced by the resonating cavities, and sustained with ease. Tonal (vocal) impurities result most frequently from tensions of the muscles of the throat and neck that interfere with the free action of the muscles of the larynx, and so of the vocal bands. Tonal impurities may arise indirectly from incorrect breathing habits which, we recall, may be associated with laryngeal tension. Tonal impurities may also be caused by inappropriate resonance.

In the absence of any structural defect of the voice-producing mechanism, a defect of hearing that makes vocal monitoring difficult, or any emotional disturbance associated with either excessive or inadequate muscular tonicity, reasonably good vocal tones should be possible for all speakers. Some speakers, we realize, will have mechanisms whose parts are so well combined that excellent voices are theirs without effort or training. Others may not be so fortunate in the structure of their vocal mechanisms. For them, effort and training are necessary to make the most of their vocal instruments. Our immediate concern will be to suggest how we can use what we have so that, without too much effort, most of us will be able to initiate and sustain good vocal tones.

INITIATION OF TONE

To initiate a good tone, the vocal mechanism must be *ready for vocalization*. Readiness implies anticipation and preparation. For voice production, this means that the vocal bands must be aligned (approximated) a moment before the column of air is forced up from the lungs to set them into action. If the column of air precedes the approximation of the vocal bands, then the vocal product will begin with a whisper or an unvocalized breath. The vocal bands must be tense enough to set up resistance to the column of air, but not so tense as to be fully successful in their resistance. With excessive tension (hypertension), the vocal bands may not be able to vibrate. With a lack of sufficient tension (hypotension), vibration may take place, but with an accompanying air leakage or breathiness.[1] What is needed is sufficient tension to require a forceful, sustained column of air to set and maintain the vocal bands in action. In brief, the tension should be just enough to permit the sustained column of air to produce an even fluttering of the vocal bands (see page 20). Although voice can be produced as the laryngeal tensions become excessive, the vocal tones become strained and generally unpleasant.

The exercises that follow will help to establish awareness of *proper laryngeal tension* as well as *readiness for vocalization*.

[1]Review the discussion on breathing for avoidance of breathiness (pages 53–56).

Exercises for Developing Readiness to Vocalize

1.   Contract the throat muscles as you would to swallow some food or water. Note the sensation of the contracted muscles. Now open your mouth as if to produce a gentle *ah* sound. Do your throat muscles feel more or less tense than they did when you pretended to swallow? Unless they are more relaxed than for swallowing, they are likely to be too tense for the initiation of a good tone. Note the sensation of the contracted muscles so that you will know what to avoid. Be sure that your *ah* production is gentle and sustained.

2.   *Yawn gently* with your mouth half open. Breathe in and out through your mouth. Note the feeling of air in the back of the throat. Now swallow, and contrast the easy breathing sensations with those in swallowing. If the yawning is gentle and the breathing easy, your throat muscles should be relaxed. This is the state of muscle tonus needed for vocalization.

3.   Sit comfortably in a chair with your feet flat on the floor. Permit your head to drop to your chest as if your head were a dead weight. Yawn gently and then breathe in and out three or four times through your mouth. Note the sensation. Now swallow, and again contrast the tonus of the throat muscles in swallowing with that in gentle yawning. Repeat the gentle yawning and easy mouth breathing until the sensation of relaxed throat muscles is fixed in your mind.

4.   Stand erect but at ease. Repeat exercise (3) in a standing position.

5.   In a standing position, with throat muscles relaxed, say the *vowels* only of the following words, each to a slow count of from one to three: *alms, all, Alps, ooze, eel.* Now vocalize from one vowel to the next without interruption. You should be able to note somewhat increased throat and laryngeal tension for the vowels of *ooze* and *eel* compared with those for *alms, all,* and *Alps.* This is proper if the different vowel values are to be produced. Try, however, to avoid excessive tension.

6.   Get ready to say *all* but do not produce any sound until your mouth is open and shaped for the vowel of *all.* Then produce the word. Now, by contrast, intentionally begin vocalizing *before your mouth is open* and you are set to articulate the word *all.* Did you hear or feel a difference? Unless your vocal habits are so good that you could not follow a direction to do the wrong thing, the first

effort should have been clearer and easier than the second. The second effort might have been characterized by initial tension and possibly by a "click" in the larynx.

7. Repeat the first half of exercise (1) with three to four successive utterances of the words *one, my, ah,* and *eel.* For each word, produce the successive utterance without intervening pauses. Check for initial tension or laryngeal click at the initiation of the effort. If your timing is right and you are prepared to vocalize before you set your vocal folds into vibration, the tone should be clear.

8. Open your mouth as though for a gentle yawn, but instead of yawning say *ha, how, ho, ha, haw, ho.* Next, try the sentence *Who am I?* These efforts should begin with some breathiness for the words which begin with an *h* sound, but the breath should not be noticeably carried over to the vowel which follows. Be sure that you maintain a relaxed throat throughout the exercise.

9. With a relaxed throat, count from one to ten, emphasizing activity of the lips and tongue. Try to become aware of oral activity in the *front of your mouth.* Now, count from one to twenty. Do not force your exhalation beyond a point of comfort. If you note any tendency to tighten the throat muscles, it may be because you are attempting too much speech on a single exhalation. Pause to inhale before excessive tension sets in.

10. Say the alphabet while emphasizing activity in the front of the mouth. Do not attempt to go beyond the letter *k* on your first attempt. On successive attempts go as far as you can in the alphabet up to the point of laryngeal or throat tension. You may note a feeling of lip fatigue. If so, it is likely that you do not habitually articulate with sufficient activity at the front of the mouth. With practice, the feeling of fatigue should disappear.

11. Read the following materials aloud, always maintaining a relaxed throat. Make certain that you are *set for vocalization* before you begin to speak. If at any time your throat muscles become tense, or you become aware of laryngeal tension, return to exercises (1)–(8).

    a. Each of us has to find his own way.

    b. For the author Carlyle, laughter was the cipher key wherewith we can decipher the whole man.

    c. Ed's weariness was seldom caused by overwork.

d. The snow fell softly in the quiet air.

e. Andrew was unfortunately not inclined to let facts get
    in the way of his opinions.

f.   But what am I?
    An infant crying in the night:
    An infant crying for the light:
    And with no language but a cry.

                           —ALFRED, LORD TENNYSON, *In Memoriam*

g. Although I enter not,
    Yet round about the spot
        Oftimes I hover:
    And near the sacred gate,
    With longing eyes I wait,
        Expectant of her.

                  —WILLIAM MAKEPEACE THACKERAY, *At the Church Gate*

h. I have had playmates, I have had companions,
    In my days of childhood, in my joyful schooldays,
    All, all are gone, the old familiar faces.

                        —CHARLES LAMB, *The Old Familiar Faces*

i. It is true, I never assisted the sun materially in his rising;
    but doubt not, it was of the last importance only to be
    present at it.

                           —HENRY DAVID THOREAU, *Walden*

AVOIDANCE OF THE "GLOTTAL ATTACK"

Several times in our discussion and in the exercises for the proper
initiation of clear tones, we referred to vocalization characterized by
a throat click. Vocalization produced with an overtense larynx is
frequently accompanied by a glottal (laryngeal) click, stop, or
shock.[2] The glottal shock frequently results from an attempt to
start vocalization when the larynx in general and the vocal bands in
particular are hypertense. The result of the hypertension is that
more than a normal amount of energy is needed for the breath column to set the vocal bands into sustained action to produce voice.

[2]The glottal click or stop is represented by the phonetic symbol [ʔ].

Unless the vocal bands are somewhat relaxed, vocal efforts are likely to be accompanied by an initial click or single, coughlike blast when the breath column succeeds in getting through between the vocal bands. Except when glottalization is an accepted characteristic of the speech of a national or cultural group—as it is among the Scots— voice accompanied by glottal clicks strongly suggests that the speaker's throat and larynx are hypertense and under strain. Added evidence of this condition is the presence of a high, narrow pitch range.

Glottal attacks are most likely to occur at the beginning of sentences or phrases with initial vowels. Some speakers, however, glottalize on almost all initial voiced sounds. The overall result tends to be detrimental to the speaker and unpleasant to listeners for whom glottalization is not an accepted speech characteristic.

For readers who are still uncertain about their tendency to initiate vocalization with a glottal attack, the following added explanation should illustrate what should generally be avoided. A glottal stop noise is normally and appropriately produced when you clear your throat with a light, unvocalized cough. You can feel this stroke, click, or flapping of the vocal bands by gently placing your thumb and index finger just below the Adam's apple as you cough. If voice is added to the light cough, the result is likely to be the production of an *ugh* sound.

The exercises to establish proper laryngeal tension, readiness for vocalization, and easy initiation of tones should be reviewed by readers who have a tendency to initiate voice with a glottal attack. In addition, the following exercises should be of help.

Exercises for Overcoming Glottal Attack

1. Produce the sound *aw* as in *awful* with intentional breathiness (semiwhisper). Repeat, prolonging the *aw* for the equivalent of a count of six. Decrease the breathiness so that on the final two counts the *aw* is fully vocalized. Maintain a relaxed throat so that there is neither glottal initiation nor tension as vocalization increases.

2. Repeat exercise (1), using the vowels of *alms, ooze, ohms, any* and *ease*. Be especially careful that on the last vowel there is no excessive strain or glottal "explosion."

3. Try to say each of the following words without initial glottalization. If you note a glottal attack, prefix a lengthened *h* before

each of the words, and move from the *h* to the word without increasing the laryngeal tension and without glottalization.

inch	arm	ohm	ale	eat	easy
instant	asp	own	at	am	east
only	all	ill	ace	and	aster

4. Repeat exercise (3), prefixing the sound *m* if there is any tendency to a glottal attack. Repeat with an initial *n*.

5. Try each of the following sentences, being especially careful to avoid glottalization on the initial vowels. Words which begin with vowels *within a phrase* should be pronounced as though they were actually linked or blended to the last sound of the preceding word. The sounds which are most likely to be glottalized are in italics.

   a. *A*ndrew *e*njoyed *a*ll *a*ctive sports.
   b. *E*very man must *a*t one time *i*nhabit his *o*wn *i*sland.
   c. *E*dward *e*njoyed cakes *a*nd *a*le.
   d. *A*n *o*hm *i*s *a u*nit *o*f *e*lectrical resistance.
   e. *I*t *i*s *e*asy to grow *a*sters *i*n the *e*ast.

6. The following phrases may be somewhat more difficult because they contain many normally tense vowels in initial positions and so provide opportunities for glottal initiation. If you initiate the vocalization with just enough tension for the proper articulation of the vowel, but with no more than that much tension, the glottal shock should be avoided.

easy access	apt and alert
up and over	apprehensive attitudes
every opportunity	insistent inclination
each event	esoteric antics
in every instance	anxious acts
any avenue	alien enemy

7. The following selections offer opportunity for additional practice.

   a. There is a feeling of Eternity in youth, which makes us amends for everything. To be young is to be as one of the Immortal Gods.

   —WILLIAM HAZLITT, *The Feeling of Eternity in Youth*

b. Inconsistencies of opinion, arising from changes of circumstances, are often justifiable.

—DANIEL WEBSTER, Speech, July 25, 1846

c. History is the essence of innumerable biographies.

—THOMAS CARLYLE, *On History*

d. I am in earnest. I will not equivocate; I will not excuse; I will not retreat a single inch; and I will be heard.

—WILLIAM LLOYD GARRISON, Speech, January 1831

e. A hen is only an egg's way of making another egg.

—SAMUEL BUTLER, *The Way of All Flesh*

The Glottal Stop As an Articulatory Fault

Although many persons initiate voice without a glottal attack, they may have a glottal quality in their speech because of an articulatory habit. The habit or fault is one of substituting a glottal grunt or click for a *t* or a *d* in words in which either of these sounds is followed by an *l* or an *n*. This sound substitution will be considered in somewhat greater detail in our discussion of specific sound improvement. For the present, we suggest that the reader test himself on the list of words and the verse that follow. If he can feel or hear himself produce a glottal explosive for the *t* or *d* on more than one or two of the words, he should make a special effort to articulate a clear but light and not exaggerated *t* or *d* to avoid giving his speech an overall glottal quality.

bottle	fettle	button	ladle
kettle	rattle	mutton	paddle
settle	written	patent	saddle
metal	bitten	mountain	hidden
little	subtle	kitten	nettle

Tender-handed stroke a nettle,
    And it stings you for your pains:
Grasp it like a man of mettle,
    And it soft as silk remains.

—AARON HILL, *Verses Written on a Window in Scotland*

CHAPTER 5

Making Yourself Heard

Adequate loudness, we pointed out earlier, is an essential attribute of an effective voice. For most of us, adequate loudness usually means being easily heard in conversation. Sometimes it means competing with surrounding noises, both human and mechanical. Occasionally, however, we must speak to a group in a physical setting that demands louder than normal conversational voice. Sometimes we must speak under conditions that demand more loudness than is ordinarily needed: we may have to yell a warning, issue a command, or address a group indoors or outdoors without the assistance of an electronic amplifier.

CONTROL OF LOUDNESS

Loudness is best regulated through breathing control. One of the ways to speak loudly is to increase the energy with which the breath stream vibrates the vocal bands. The greater the amplitude, or the more extensive the swing of the vocal bands, the louder the vocal tone. In addition, loudness is also related to the way our resonating cavities reinforce our vocal tones. It usually requires less energy than we think to vocalize loudly enough to be readily heard.

67

If we recognize that the vocal attribute we think of as loudness is a result of the amplitude or swing of the vocal bands *and* the amount of reinforcement afforded the initiated tone by the resonating cavities acting as reinforcers, we will not overstress the force or energy it takes to speak as loudly as the occasion requires. The danger in using added energetic action to produce loud tones is that a strain of the pharyngeal and laryngeal walls is likely to result. The effect of such strain is to reduce the efficiency of the cavities of the pharynx and larynx as reinforcing cavities. Because of this the vocal tones are less loud than they might otherwise be. In carrying out the suggestions for increasing loudness, the reader should avoid increasing tensions of the larynx or throat. In addition to the physical feeling of strain, listen for elevation of pitch. If the vocal tones are higher in pitch than normal for you, the likelihood is that the muscles (walls) of your resonating cavities are excessively strained.

To understand the change in action of the abdominal wall for loud vocalization, place your hands on the abdomen and shout aloud "All out!" You will (or should be able to) note that there is a sudden pulling in of the abdominal muscles and that the pulling in is greater than for normal conversation. If this does not occur, and you are not readily able to speak as loudly as you would like to and should reasonably expect to, then the following exercises should be of help in establishing adequate loudness.

Exercises for Developing Adequate Loudness

1. Review the exercises for proper breath control (see pages 44–56). This should create awareness of abdominal action established for conversational voice needs.

2. Place your hands on the abdomen and say *ah* as you might for a throat examination. Then take a moderately deep but comfortable breath and again begin to say *ah*. This time apply pressure suddenly with your hands. The tone should increase in loudness. If you have not caught yourself by surprise, and exhaled without vocalization, the *ah* should have become appreciably louder. Whether or not you have caught yourself by surprise, repeat the exercise and produce a loud *ah*.

3. Repeat exercise (2), producing three loud *ah*'s without straining. Breathe in if necessary after each *ah*. Loud voice production

requires more breath than normal conversation, so that more frequent inhalation becomes necessary to maintain a loud voice without strain. Try again, this time with *aw*.

4. Repeat, except this time exert direct control over the abdominal muscles as you produce your loud *ah*'s and *aw*'s.

5. Say the following short commands, each on a single breath, without strain and without an increase in pitch level toward the end of the phrase.

    a. Let's go!
    b. Time out!
    c. You go!
    d. Stop him!
    e. Look lively!
    f. Give him a hand.
    g. Lower away!
    h. Let him go!
    i. Turn around.
    j. Silence, please!

6. Try the following sentences on a single breath if possible. Speak as if there were a need to use a loud voice to assert yourself.

    a. This will never do.
    b. Let's waste no more time.
    c. Certainly, I meant what I said.
    d. Old fellow, just pack up and go.
    e. We'll talk about this matter later.

The following exercises are intended to help in the building up and control of degrees of loudness rather than in the sudden production of loud voice. Such practice is closer to the normal use of loudness for emphasis and vocal variety in speaking.

Exercises for Controlling Loudness

1. Initiate an *ah* in a tone which is barely audible; gradually increase the loudness of the *ah* until it is louder than your usually conversational voice, and then reduce the loudness until the tone is again barely audible. Do not change the pitch or force the length of exhalation beyond a point of comfort.

2. Count from one to five increasing the loudness on each num-

ber. Begin with a barely audible *one* and end with a *five* which can easily be heard across a forty-foot room.

3. Count to seven, increasing the loudness up to four and then decreasing loudness from five through seven. Maintain the same pitch level throughout the count.

4. Say each of the following phrases or sentences three times, increasing loudness from a normal conversational level to one which can easily be heard across a forty-foot room.

  a. I'll go!
  b. Come back!
  c. Please!
  d. No!
  e. I won't!
  f. Enough!
  g. Who's there?

5. Lengthen the vowel in each of the following words and maintain uniform loudness throughout the lengthened production of the vowel. Do not, however, distort the vowel by excessive lengthening.

alms	gnaw
bomb	thaw
father	walk
pause	tall
awe	mall

6. Lengthen and maintain the force for the vowels or diphthongs of the stressed syllables in the following phrases. Again, avoid distorting the vowel or diphthong to a point where a listener would not be certain of the words you are saying.

loud laughter	hearty applause
come on time	honest and true
almost always	large house
bounce the ball	ardent author
worthy cause	gone yonder

7. Read each of the following sentences, first in an ordinary conversational tone and then as if you were trying to address a person in the tenth row of a crowded room.

  a. Is that you, Tom?
  b. I'll go in a few minutes.

c. The time is now.
d. I'll say this for the last time.
e. Listen if you wish to understand.
f. Are you John Jones?

Strengthening the Voice

Up to this point our discussion of loudness has been based on the assumption that the speaker could make himself heard under normal conditions but might be in need of help to make himself readily heard under difficult conditions. Occasionally, however, we find persons whose habitual loudness levels are too weak for easy hearing even under relatively good speaking conditions. Such speakers need help to be heard even in quiet conversation.

In some instances, the cause of a weak voice is physical and may be attributed to a structural disturbance or anomaly of the vocal mechanism. Such instances are comparatively rare and require specialized treatment rather than self-help to improve the voice as much as possible. Sometimes a weak voice is a carry-over from a physical state during sickness or the subsequent period of convalescence. A sick person may not have the energy to make himself heard, and in the early stages of recovery he may not care whether or not he can be heard. When the patient is finally well enough to care, he may somehow decide that perhaps making others strain to hear him is not without advantage. So a habit of weak vocalization may persist. There is also a possibility that as a child the speaker was brought up in a home with an ill relative, or a crotchety one who believed that children should be seen, if necessary, but were not ordinarily worthy of being heard. The barely audible voice may then have become the safer one, the one that did not bring isolation or a scolding.

Occasionally, the weak or barely audible voice characterizes the individual who feels that what he has to say is unworthy of a listener or that as a speaker he lacks value. His weak sounds may be interpreted as apologetic noises or noises that are produced because he feels a social need to say something but at the same time fears that if he is heard he may be held responsible for what he says.

Such physical and mental conditions, however, are not the usual causes of weak voice. Much more frequently, a weak voice is the result of poor vocal habits such as poor breath control, habitual breathiness, excessive tension of the vocal mechanism, inappropriate pitch, or improper use of the resonating cavities to reinforce vocal tones. If the reader has no reason to believe that there is anything physically wrong with his vocal apparatus, if he is not longing for the advantages and immunities of the sickbed or the attentions associated with his convalescence, if he is a reasonably well-adjusted person, audible voice should be his for the trying.

The earlier discussion on how to control loudness through breath control obviously holds for the person with a weak voice. In addition, the following exercises should be of help.

Exercises for Strengthening a Weak Voice

1. Drop your jaw for a gentle but open-mouthed yawn. Inhale with your mouth open, and then pull in slowly but firmly on the abdominal muscles. Now permit a yawn to escape as you exhale as a "by-product" of the position of mouth and the controlled breathing.

2. Repeat exercise (1) five times, making the yawn louder each time but maintaining the same pitch.

3. Now, instead of yawning, prepare to say *aw* as in *awful*. Maintain an even pitch. Repeat five times.

4. Repeat exercise (3), but this time with the sound *oh*.

5. Say *oh* as follows: (a) as if surprised, (b) as if horrified, (c) as if pleased, and (d) as if you are shouting a warning.

6. Pretend you are imitating a siren on a fire truck, increasing and decreasing the loudness of your voice on the sound *oh*. Repeat, using the sound *aw*. Avoid any feeling of tension of the throat or larynx, and do not extend the length of vocalization to a point of discomfort.

7. Imagine yourself a drill sergeant and give your platoon the following orders.

    a. Forward, *march!*
    b. Platoon, *halt!*
    c. About *face!*
    d. At *ease!*
    e. To the rear, *march!*
    f. Fall *out!*

8. Count from one through five, increasing the loudness on each count but maintaining the same pitch level. Repeat three times.

9.   Practice each of the following in a voice loud enough to be readily heard across the length of your living room.

a.   Blow, blow, thou winter wind,
Thou art not so unkind
   As man's ingratitude:
Thy tooth is not so keen,
Because thou art not seen,
   Although thy breath is rude.

—WILLIAM SHAKESPEARE, *As You Like It*

b.   Out of the night that covers me,
   Black as the Pit from pole to pole,
I thank whatever gods may be
   For my unconquerable soul.

—WILLIAM E. HENLEY, *Invictus*

c.   Give me your tired, your poor,
Your huddled masses yearning to breathe free,
The wretched refuse of your teeming shore,
Send these, the homeless, tempest-tossed, to me:
I lift my lamp beside the golden door.

—EMMA LAZARUS, *The New Colossus*

d.   Give a man a horse he can ride,
   Give a man a boat he can sail;
And his rank and wealth, his strength and health
   On sea nor shore shall fail.

—JAMES THOMSON, *Gifts*

e.   And we are here as on a darkling plain
Swept with confused alarms of struggle and flight,
   Where ignorant armies clash by night.

—MATTHEW ARNOLD, *Dover Beach*

f.   Roll on, thou deep and dark blue Ocean—roll!
Ten thousand fleets sweep over thee in vain;
Man marks the earth with ruin—his control
Stops with the shore;

—LORD BYRON, *Childe Harold's Pilgrimage*

g.   If a word
Our orators let fall, save what pertains

To peace, I'll raise a storm of words, and rain
A very tempest of abuse upon them!

—ARISTOPHANES, *The Acharnians*

h. Let the great world spin forever down the ringing
grooves of change.

—ALFRED, LORD TENNYSON, *Locksley Hall*

i. He flung himself from the room, flung himself upon his
horse and rode madly off in all directions.

—STEPHEN LEACOCK, *Gertrude the Governess*

j. Shrill and high, newsboys cry
The worst of the city's infamy

—WILLIAM VAUGHN MOODY, *In New York*

k. Lay on, Macduff
And damn'd be him, that first cries,
"Hold, enough!"

—WILLIAM SHAKESPEARE, *Macbeth*

l. Pour the sweet milk of concord into hell,
Uproar the universal peace, confound
All unity on earth.

—WILLIAM SHAKESPEARE, *Macbeth*

m. "My name is Ozymandias, King of Kings.
Look on my works, ye Mighty, and despair!"

—PERCY BYSSHE SHELLEY, *Ozymandias*

n. The cataract strong
Then plunges along,
Striking and raging
As if a war waging
Its caverns and rocks among—

—ROBERT SOUTHEY, *The Cataract of Lodore*

10. If you have no difficulty making yourself heard across your
living room, try the same selections again but this time pretend that
your room is forty feet long and as many feet wide. If you are successful in this exercise, then repeat the selections as if you were
addressing an audience from the stage of moderate-sized theater.

11. Read the following as if your were addressing four hundred
persons waiting for your announcements in an auditorium that has
no public address system.

a. The meeting is adjourned. Return in two hours.
b. Tomorrow's meeting will begin at 9 A.M.
c. Refreshments will be served in the recreation hall.
d. John Smith is the winner.
e. There will be no school tomorrow.
f. Please leave by the nearest exit.

FORCE

In our earlier discussion of loudness and force, our emphasis was on producing voice so that it is audible in varying speaking situations. At this time we shall assume that the speaker has no problem in making himself heard and is controlling the loudness of his voice so that it is adequate to meet the needs of a small conversational group or of a larger formal audience. The speaker is now concerned with the use of loudness or force to give color and meaning to what he wishes to say.

Syllable Stress

Differential syllable stress is a feature of English speech. We use differential stress or accent in the pronunciation of polysyllabic words so that "normally" a word such as *rainy* or *beautiful* would be uttered with primary stress or accent on the first syllable. In the word *beautiful* a secondary stress may be heard on the final syllable. In a word such as *unkind,* the "normal" syllable stress is on the second syllable. In some contexts, however, a speaker may intentionally stress the first syllable of the word *unkind* to communicate his meaning; for example, "Yes, he certainly is an *un*kind man." Syllable stress for polysyllabic words is characterized by increased force or loudness associated with relatively longer duration and higher pitch than for the unstressed syllables of the words.

There are some words which differ in parts of speech, and so in meaning, according to their syllable stress. What are the differences in meaning for the following words when the accent or syllable stress is shifted from the first to the second syllable?

*con*duct	con*duct*
*con*vict	con*vict*
*di*gest	di*gest*

*dis*charge   dis*charge*
*ex*tract   ex*tract*
*fre*quent   fre*quent*
*ob*ject   ob*ject*
*per*mit   per*mit*
*re*bel   re*bel*
*sur*vey   sur*vey*

Stress in Compound Words

In general, compound words[1] differ from polysyllabic words in stress. For compounds, the stress is "normally" equal or almost so for each of the components. Compounds are similarly distinguished in stress from the components of the compound by relatively equal stress for the two parts of the former. Thus we may distinguish the meaning of "Jack is in the white house" from "Jack is in the White-house," or "After a half hour of fishing, I hauled in a weak fish" from "After a half hour of fishing, I hauled in a weakfish."

Indicate the differences in meaning for the following compounds and the paired words by incorporating them into sentences—e.g., "Joe made the doorstop" and "Joe made the door stop." Besides differences in stress, what other vocal feature do you detect in the utterances of the compound words as distinguished from the sequence of words that comprise the compound?

birthday	birth day
blowout	blow out
bluebell	blue bell
breakthrough	break through
campground	camp ground
greenhouse	green house
hideout	hide out
Irishman	Irish man
lightmeter	light meter

[1]Although many compound words suggest a single concept formed by the "wedding" of the two component words of the compound so that a distinction may be made between a *blackfish* and a *black fish*, this semantic feature is by no means consistent. For reasons other than semantic, some unfortunate persons may have *kidney stones* while others have *gallstones*.

L. B. Solomon's "The Game of Words," *Harpers* (November, 1961), pp. 40–42, is an informative and entertaining article on the subject of compound words.

middleman   middle man
paperback   paper back
sometime   some time

Variety

Except for public speaking situations in which the speaker does not have the help of mechanical amplification, large differences in force are rarely necessary. Change in the use of force rather than amount of force is the factor of variety which permits the speaker to give import to one idea and to subordinate other related ideas. Sometimes a desired effect in giving special meaning is better achieved when the significant words are spoken with reduced rather than increased loudness. Such would be the case for the sentence, "Please, my love, *be still.*" If the words *be still* are spoken so that they are barely audible, they are given more complete meaning than might otherwise be possible.

Change in force may be used to achieve dramatic as well as subtle, intellectual effects. A deliberate, degree-by-degree increase in force from a low to a high level helps to produce a dramatic effect. So also may a reduction in force from a moderately high to a low level. It may be both dramatic and sophisticated if the content is worthy of the technique.

Exercises for Change in Force

1. Read the following sentences, changing the stress from the first word of the sentence to each succeeding word. Do not, however, stress articles, conjunctions, or prepositions. How do the meanings of the sentences change with the differences in word stress?

    a. John and I will go.
    b. Ted was poor but honest.
    c. One or the other must leave.
    d. Mary is fond of Bill.
    e. Is he the man you like?
    f. What is your answer?
    g. This is your reward.
    h. Joe is indeed a brilliant fellow.
    i. We thought he had returned.

j. He is not long for this world.
k. Thursday was the day of reckoning.
l. She alone can do anything.
m. Fred was almost run down.

2. Read sentences (*a*), (*b*), and (*c*) of exercise (1) stressing the conjunction. What are the changes in meaning?

3. Use controlled and moderate stress to bring out the flavor and meaning of the wit and wisdom of the following items from Benjamin Franklin's *Poor Richard's Almanac.*

a. The worst wheel of the cart makes the most noise.

b. Genius without education is like silver in the mine.

c. He that would live in peace and at ease, must not speak all he knows, nor judge all he sees.

d. A man in a passion rides a mad horse.

e. None but the well-bred man knows how to confess a fault, or acknowledge himself in an error.

f. Seven wealthy towns contend for Homer dead,
Thro' which the living Homer beg'd his bread.

4. The same approach—the use of controlled and moderate stress —should be used in bringing out the essential meanings of the following passages.

a. What I must do is all that concerns me, not what the people think. This rule, equally arduous in actual and intellectual life, may serve for the whole distinction between greatness and meanness. It is the harder because you will always find those who think they know what is your duty better than you know it. It is easy in the world to live after the world's opinion; it is easy in solitude to live after our own; but the great man is he who in the midst of the crowd keeps with perfect sweetness the independence of solitude.

—RALPH WALDO EMERSON, *Self-reliance*

b. A foolish consistency is the hobgoblin of little minds, adored by little statesmen and philosophers and divines. With consistency a great soul has simply nothing to do.

He may as well concern himself with his shadow on the wall. Speak what you think now in hard words and to-morrow speak what tomorrow thinks in hard words again, though it contradict everything you said today—"Ah, so you shall be sure to be misunderstood."—Is it so bad, then, to be misunderstood? Pythagoras was misunder-stood, and Socrates, and Jesus, and Luther, and Coper-nicus, and Galileo, and Newton, and every pure and wise spirit that ever took flesh. To be great is to be mis-understood . . .

—RALPH WALDO EMERSON, *Essays*

5. Use more marked changes in force to communicate the mean-ings of the following passages.

a. Four freedoms: The first is freedom of speech and expres-sion—everywhere in the world. The second is freedom of every person to worship God in his own way—everywhere in the world. The third is freedom from want . . . every-where in the world. The fourth is freedom from fear . . . anywhere in the world.

—FRANKLIN D. ROOSEVELT, Message to Congress, January 1941

b. Death and sorrow will be the companions of our journey; hardship our garment; constancy and valor our only shield. We must be united, we must be undaunted, we must be inflexible.

—WINSTON CHURCHILL, Report on the War Situation, October 1940

c. Today the guns are silent. A great tragedy has ended. A great victory has been won. The skies no longer rain death—the seas bear only commerce—men everywhere walk upright in the sunlight. The entire world is quietly at peace. The holy mission has been completed, and in reporting this to you, the people, I speak for the thousands of silent lips, forever stilled among the jungles and the beaches and in the deep waters of the Pacific which marked the way. I speak for the unnamed millions home-ward bound to take up the challenge of that future which they did so much to salvage from the brink of dis-aster. . . .

We have known the bitterness of defeat and the exultation of triumph, and from both we have learned there can be no turning back. We must go forward to preserve in peace what we won in war.

—DOUGLAS MACARTHUR, *The Surrender of Japan,* September 2, 1945

d. John Milton asked, "What is strength without a double share of wisdom? Vast, unwieldy, burdensome, proudly secure, yet liable to fall by weakest subtleties; strength's not made to rule, but to subserve, where wisdom bears command."

e. Read the following stanza with increased but controlled force up to the next to the last line; try reading the last line with a marked reduction in force to achieve dramatic contrast.

O masters, lords and rulers in all lands,
How will the future reckon with this man?
How answer his brute question in that hour
When whirlwinds of rebellion shake the world?
How will it be with kingdoms and with kings—
With those who shaped him to the thing he is—
When this dumb terror shall reply to god,
After the silence of the centuries?

—EDWIN MARKHAM, *The Man with the Hoe*

CHAPTER 6

Reinforcement of Tone Through Resonance

The material and exercises in the preceding chapter stress the well-controlled and, when necessary, energetic use of breath for the purpose of making ourselves readily heard when more than conversational loudness is required. As we recall (see pages 25–31), the loudness of our voice is also determined by resonating cavity reinforcement. Because of this effortless and energy-conserving physical phenomenon, most of us are able to speak at length, even under less than optimum conditions, without experiencing fatigue. With the mechanical assistance of microphones and electronic amplifiers, we seldom need to speak at more than conversational level. But even conversational voice level would be difficult for all of us to maintain, as it is for some of us, without resonating cavity reinforcement.

The chief resonators, we recall, are the cavities of larynx, pharynx (throat), mouth, and nose.[1] If these cavities are not temporarily irritated or inflamed by a respiratory ailment or obstructed by organic growth such as enlarged tonsils or adenoids, good reinforcement of tone should be possible. Muscular tension may also impair

[1]This is a good point to review our earlier discussion of the resonating cavities (see page 21 ff.).

tone, but unless such tension is chronic or regularly associated with some speech efforts, the effect of tension is likely to be transitory.

IMPROVEMENT OF RESONANCE

The manner in which the combination of our resonators reinforces our vocal tones produces that attribute of speech by which the quality or timbre of our voices is identified. Unless we make a conscious attempt to disguise our voice, and frequently despite such an attempt, we are revealed by our vocal tones. Some of us are fortunate and have voices that are naturally pleasant to hear. A few of us, by misuse, do harm to our vocal apparatus. A very few may not have been generously endowed by nature and have mechanisms that at best are only fair. In this small number may be persons whose combination of laryngeal, pharyngeal, oral, and nasal cavities do not adequately reinforce the basic tones to produce acceptable vocal qualities. Fortunately, most of us, including the members of the last group, can learn to treat our mechanisms with respect. By doing so we can make the most effective use of what we have. The discussion that follows should be helpful.

In our earlier discussion of the initiation of tones we considered the relationship of physical and emotional tension to voice production. Specific suggestions and exercises were presented to establish proper initial vocalization. Our present concern will be to create awareness of resonance as one of the objectives for voice improvement. As we continue our discussion of resonance, we must bear in mind that none of our resonating cavities acts independently of the others. Changes of the oral cavity are likely to affect the pharynx, and changes in the pharynx are likely to affect the oral cavity, larynx, and/or the nasal cavity. Despite this interdependence, specific modifications in one of the resonating cavities can result in vocal qualities which may be described by such terms as oral, guttural, and nasal.

Pharyngeal Resonance

Earlier we described the pharynx and its characteristics as a cavity resonator (see pages 29–30). We pointed out that this large resonating structure may enable the voice to sound full and rich if it is open and relaxed, or strident and metallic when the walls of the pharynx are tense. The implications of abnormal tissue growth or of infection relative to the damping of tone were also suggested. We shall now expand on this discussion.

Because the pharynx is a large resonator it is best suited to the reinforcement of our lower vocal tones. Normally, also, the relatively "soft" or relaxed tissue of the pharynx damps out the higher-pitched tones and reinforces the lower or fundamental vocal tones. If, therefore, the pharynx is relaxed and "open" the full potentialities of the pharynx are exercised for the reinforcement and coloring of the low vocal tones. If, however, as a result of tension or pathology the pharyngeal walls are tense, the potentialities of the pharynx as a resonator are not realized. The tense or "hardened" surface reinforces the higher pitches, or the vocal overtones.

If a physical pathological condition accounts for abnormal pharyngeal tension, then medical treatment is in order. If, however, the pharyngeal tension is a product of habit, or of temporary mental tension, or of the residual effects of mental tension that once influenced the behavior and control of the pharynx, then a change may take place as a result of our own efforts. We may accept as a basic truism that a throat that is constricted, that is associated with a sensation of tightness, will produce a tense and strident voice. An open, relaxed throat is more likely to produce a full, rich, and mellow voice.

Because of the relationship between the continuous and coupled oral and pharyngeal cavities, suggestions and exercises for optimal pharyngeal resonance will be presented following our discussion of oral resonance.

Oral Resonance

Oral resonance is likely to be improved if the speaker makes a conscious effort to emphasize lip and tongue activity while speaking. Such activity helps to accomplish the objective of the singing teacher who directs his student to "place his tones forward in the mouth." In our attempt to achieve oral resonance, however, we must not so exaggerate articulatory activity as to make it obvious to our listener-observer, and so make us self-conscious. Nor should we create a condition of excessive articulatory tension that will carry over to the muscles of the throat.

Optimum oral resonance can be obtained only when the back of the oral cavity is open and relaxed so that we are able to initiate and maintain vocalization with an open throat. The following exercises should be of help for this purpose.

Exercises for Oral and Pharyngeal Resonance

1. The optimal use of the pharynx as a resonator presupposes proper breath control and the avoidance of any tension that might result from forced breathing or vocalization with residual air. The first step, therefore, is a review of the exposition and the exercises for breathing for effective vocalization (see pages 43–56).

2. Establish a feeling of overall bodily relaxation, as follows: (a) Slowly clench your hands to make tight fists. Note the related tension in the arms as well as the fingers. Note also the associated tension of the jaw as your fingers are clenched into fists. (b) Relax slowly and gently until your fingers are extended. Do not, however, extend your fingers so that they become tense. Now note the associated relaxation of your arms and the muscles that control the jaw. Note also the easing of the muscles of the throat.

3. Breathe in gently and then exhale with a "soft" sigh. Note the relaxed feeling in your throat. If your throat is not relaxed, it is likely that either your inhalation or your exhalation was not sufficiently gentle. Try again until you achieve a gentle, sustained, vocalized sigh. Be certain also that your tongue lies almost completely flat at the bottom of the mouth, with a minimum of back of the tongue elevation.

4. Inhale deeply, but not to a point of discomfort, and then yawn as if you were sleepy. Open your mouth wide, but avoid any feeling of tension of the muscles of the face or jaw. Your throat should feel relaxed if the yawn was convincingly produced.

5. Optimum pharyngeal resonance is inconsistent with excessive back of the tongue tension. Were you aware of any inclination toward such tension in any of the preceding exercises? Recall that the mouth and throat are continuous, coupled resonating cavities. If the back of the tongue is buckled or humped, the result is a narrowing of the coupling passage. The effect is a narrowed resonator, constriction, and a loss of reinforcement of the low-pitched tones. So, produce a free, open, and sustained *ah*. Note the state and feeling of the back of the tongue. The back of the tongue

should be elevated slightly, but not enough to block the view of the pharynx. Use a mirror, preferably a hand mirror, so that you can see the position of the back of the tongue and the throat. Associate the tongue position and the feeling of an almost flattened tongue and an open, easy-to-view throat.

6. Drop your head to the chest, and vocalize an easy, sustained *aw*. Now roll your head gently and smoothly from shoulder to shoulder while sustaining the *aw*. Repeat with a long *ah*.

7. Begin as in exercise (5), but this time add an *m* to the *ah* so that the result is *ahm*. Repeat five times.

8. With an open throat and relaxed lower jaw, say each of the following three times. Say each slowly, and stop for a breath between vocalizations.

mah, bah, dah, nah, hah, pah, fah, thah, shah, yah

In the immediately succeeding exercises, it will not be possible to keep your throat as relaxed as for exercises (1)–(5). Make certain, however, that your throat and mouth muscles are as relaxed as they can be while producing the indicated sounds. The exercises will emphasize oral activity and articulation in the front of the mouth.

9. Observe your mouth in a mirror as you say the following words in pairs. Note the change in lip and jaw positions.

he	who	elf	off
it	hook	am	ought
ate	oat	alp	alm

10. Observe lip and tongue activity as you say each of the following:

temper tantrum	calm and balm
do or die	petty person
tense times	polished pewter
twice told tales	pretty polly
tip to toe	winsome wiles

11. Say the following, with proper regard for tongue and lip activity.

a. Tic, tac, toe, away we go.
b. Peter was fond of picking peppers.

   c.   Who are you and who am I?

   d.   Jeanie tiptoed up the hill.

   e.   The wind whistled a tune in the trees.

   f.   The silvery moon shed its light on the lake.

   g.   A wag once defined an American college as a football stadium with a few associated academic buildings.

   h.   Is basketball replacing baseball as the most popular American sport?

   i.   Poets are fond of picking on December as a dreary time of the year.

   j.   A university must be both a place and a state of mind for ideals and ideas and opportunities to put them into practice.

12.   The following selections should be read with emphasis on articulatory action in the front of the mouth.

   a.   Two barrels of tears do not heal a bruise.

                      —Chinese Proverb

   b.   In *The Magic Mountain* Thomas Mann observes: "Order and simplification are the first steps toward the mastery of a subject—the actual enemy is the unknown."

   c.   The grey-ey'd morn smiles on the frowning night,
        Chequ'ring the eastern clouds with streaks of light.

             —WILLIAM SHAKESPEARE, *Romeo and Juliet*

   d.   And, after all, what is a lie?
        'Tis but
      The truth in masquerade.

                  —LORD BYRON, *Don Juan*

   e.   Man passes away; his name perishes from record and recollection; his history is as a tale that is told, and his very monument becomes a ruin.

             —WASHINGTON IRVING, *The Sketch Book*

   f.   Admirers of cats insist that all kittens and cats, whether they be of low estate or of Royal Persian blood, resent, reject, and ignore human patronage.

   g.   I speak severely to my boy,
        I beat him when he sneezes,

For he can thoroughly enjoy
The pepper when he pleases.
—LEWIS CARROLL, *Alice's Adventures in Wonderland*

Nasal Resonance

We have already suggested that the importance of the nasal cavities for vocal reinforcement can be appreciated when we are suffering from a head cold. This condition not only deprives us of the ability to produce proper nasal sounds but generally and adversely affects all vocal efforts. We become especially aware of the need for nasal reinforcement when we try to produce the nasal sounds *n, m,* and *ng* [ŋ]. These nasal consonants are articulated orally, but they are reinforced in the nasal cavities and emitted through the nose. In order for the sound to enter the nasal cavities, the soft palate must be relaxed and lowered. Lowering the soft palate produces a large opening at the posterior entrance of the nasal cavities (the nares) and a narrow avenue through the nares for the sound to be resonated as it emerges from the nostrils. The characteristic differences in the three nasal consonants result from modification in the oral cavity. For the sound *m,* the entire cavity is used because the tongue lies comparatively flat at the floor of the mouth; for *n,* the tongue is raised so that a smaller part of the mouth is used; for the *ng,* only a narrow area at the back of the mouth behind the raised tongue is used as a supplemental reinforcer.

Although there are only three English sounds which are characteristically (predominantly) nasal, there is little doubt that, in connected speech, sounds in close proximity to the nasals are also partly reinforced nasally. It is virtually impossible to avoid some degree of nasality on the vowels of words such as *nine, mine,* and *ring.* How to avoid inappropriate and excessive nasalization of vowels will be considered later. At the present time we prefer to make a case for proper nasal reinforcement, rather than to create anxiety about excessive nasality as a defect of vocal production.

Appropriate nasal reinforcement provides both roundness and carrying power to the voice. It permits us to be heard with relatively little expenditure of energy. We can become aware of these effects by sustained, easy humming. To hum easily, make certain that the throat muscles, the tongue, and the soft palate are relaxed.

The jaws should be almost but not quite together. The lips should barely touch so that a slight tickling sensation is experienced when humming. An easy, properly produced hum should be felt as well as heard. You should be able to feel it not only on the lips but at the sides of the nostrils if your thumb and index finger are placed gently at these areas.

The fullness of tone and vibrating effects associated with proper nasal reinforcement can be appreciated by contrasting a phrase or sentence with many nasal sounds with another containing no nasals, such as the following:

1. Amanda enjoys candy. Tilly likes fish.
2. Mabel may marry. Bill will tarry.
3. Mary murmured in the moonlight. Ted was tight-lipped.
4. No moaning, my man. Please, stop the tears!
5. MacDonald was the canniest member of his clan. Teasdale was the brightest of all his relatives.

The following exercises should help to create awareness of nasal resonance as well as to afford an appreciation of the fullness of tone and carrying power which may be obtained with the careful production of nasal sounds. At first exaggerate the length of each nasal sound, but avoid any intentional increase of energy in vocalization. Also be certain that each exercise is performed with a relaxed throat and jaw. Sustain your tones evenly through controlled, gradual abdominal contraction on exhalation.

Exercises for Awareness and Improvement of Nasal Resonance

1. Hum up and down the musical scale. Then sing the musical scale with the conventional *do—re—mi.* . . . Compare the two vocal efforts. Request a friend to do the same while you listen to the vocal efforts. Which sounds fuller? Was humming easier than the conventional singing? If your humming was done with lips barely touching, the result should have been the production of a series of full or relatively full, easy-to-produce tones.
2. Occlude your nostrils and count from one through ten. Which numbers were not normally produced? Why?
3. Hum gently for the equivalent of a count of four on a sustained breath. Repeat five times.

4. Drop your jaw and bring the tip of the tongue in position for *n*. Produce *n* for the equivalent of a count of four. Repeat five times. Repeat with the sound *m*.

5. Blend a hum with the sound *ah* (*mah*). Make certain that the soft palate is raised for the *ah*. Repeat five times.

6. Blend a lengthened *n* with *ah*, then do the same for *n* and *aw*. Repeat each five times.

7. Blend a lengthened *m* with *ah* and follow by another *m* (*mahm*). Do the same for *m* and *aw* (*mawm*). Repeat each five times.

8. Repeat exercise (5) with *n* before and after the sounds *ah* and *aw* (*nahn* and *nawn*). Repeat each five times.

9. Exaggerate the length but *not the intensity* of the nasal sounds for the materials that follow:

a.
mountainous moon	ominous thunder
mineral mining	nine numbers
mindful of manners	no man's land
manna from heaven	noisome nomads
memorial monuments	normal nonsense
mundane happenings	winsome maiden

b. —Many Canadians speak both English and French.

—In the Northern Hemisphere, November is an autumn month.

—Mason was known for his mathematical acumen.

—Norton was fond of mountain climbing.

—A monody is a poem or a song in which one person laments the demise of another.

—Amanda was fond of meandering through winding lanes.

—The Ming dynasty is considered by some historians to be the last one of true Chinese origin.

—Manganese is a chemical element employed in the making of steel to give it hardness and toughness.

—Melvin wanted to be known as a man about town.

—Nicaragua is a Central American nation.

c. Tranquility! thou better name
Than all the family of Fame.

—SAMUEL TAYLOR COLERIDGE, *Tranquility*

d. When, musing on companions gone,
We doubly feel ourselves alone.

—SIR WALTER SCOTT, *Marmion*

e. Voltaire maintained that doctors are men who prescribe medicine of which they know little, to cure diseases of which they know less, in human beings of whom they know nothing.

f. If the mountain won't come to Mohammed,
Mohammed must go to the mountain.

—English proverb

g. In a wonderland they lie,
Dreaming as the day goes by,
Dreaming as the summers die.

—LEWIS CARROLL, *Through the Looking Glass*

h. I bring fresh showers for the thirsting flowers,
    From the seas and the streams;
I bear light shade for the leaves when laid
    In their noonday dreams.
From my wings are shaken the dews that waken
    The sweet buds every one,
When rocked to rest on their mother's breast,
    As she dances about the sun.
I wield the flail of the lashing hail,
    And whiten the green plains under,
And then again I dissolve it in rain,
    And laugh as I pass in thunder.

—PERCY BYSSHE SHELLEY, *The Cloud*

i.   The end crowns all,
And that old common arbitrator, Time,
Will one day end it.

—WILLIAM SHAKESPEARE, *Troilus and Cressida*

j. A man so various, that he seem'd to be
Not one, but all mankind's epitome:
Stiff in opinions, always in the wrong,
Was everything by starts, and nothing long;

But, in the course of one revolving moon
Was chemist, fiddler, statesman, and buffoon.

—JOHN DRYDEN, *Absalom and Achitophel*

NASALITY

Our orientation in this book has been to emphasize the positive.
We preferred, for example, to explain how vocal tones could be
produced clearly, with adequate loudness and proper breath control, rather than to discuss how to overcome hoarseness, breathiness,
or any other vocal inadequacy or defect. This was also our approach
in considering resonance and the reinforcement of tone by the nasal
cavities. As a precautionary measure, however, we believe it ad-
visable at this point to discuss separately the prevalent fault of
excessive nasality. Fortunately, when we have learned either to avoid
or to overcome excessive nasality, we shall also have attained the
positive objective of establishing appropriate nasal reinforcement.

Causes of Excessive Nasality

The most common cause of excessive nasality is failure of the
soft palate to rise when necessary to block off the stream of breath
(sound) as it enters the oral pharynx. If the soft palate is elevated,
the sound is directed forward and emitted orally. A relaxed soft
palate permits the sound to enter the nasal cavities where it is reinforced to become qualitatively nasal.

If failure to elevate the soft palate has a physical basis, medical
attention is in order. If the failure is caused by a general indiffer-
ence to speech efforts, to listener reactions, and superficially at least
to the world in general, psychotherapy may be indicated. Excessive
nasality is frequently associated with articulatory sluggishness.
Often the jaw, lips, and tongue as well as the soft palate move
without precision and alertness. The overall result is speech that
sounds slovenly and voice that sounds tired, monotonous, and nasal.

For the most part, excessive nasality is a manner of speech that
has been learned unconsciously. Even if this manner of speaking
reflected at one time an attitude of thinking or of behavior, change
for the better can take place if the will to change is present.

The following exercises are based on the assumption that there is no organic basis for the excessive nasality and no psychological need for its persistence.

Exercises for Awareness of Palatal Action

1.   Stand before a mirror and yawn with a wide-open mouth. Note the upward movement of the soft palate and uvula while the yawn is maintained. Stop the yawn and relax. Repeat and note the feeling as well as the action of the elevated palate.

2.   Hum gently, then think but do not vocalize a lengthy *ah*. Be certain that your mouth is open and the tongue almost flat. Observe the action of the soft palate as it is elevated and maintained for the *ah*. Now, by way of contrast, permit the soft palate to relax and produce a nasalized *ah*. Again, raise the soft palate for an appropriately vocalized *nonnasal ah*. Capture the feeling of the elevated soft palate when the *ah* is properly vocalized and orally reinforced. Repeat for the vowels of *all* and *ooze*.

3.   Close your nostrils by pinching them. Say *ah*. Repeat with open nostrils. Whether the nostrils are pinched or free there should be no identifiable nasality for the sound. Repeat for the vowels of *whose, hull, home, haw, hog, harm*.

4.   Say *n* while noting (feeling) the action and position of a relaxed soft palate. Then say *ah* and again note the action and position of the elevated palate. Alternate between the two sounds until you have an immediate awareness of the difference in palatal position.

5.   Place a clean, cold hand mirror under your nostrils and produce a lengthy *ah*. If the soft palate is elevated, there should be no clouding of the mirror. Practice until there is no clouding, then repeat for all the vowels of exercise (3).

6.   Repeat exercise (5) with the vowels of *eel, if, ail, elf, at, ask*. Check with a mirror for nasalization. Be especially careful about the vowels of *elf* and *ask*.

7.   Pinch your nostrils closed as you say each of the following sentences. (If you note a feeling of stuffiness in your nose, or a feeling of pressure in your ears, then you are being excessively nasal. Lift your soft palate to block off the entrance of air to the nasal cavity.)

a. The beagle chased the fox up the tree.
b. The boy walked the dog through the field.
c. The fog rested at the top of the hill.
d. What is it you wish to see?
e. Peter helped Pat pick the flowers.
f. For Shakespeare brevity was the soul of wit.
g. Paula preferred tea to coffee for supper.
h. Ted liked to tell droll stories.
i. All causes have effects; all effects have causes.

8. Say the following pairs of words with your attention focused on the avoidance of nasality in the second member of each pair. Make certain that your palate is elevated immediately after the nasal consonant is produced in the first member of each pair and through the production of the second member. It may also help to lessen any tendency toward nasality if you exaggerate the articulatory activity of the lips and the front part of the tongue.

me	be	new	do	nest	lest
knit	lit	nook	book	knife	life
nail	dale	note	dote	meat	beat
met	wet	nought	bought	more	bore
mat	bat	not	dot	may	bay
mask	bask	man	ban	my	bye
need	bead	mare	bare	mean	bean
mud	bud	near	dear	male	bale
mile	bile	maze	daze	mike	bike
nice	dice	new	due	mob	bob

Associated or Assimilated Nasality

Earlier we learned that there are three sounds in American and English speech that appropriately require nasal reinforcement for their production. These sounds are m, n, and ng [ŋ]. In connected speech, unless there is almost anxious care to avoid the effect, sounds in close proximity to nasal consonants are likely to be slightly nasalized. The nasalization is a "contamination by association" resulting from the manner of the articulation of the nasal sounds. Specifically, one of the following may happen.

1. The lowered soft palate may not be raised in time to prevent the following sound from being somewhat nasalized. Delay in raising the soft palate after the production of a nasal consonant probably accounts for the nasalization of the vowels that succeed the nasals in words such as *my, may, mate, new,* and *note.*

2. The soft palate may be lowered while the sound preceding the nasal is articulated as in words such as *aim, and, whom, only, sing,* and *young.* Here the nasalization is in anticipation of required articulatory movement (the lowering of the soft palate for appropriate reinforcement of a succeeding nasal sound).

3. The soft palate may not be sufficiently elevated because of the influence of preceding as well as succeeding nasal consonants as in *name, man, among, number, singing, ringing,* and *longing.*

There is no reasonable objection to some traces of nasalization resulting from the assimilative influence of nasal consonants. *What needs to be avoided is an overall effect of dominant nasality* merely because some nasal sounds are present.

The exercises recommended earlier for gaining awareness and control of the soft palate are, of course, applicable for overcoming the effects of excessive nasalization resulting from the influence of nasal consonants. Here also emphasis on front of the mouth (tongue and lip) activity is important. The following additional exercises should also be helpful.

Exercises for Avoidance or Reduction of Assimilative Nasality

1. When the nasal consonant precedes the vowel, lengthen the nasal consonant. Lengthening the consonant will afford you the extra moment of time needed to elevate the soft palate. This should reduce the "contaminating" assimilative effect of associated nasality and permit you to give appropriate reinforcement to the nasal sound in the given context.

    a. Practice on the following sound combinations. At the outset, exaggerate the length of the nasals to a marked degree. Then reduce the degree of exaggeration, but maintain the actual duration of the nasal sound for a time you consider about twice as long as normal. Finally, reduce the length of the nasals so that they are of normal duration, or as close to normal as possible, without nasalizing the succeeding sounds.

m	ee	n	ee
m	oo	n	oo
m	ay	n	ay
m	ah	n	ah
m	aw	n	aw

b. Practice saying the following words, at first exaggerating the length of the nasal sounds. Then practice with the same words, this time with as little exaggeration as possible consistent with the avoidance of assimilated nasality.

meek	mock	need	nick
meal	mood	neat	noose
mill	mull	nill	nook
mell	mode	nail	note
mate	maul	never	nought
mat	mob	nack	not
mask	moth	nap	nock
mud	mirth	nut	nerve

c. Practice with the following phrases, being careful at first to lengthen the nasal sounds and to avoid excessive nasality on the sounds that follow. Go over the same phrases, this time lengthening the nasals only as much as necessary to avoid assimilated nasality.

a man of moods	not my meat
more and more	now or never
new to me	native of Norway
no news	many a moon
move the map	next-door neighbor

d. Practice with the following sentences, observing the same precautions as in the preceding exercise.

—Matt enjoyed his work as a mailman.

—Noah Webster believed that language as well as speech were immediate gifts of God.

—Ben Franklin observed that laws which are too gentle are seldom obeyed and those which are too severe are seldom enforced.

—Seneca advised that men learn best when they teach.

—In *Don Juan,* Byron remarked that the night shows stars and women in a better light.

—According to a Chinese proverb, it may be easier to rule and control a nation than a son.

2.   Emphasize oral activity for the sounds that precede the nasal consonants in the following exercises.

am	rant	lounge	turned
aim	town	lunch	joined
end	any	round	found
own	only	yearn	haunt
on	anger	hunger	penny

3.   Incorporate the words of the preceding exercise into short sentences such as the following:

a.   There is nothing without an end.
b.   Big Jim owned the town.
c.   Courage is not only for the strong.
d.   We joined the group in song.

4.   The following exercises emphasize combinations in which the nasal consonants both precede and follow vowels or diphthongs. They therefore provide an opportunity for careful control to avoid temptation and inclination to excessive assimilative nasality. Nasality of the nonnasal sounds can be minimized if you lengthen the first nasal consonant and emphasize oral activity for the succeeding vowel or diphthong. Your objective should be only as much lengthening of the nasals as is necessary to avoid assimilated nasality.

a.   Practice on words such as the following:

mine	noon	innumerable	murmuring
mean	nine	rumbling	Neanderthal
nimble	meander	underneath	known
main	numerous	crowning	mentor
meant	numb	ambition	mince
moan	mournful	grinding	minnow
moon	meaningful	reminding	muttering

b.   In sentence contexts, the tendency for assimilative nasality is increased. Practice careful enunciation of the following:

—Living language undergoes constant change.

—Martin, in common with most men, was more mindful of his own misfortunes than those of his next-door neighbor.

—The winter snows were followed by spring rains.

—If Benson had any inclination toward genius, it was in his ability to ignore any suggestion that he might resist temptation.

—Anthony was against any position initially taken by another. This inclination earned him the nickname of Contrary Tony.

—Samuel Johnson's famous *Dictionary* included a number of personalized definitions. One example is for the term *pension*, which Johnson defined as "An allowance made to anyone without an equivalent. In England it is generally understood to mean pay given to a state hireling for treason to his country."

—"And all the days of Methuselah were nine hundred sixty and nine years," says Genesis IV:27.

—"One precedent creates another. They soon accumulate and constitute law" is a principle in *The Letters of Junius*.

5. The following provide additional combinations in which the nasal consonants both precede and follow vowels or diphthongs.

    a. American football teams consist of eleven men.

    b. Dreams furnish opportunities for persons who are meek to become strong and to crown their unconscious ambitions and strivings with neither qualms nor anxieties about consequences.

    c. Mournful sounds are often made by nonmournful minstrels.

    d. According to a Persian maxim, a person endowed with a long tongue may have a shortened life.

    e. Morton's farm background did not prepare him for employment on Madison Avenue.

    f. Anne preferred a short plane trip to a long one by train.

    g. Man is a subject of thought, of scorn, of controversy, and of near divinity. Poets and thinkers through ancient times to the present have expressed their views. Here are some of them.

—Carlyle maintained that man was the miracle beyond all miracles, "the great inscrutable mystery of God."
—Mark Twain, not entirely in humor, once proclaimed: "There are times when one would like to hang the whole human race, and finish the farce."

6.   As a test of your ability to resist the temptation of assimilated nasality, use the materials of exercises (1), (2), and (4), intentionally exaggerating the overall nasality of your speech. Then, to demonstrate your control, go over the exercise materials without yielding to the temptation to commit assimilated nasality. By way of variety, try the same techniques for the following:

a.   The strongest is never strong enough to be always the master, unless he transforms strength into right, and obedience into duty.

—JEAN JACQUES ROUSSEAU, *The Social Contract*

b.   So long as a man imagines that he cannot do this or that, so long is he determined not to do it; and consequently, so long it is impossible to him that he should do it.

—BENEDICT SPINOZA, *Explanation*

c.   What man has assurance enough to pretend to know thoroughly the riddle of a woman's mind, and who could ever hope to fix her mutable nature?

—CERVANTES, *Don Quixote*

d.   There is no man so good, who, were he to submit all his thoughts and actions to the laws, would not deserve hanging ten times in his life.

—MONTAIGNE, *Of Vanity*

e.   Hereby, too, I shall indulge the inclination so natural in old men, to be talking of themselves and their own past actions; and I shall indulge it without being tiresome to others, who, through respect to age, might conceive themselves obliged to give me a hearing, since this may be read or not as any one pleases. And, lastly (I may as well confess it, since my denial of it will be believed by nobody), perhaps I shall a good deal gratify my own vanity.

Indeed, I scarce ever heard or saw the introductory words, "Without vanity I may say," etc., but some vain thing immediately followed.

—BENJAMIN FRANKLIN, *Autobiography*

f. No nightingale did ever chaunt
    More welcome notes to weary bands
    Of travelers in some shady haunt,
    Among Arabian sands.

—WILLIAM WORDSWORTH, *The Solitary Reaper*

7. Review the discussion and practice the exercises on nasal resonance (see pages 87–90).

CHAPTER 7

Pitch and Voice Improvement

In our discussion of the mechanism for voice production the point was made that vocal pitch should be related to properties inherent in the individual's mechanism. We are not free to choose a habitual pitch level or pitch range according to our attitudes, tastes, or whims or to change the pitch level and range according to mood or fashion. An essential task for a speaker who wants to be certain that he is making the best use of his vocal instrument is to determine the pitch level and range most appropriate for him. Fortunately, most speakers normally vocalize at pitch levels and within pitch ranges that are appropriate for them. Under abnormal conditions, with or without conscious awareness of the pitch level and range which we shall consider optimum, vocalization may suffer because control is lost. A teacher may vocalize quite well, except when annoyed by her pupils, at which time her pitch may rise beyond the range of easy vocalization. If the occasions for annoyance are frequent, so are the opportunities for inappropriate vocalization. A salesman may have no cause for thinking about his voice until he becomes anxiously concerned while talking to a sales prospect. On such occasions he may phonate within an elevated pitch range, with accompanying strain and excessive effort. The resultant effects may be both displeasing and potentially harmful to his laryngeal mechanism. A few persons, however, may habitually vocalize at pitches which are not natural or optimum, and so their voices are less effective, less pleasant, and frequently much less comfortable than they could be. Before discussing how to determine the optimum pitch level and the most suitable pitch range, we shall present a few working definitions.

Optimum or *natural pitch* is the level at which voice can be initiated with greatest ease and effectiveness. It is the pitch at which one can achieve the best quality and the necessary loudness with the least expenditure of energy. It is the pitch at which the individual's vocal mechanism functions with greatest efficiency. Because optimum pitch is related to the structure of the vocal apparatus, it is sometimes referred to as the *structural pitch*. Because optimum pitch would be the likely product of "doing what comes naturally" if there were no contrary internal or external physical, emotional, or cultural pressures, the term *natural pitch* is also used.

Habitual pitch is the level at which an individual most often initiates vocalization. *Habitual range* refers to the pitch levels most frequently employed in speaking. *Range* itself refers to the pitch levels which a speaker is capable of producing below and above his habitual pitch level. It is obviously desirable that the speaker's optimum pitch and optimum range be the ones habitually used. If this is not the case, then changes need to be made. The changes will be directed toward (1) becoming aware of optimum pitch and learning to produce this pitch level at will, (2) establishing this pitch as a habit, and (3) developing a pitch range with optimum pitch as the basic level.[1]

DETERMINATION OF OPTIMUM PITCH

For most speakers, optimum pitch is likely to be the level one fourth to one third above the lowest level within the entire pitch range. If, for example, the speaker has a twelve-level pitch range (musical tones and half-tones according to the scale), his optimum pitch would probably be the third or fourth level above his lowest. If his pitch range were wider and were to include fifteen levels, his

---

[1] G. Fairbanks, *Voice and Articulation Drillbook* (2nd ed.; New York: Harper & Row, 1960), p. 122, says: "It is proposed that each speaker has an individual level determined by such characteristics of his vocal mechanism as size, manipulability, etc., at which his voice is most efficient for speech; for this we shall use the term natural level."

optimum pitch would most likely be about level five. For a speaker with a twenty-one–level pitch range, optimum pitch would be about level six.

There are several approaches and techniques that may be used to arrive at optimum pitch. Ultimately, the best technique is the one which works successfully for the individual; it should not be limited by any voice or speech teacher's personal prejudices. We shall consider the techniques[2] we personally have found useful and easily demonstrable without any pretense of having a monopoly on all the workable ones. For most cases, the first of the techniques is usually sufficient to establish awareness of optimum pitch.

Techniques for Achieving Optimum Pitch

1. Relax the throat muscles. Take a moderately deep breath and vocalize an evenly sustained *ah* at whatever pitch comes out naturally. Do not think of the pitch until after you hear yourself produce it. Do not attempt to modify the tone once it has been initiated.

2. Relax, and vocalize, but this time intentionally do so at a level lower than in exercise (1).

3. Continue, going down the scale, until you have produced the lowest-pitched tone you are capable of vocalizing. It may help to think of a descending musical scale in going from your initial pitch level to your lowest. Do not strain for an abnormally low pitch. Stop at the level at which your voice becomes a low-pitched whisper.

4. Return to the initial pitch you produced in step (1). Now produce tones on an upward scale until you reach the highest-pitched falsetto. If you started vocalization at your natural pitch, you should be able to go up in pitch above twice the number of tones you were able to descend below your initial level. If this is the situation, then you are probably initiating vocalization at or very close to your optimum or natural pitch.

An alternate technique for determining optimum pitch is through the matching of vocal and piano tones throughout the pitch range including the first low and first high falsetto tones.

1. Sing or chant from your lowest to your highest tone, matching

[2]Other approaches for arriving at *optimum pitch* are presented by G. Fairbanks, *Voice and Articulation Drillbook* (2nd ed.; New York: Harper & Row, 1960), pp. 123–129.

each tone with a corresponding one on a well-tuned piano. If your own sense of pitch discrimination is not reliable, obtain the help of a friend with a reliable ear to establish your vocal range.

2. Repeat the singing or chanting several times so that you are certain that you have established your entire range. Your optimum or natural pitch is likely to be between one-fourth and one-third above the lowest tone you can produce.

3. Reproduce this tone until it is firmly fixed in your mind and you can initiate it without the help of the piano.

This approach should be repeated at different times during a day and on several different days. Pitch range may vary somewhat under conditions of fatigue or tension, but unless the variation is great, the optimum pitch level should not deviate by more than a single level.[3]

HABITUAL PITCH

In order to know whether there is any need to make a conscious effort to initiate voice at the optimum pitch level it is necessary to compare your habitual pitch with your optimum pitch. If the two are the same, or no more than a single pitch level (a half or a full tone) apart, then there is no need to think about your initial pitch. For most persons who have had no physical ailment or emotional trauma, the likelihood is that habitual pitch and optimum pitch are

[3]Another approach for arriving at optimum pitch is through a technique of vocalizing while chewing. Dr. Froeschels, who is largely responsible for the discovery and popularization of the chewing technique for vocal therapy and vocal improvement, recommends the following as an approach: "... the patient is asked to chew as usual with closed lips, but without anything in his mouth, and to observe his tongue, which moves continually during the chewing. Immediately afterward he is asked to chew like a savage, that is, by opening the mouth, and with extensive movements of the lips and tongue.... If the chewing is done correctly, that is with vigorous movements of the lips and the tongue, a great variety of sounds escape the mouth. If uniform sounds, like *ham-ham-ham* are heard, the movements of the lips and tongue do not vary sufficiently." (E. Froeschels, "Hygiene of the Voice," *Archives of Otolaryngology*, August, 1943, 38:122–130.)

Our experience has been that persons who chew and vocalize in the manner described by Froeschels reflexively produce vocal tones at or close to their optimum pitch. For persons who have a poor sense of pitch discrimination and who are not excessively self-conscious, chewing may be used successfully as a technique for arriving at optimum pitch. It is not, however, a cure-all for all vocal ills.

close enough so that no special concern is necessary. Just to be certain, however, all who are interested in producing voice according to their maximum capabilities might observe the suggestions which follow for determining habitual pitch and comparing it with optimum pitch.

Look over several easy prose passages and select one containing material that is neutral in affective (emotional) content and not particularly challenging in intellectual content. (Three such selections are provided under "Reading Selections to Determine Habitual Pitch," following.) Make sure also that the selected passage includes no words that cause you uncertainty as to pronunciation. First read the selection aloud in as natural and conversational a manner as you can. On the second and third readings, when the thought content has been reduced to insignificance because of repetition, level off toward a monotone in pitch. You can accomplish this by intentionally avoiding inflectional changes. The final reading—fourth or fifth— will begin to sound like a chant. When this happens, you have probably arrived at a single level, or at least a narrow pitch range, at or close to your habitual pitch. At the conclusion of your chanted passage, vocalize a sustained *ah* at the same pitch level.

Locate the last level on a piano. Then say a series of *ah*'s, matching your voice with the piano note. Count from one to ten on this level. Then say the alphabet on this level. If possible, have a companion listen to you to help you locate the level.

Compare your optimum pitch with your habitual pitch. Are the two nearly the same or no more than a tone or two apart? If they are, then you need not be further concerned about the matter of initial pitch. If not, then work to bring your habitual pitch closer to your optimum pitch. This accomplishment will pay large dividends if you are interested in good voice production. The most generous permissible margin of error between habitual and optimum pitch should not exceed two levels for persons with a narrow pitch range. This may be extended to one third of an octave for individuals with a wide (two or more octaves) pitch range. In general, the closer habitual pitch is to optimum pitch, the better the voice is likely to be.

Reading Selections to Determine Habitual Pitch

1. A continent may be defined a the largest unit of land mass. The continents of the earth are North America, South America, Aus-

tralia, Africa, Eurasia (Europe and Asia combined), and Antarctica. The combined continental surface areas constitute about 29 per cent of the total surface area of the earth. The Northern Hemisphere contains more land mass than the Southern Hemisphere. The continental masses properly include the elevated or exposed areas above the sea level and the underwater shelves or ledges. The continental shelves slope from the exposed land surface into the depths of the oceans.

2.   An index is a listing, almost always in alphabetical order, of the topics treated in a book or periodical. In most books the index is in the back. The purpose of a book index is to help the reader to locate the pages of subjects and names about which information is provided. The subject and the number or numbers of the pages on which the information is found is called the entry. A good indexer is able to anticipate where, in the listing of topics, a reader is likely to look for an item of information or a subject treated in the book. Some books have one index for proper names and another for other entries.

3.   The French consider a sauce the foundation of good cooking. Sauces may be made with butter, with oil and vinegar, with wine, and with bones and vegetables as basic ingredients. Although French chefs accept the need to spend hours in the preparation of a sauce, most American cooks are less patient. For example, a French housewife may spend half a day selecting, preparing, and cooking a combination of vegetables and bones to make a brown sauce. The American housewife is much more inclined to use canned beef gravy for the same purpose.

WIDENING THE PITCH RANGE

How wide a pitch range should we have? Practically, the answer is *wide enough to be effective as a speaker,* but not at the expense of strain or discomfort. Some persons with a demonstrably wide pitch range tend to speak habitually only at the lower end of their range. Others, especially when under emotional stress, may confine their vocalizations to the higher end of their range. The result for both types of speakers may be inefficient vocalization. For the listeners the result may be unpleasant exposure to monotonous or to strained vocal efforts. Although experimental evidence is not consistent, some studies have shown that effective speakers and male speakers considered to have good voices tend to use both greater variability and a wider range than do less effective speakers.[4] Better speakers, by and large, make greater use of the upper part of their pitch ranges, and their pitch ranges generally cover at least an octave and a half. Poor speakers, in contrast, tend to have pitch ranges limited to about half an octave.

Extending Pitch Range Upward

Since optimum pitch is at the lower end of the pitch range, it follows that the direction for extending pitch range for most persons is likely to be up rather than down. With this in mind, the following exercises should be undertaken.

Exercises for Extending Pitch Range Upward

1. Review the discussion of optimum pitch. Check your optimum pitch and your total pitch range.
2. Count from one through ten at your optimum pitch level. Now count to ten in a monotone three tones above your optimum pitch. Raise the pitch level three more tones, and repeat the count. Finally, count to ten at the very top of your normal pitch range.
3. Say the sentence "We're going for a walk" at your optimum pitch. Practice the same sentence, initiating the first word on successively lower levels until you reach the lowest comfortable pitch level. Start again from your optimum pitch and now initiate the first word of the sentence at successively higher pitch levels until you have reached the top of your range.
4. Read the following sentences and paragraphs first in a manner natural or habitual for you and then intentionally extending the pitch range upward.

   a. Washington Irving believed that though little minds are tamed and subdued by misfortune, great minds rise above it.

[4]See J. W. Black and W. E. Moore, *Speech* (New York: McGraw-Hill, 1955), p. 56. Fairbanks, *op. cit.,* p. 129, says: "A good speaker usually distributes his pitches over a *pitch range* of about two octaves while reading a short (75–100 words) sample of factual prose."

b. According to Balzac, true modesty is the conscience of the body.

c. Hazlitt, the English essayist and critic, advised that the art of pleasing consists in being pleased. Hazlitt believed that to be amiable is to be satisfied with one's self and with others.

d. A wit once observed that though the race is not always to the quick, nor the battle to the strong, that nevertheless is the way to place your bets.

e. A gentleman has been characterized as a man who can disagree without being disagreeable.

f. Benjamin Franklin held that "There are two ways of being happy: we may either diminish our wants or augment our means. Either will do, the result is the same. And it is for each man to decide for himself and do that which happens to be the easiest...."

g. Young men are fitter to invent than to judge; fitter for execution than for counsel; and fitter for new projects than for settled business.

—FRANCIS BACON, *Of Youth and Age*

h. There is no season such delight can bring,
As summer, autumn, winter, and the spring.

—WILLIAM BROWNE, *Variety*

Extending Pitch Range Downward

If, after determining your optimum pitch and your habitual pitch range, it becomes apparent that little use is made of your lower pitch levels, some practice is in order. Do not, however, go so low in your range that your voice becomes throaty, excessively breathy, or barely audible. Avoid strain or any low tone that seems to be lacking in substance or is difficult to sustain. In general, try to incorporate tones into your pitch range that are one or two levels above your lowest tone within your pitch range. The following exercises, which present material on sober matters, should provide opportunity for emphasizing tones at the lower end of your pitch range.

Exercises for Extending Pitch Range Downward

1. Sadness is a wall between two gardens.

    —KAHLIL GIBRAN, *The Prophet*

2. We must anticipate that some days of our lives, like the weather, must be dark and dreary.

3. The deeper the sorrow, the less tongue it hath.

    —*The Talmud*

4. The nurse of full-grown souls is solitude.

    —JAMES RUSSELL LOWELL, *Columbus*

5. The history of the world is but the biography of great men.

    —THOMAS CARLYLE, *Sartor Resartus*

6. Man is his own star; and that soul that can
   Be honest is the only perfect man.

    —JOHN FLETCHER, *Upon an "Honest Man's Fortune"*

7. People who make no noise are dangerous.

    —JEAN DE LA FONTAINE, *Fables*

8. Time does not become sacred to us until we have lived it.

    —JOHN BURROUGHS, *The Spell of the Past*

9. A man in armor is his armor's slave.

    —ROBERT BROWNING, *Herakles*

10. Many of us have learned in sadness, if not in sorrow, that when we return to a place of youthful joy we seldom relive even one moment of that joy.

SPEECH MELODY (INTONATION)

Speaking and Singing

All of us, including those who are resigned to being classed among the nonsingers because of the violence we do to the melody of a song, use melody in our speech. The music of speech, however, is usually subtle, and the changes in pitch may not be as wide or as distinct as they are in singing. When speaking, our voices glide from sound to sound with an almost continuous change in pitch.

In singing, changes in pitch are usually more clear-cut and usually take place in discrete steps equivalent to musical tones. Some of us, without intention, somehow manage to sing between the tones and our voices fall "flat" into the cracks between the piano keys. A few singers have earned a reputation by doing intentionally and under control what seems to have come naturally, accidentally, and inconsistently for others.

Intonation

Patterned vocal variation or intonation is an inherent feature of almost all spoken languages. In some languages, the changes in vocal tones are relatively slight, whereas in others, such as Chinese, the changes are marked. Some languages, such as Norwegian, Swedish, and Lithuanian, have relatively fixed patterns of pitch changes. English pitch variation is relatively free. The melody of English speech is determined in part by conventions of sentence formation and in part by the mood and subjective responses of the speaker to the content of his speech and the overall speech situation. Despite this highly individual determinant of American-English speech melody, there are several features that characterize the direction of inflectional changes (pitch changes that occur without interruption of phonation) for sounds of words. There are also characteristic pitch changes within word groups which constitute recognizable intonation patterns in our language.[5]

Types of Pitch Changes

There are two categories of pitch changes that together constitute the overall pitch variation or *intonation* of American-English speech. These are inflections and shifts or steps. Inflections are modulations of pitch that occur during phonation. *Shifts* are changes of pitch and occur between phonations. Inflections may be subclassified according to contour or "direction" of change as downward, upward, and circumflex. For any but very short uninterrupted phonatory efforts or flows of utterance we are likely to have several inflectional

[5]See R-M. S. Heffner, *General Phonetics* (Madison, Wisc.: University of Wisconsin Press, 1949), pp. 216–223, for a review of basic tendencies relative to intonation patterns and alternate systems for their representations.

changes. Because shifts properly occur only between subunits of utterances when the speaker takes a moment to pause to indicate a unit of thought or a "phrase," inflectional changes will almost always outnumber shifts. The uses and implication of pitch changes will be considered in the discussions that immediately follow.

Shifts

Shifts, or steps in pitch, indicate the importance we give to a unit of thought within an utterance or phonatory effort. If we regard a phonatory effort as a sentence, even a two-word sentence may have two related subunits of thought, each appropriately uttered at a different pitch level. Thus, sentences such as "Go now" or "Come here" may be uttered for effect with a momentary pause at the end of the first word and a shift in level of pitch from the first to the second word. In both of the examples given, the "normal" shift in level of pitch would be upward, so that we might represent the sentences as:

$$\overrightarrow{\text{Go}} \ || \ \overrightarrow{\text{now}}$$

$$\overrightarrow{\text{Come}} \ || \ \overrightarrow{\text{here}}$$

Exercises for Change in Pitch Level

1. Practice the following sentences using a higher pitch level on the second word-phrase than on the first.

Please don't.	Wake Joe.
Don't complain.	We chatted.
Had enough?	Mary cried.
You're out.	Joe listened.
Birds fly.	Type this.
Jill stumbled.	Move away.
All safe.	Bill ran.
Go home.	I laughed.
Come alone.	Frank slept.
Return soon.	Tom sang.

2. What would be the effect on the meaning of the utterance if the second word-phrases were produced on a lower pitch level than were the first?

3. Practice these longer sentences changing the level of pitch as indicated by the direction of the arrow:

    a.   Winter came— |↑| wind, freeze, and snow.
    b.   He stopped suddenly, |↑| then turned to the right.
    c.   Why Tom did it, |↓| he could not tell.
    d.   Our team lost, |↓| but the game was close.
    e.   Will you |↓| or won't you?
    f.   It can't be done, |↑| no matter how you beg.
    g.   Come now, |↓| that's enough.
    h.   We're tired, |↑| much too tired.

4. How would you be inclined to shift the pitch for the following sentences after the indicated places for pause? What changes in meaning would you imply by reversing the direction of the pitch change? By using the same general level on the second part of the sentence as the first?

    a.   It's late, || perhaps too late.
    b.   Come early, || come often.
    c.   Did you care || or just pretend?
    d.   It can be done || if you really try.
    e.   Waste not, || want not.
    f.   He spoke quietly || but with certainty.
    g.   He stopped || just in time.
    h.   Don't write, || phone him.
    i.   He sped away || out of sight.
    j.   Look out, || look out!

Downward or *falling inflections* (↘) are generally used to indicate the completion of a thought, and to give emphasis to an idea. The sample sentences that follow would end with falling inflections. The second sentence would probably have falling inflections on both italicized words.[6]

1. This is your *pen*.
2. *Certainly*, this is your *pen*.

Command statements also end with falling inflections.

3. Stop *now!*

---

[6]In the examples to be presented the italicized words are those on which inflectional changes might be anticipated.

A question that begins with an interrogative word—*when, where, who, why, how, whom*—for which an answer other than the single word "Yes" or "No" is anticipated, also ends with a falling inflection.

4.   Why did Bill *go?*
5.   Why did you read this *book?*

Upward or *rising inflections* (↗) are generally used to suggest doubt, uncertainty, or incompleteness. It is also used for questions that call for a simple "Yes" or "No" answer. And we are likely to use rising inflections in statements that enumerate a series of items until the last item is stated. The last item would be spoken with a falling inflection.

6.   It apparently didn't occur to *us* that this was your *book.*
7.   Is this your *book?*
8.   We bought *groceries, meat,* and *fruit* at the supermarket.

Circumflex Inflections

We would get into great difficulty if we attempted to illustrate how irony, innuendo, sarcasm, cynicism, skepticism, or surprise combined with disbelief or incredulity are expressed in pitch. These intellectual states and attitudes all have marked degrees of feeling. Most native Americans would probably employ some form of circumflex (down-up, up-down, or down-up-and-down) inflection to express them. If, for example, surprise and "I can't believe it" were to be expressed at the choice of a candidate through the use of the single word *Him!*, the inflection might be:

Him! ⤵↗

A longer statement such as "Of all persons, to choose—him!" in which a related sentiment might be expressed relative to the same person might employ a series of circumflex inflections. The specific form of inflection is likely to be even more individualized than in the illustrations previously presented.

The examples presented below, and the generalizations we are about to make, might serve as guides for a speaker who has somehow not been able to get the tune of American-English speech. Once the basic tune is learned, the speaker should feel free to indulge in variations from the fundamental melodic theme or pattern.

1. Pitch change to some degree is almost continuous in normal conversational speech.

2. Major pitch changes occur at the end of phrases and sentences and on the most significant words within the phrase or sentence.

3. Falling or downward inflections are used when we make definite or positive assertions and when we wish to indicate the completion of a thought (examples 1, 2, and 3 on page 112). A falling inflection is also used on the final word of a question which begins with an interrogative word (examples 4 and 5, page 113).

4. A rising inflection is used to suggest incomplete or dependent thoughts and to express doubt or uncertainty. The rising inflection is also used in questions which may logically be answered by the words "Yes" or "No" (examples 6, 7, and 8, page 113).

5. The pitch level of the most important word within a phrase or unit of thought is likely to be at a different level from the other words of the unit. Most frequently, it will be higher in level, but occasionally the emphasized word may be uttered at a distinctively lower level than the other words of the unit.

6. The stressed syllable of a word is usually spoken on a higher pitch level than the unstressed syllable or syllables of the word.

The exercises that follow afford opportunity for application of the generalizations relative to inflectional changes and intonation patterns of American-English speech.

The first group of sentences would ordinarily end with falling inflections unless special meanings are read into them. For the present, avoid special meanings and read the sentences "straight" to indicate assertions and completed thoughts.

Exercises for Falling Inflections

1. Tom starts today.
2. This tastes good.
3. I like to skate.
4. This is enough.
5. Bill enjoys hiking.
6. Sue likes to sew.
7. Spring comes in March.
8. It's good to be through.
9. Good lawns require care.

10. Not all roses are red.
11. Joe is always hungry.
12. Ned is a good golfer.
13. Ted is a fast reader.
14. Come when you're ready.
15. This is the path.
16. That's not so!
17. It's time for tea.
18. Now we're done.
19. Take your time.
20. Dan found the book.

Many of the items in the next group, if read straight, would normally employ falling inflections on the last words. If read to suggest doubt or uncertainty or to express an incomplete thought, rising inflections are employed. The questions ordinarily answered by a "Yes" or "No" also end with rising inflections.

Exercises for Rising Inflections

1. I'm just not sure.
2. Well, perhaps.
3. You're going to ski?
4. I guess that's right.
5. Well, we'll see.
6. Is Tom going?
7. Do you like pie?
8. Shall we dance?
9. Do you like fishing?
10. Is this Ben's?
11. Can you wait?
12. Is Bill late?

All questions, we recall, do not end with rising reflections. Those which begin with interrogative words usually end with falling inflections when the questions are intended to elicit information. When a rising inflection is used for questions beginning with interrogative words, some special implication or meaning is intended other than the asking of information. Read the following sentences first with the expected falling inflection and then with a final rising inflection and note the change in meaning.

1. What is today's date?
2. What's your name?
3. Who came late?
4. Where are we going?
5. When shall we leave?
6. Why should we go?
7. Who knows his lines?
8. What does this cost?
9. How long is the road?
10. What time is it?
11. How did you know?
12. What makes this right?

As indicated in some of our earlier sample sentences, inflectional changes may take place within sentences, normally on the last word of a phrase as well as at the end of a sentence. By and large, the nature of the inflectional change will be determined by the intended meaning and will be consistent with the generalizations previously listed relative to inflectional changes and intonation patterns.

Read the following sentences according to the indicated inflectional changes. What are the differences in implied meanings?[7]

1. Give me liberty,↗ or give me death.↘
2. Give me liberty,↘ or give me death.↗
3. Give me liberty,↘ or give me death.↘
4. While there is life ↗ there is hope.↘
5. While there is life ↘ there is hope.↘
6. Please give me the bread,↗ butter,↗ and jam.↘
7. Please give me the bread,↘ butter,↘ and jam.↘
8. Please give me the bread,↗ butter,↗ and jam.↗
9. She came,↗ he saw,↗ she conquered.↘
10. She came,↘ he saw,↘ she conquered.↗
11. She came,↘ he saw,↘ she conquered.↘

Exercises for Practice of Inflectional Changes

1. Say the word *yes* to indicate (*a*) certainty, (*b*) doubt, (*c*) indecision, (*d*) sarcasm.

[7] See G. Fairbanks, *Voice and Articulation Drillbook* (2nd ed.; New York: Harper & Row, 1960), Chap. 14, for additional exercise materials on inflectional changes.

2.   Say the word *no* and, by changes of inflection, indicate the following:

    a.   "Definitely not."
    b.   "Well, maybe."
    c.   "I'm surprised to learn that."
    d.   "I'm annoyed to learn that."
    e.   "I'm pleased and surprised to learn that."

3.   Say the sentence *I shall come* so that the following attitudes are implied:

    a.   Determination.
    b.   Pleasant agreement.
    c.   Surprise.
    d.   Annoyance.

4.   Say the sentence *He's a fine fellow* to bring out the following meanings:

    a.   You admire the person about whom you're talking.
    b.   You dislike the person.
    c.   You are surprised at the newly discovered qualities of the person.

5.   Speak the sentence *I like Bill* to bring out the following:

    a.   A direct statement of fact. (You mean literally what the words say.)
    b.   A contradiction of the literal meaning of the words. (You definitely do not like Bill.)
    c.   Irritation and surprise that anyone could conceivably accuse you of liking Bill.
    d.   Indecision as to your feelings about Bill.
    e.   Specific indication that your liking is for Bill and not for anyone else who may be present.
    f.   Your answer to the question "Who likes Bill?"
    g.   An aggressive, emphatic answer to the question "Who could possibly care for a fellow like Bill?"

Avoidance of Monotony

In discussing the differences in pitch variation between singing and speaking, we pointed out that most pitch changes in song melody are discrete and take place in distinct steps. Each song syllable is likely to be maintained on a recognizable pitch level (note) longer than is likely to be the case in either conversational or public speech. Variation in speaking is almost continuous. Distinctive changes, however, should be noted when pitch is used for purposes of emphasis. For emphasis, pitch change is likely to be on a higher rather than on a lower level than the preceding or following words. When the pitch change is to a lower level, the speaker must maintain or increase the volume of his voice to give the word or phrase the desired emphasis.

Repetition of pattern in singing constitutes melody. This is considered a desirable characteristic of classical song. In speaking, where verbal content rather than pitch pattern is usually important, repetition of pitch pattern should be avoided. In American and English speech subtleties of ideational content, we now appreciate, are expressed through pitch change. If pitch changes become patterned and repeated, shades of meaning cannot readily be communicated. Beyond this, pitch changes, if they can be anticipated, no longer command attention and tend to work against rather than for the maintenance of interest. For these reasons the effective speaker not only uses as wide a range of pitch as he can within his normal pitch range but is careful to avoid pitch patterning and its consequent monotony.

Pitch Variation in Content Characterized by Strong Feelings

Speech content characterized by strong feelings, which is more significant for the emotional than for the intellectual content, tends to use less pitch variation than most conversational speech. When we wish to establish a dominant mood, or to share a strong feeling with a listener, we begin to approximate the melody of song or the relatively sustained pitch of lyrical poetry. A passage from the Bible should not be read as one reads an item from the day's news. Neither should it be read with an unvarying cadence and stereotyped intonations. It follows also, despite the tendency of some news commentators, that a news item should not be spoken as one should read a passage from the Bible.

In general, the pitch changes for an effective reading of poetry or emotional prose are individually more extensive but collectively less varied and longer sustained than for an effective reading of intellectual material. The exception is content of heightened feeling when the gay rather than the lofty is to be expressed. Then changes are likely to be more sweeping and to occur as often as or more often than for predominantly intellectual material. Anger is also likely to be expressed with relatively wide pitch changes and in the upper pitch range. With these points in mind, the following passages should be read. Use pitch variation to emphasize changes in thought and feeling. Sober and solemn moods are probably best expressed through the use of relatively low, sustained pitch levels.

Exercises for Using Pitch Variation

1. Goethe reminded us that "We know accurately only when we know little; with knowledge doubt increases."

2. No one can draw more out of things, books included, than he already knows. A man has no ears for that to which experience has given him no access.

—FRIEDRICH WILHELM NIETZSCHE, *Ecce Homo*

3. Fame has also this great drawback, that if we pursue it we must direct our lives in such a way as to please the fancy of men, avoiding what they dislike and seeking what is pleasing to them.

—BENEDICT SPINOZA, *Ethics*

4. The happiness of life is made up of minute fractions—the little soon forgotten charities of a kiss or smile, a kind look, a heartfelt compliment, and the countless infinitesimals of pleasurable and genial feeling.

—SAMUEL TAYLOR COLERIDGE, *The Friend*

5. But they that wait upon the Lord shall renew their strength; they shall mount up with wings as eagles; they shall run, and not be weary; they shall walk, and not faint.

—Isaiah 40:31

6. In your reading, level, sustained tones will help to establish the solemnity and reverence of your thought. Do not, however, fall into a patterned, unchanging reading.

The Lord is my shepherd; I shall not want. He maketh me to lie down in green pastures: he leadeth me beside the still waters. He restoreth my soul: he leadeth me in the paths of righteousness for his name's sake. Yea, though I walk through the valley of the shadow of death, I will fear no evil: for thou art with me; thy rod and thy staff they comfort me.

—Psalm 23

7. Golden lads and girls all must
    As chimney sweepers, come to dust.

—WILLIAM SHAKESPEARE, Cymbeline

8. I was angry with my friend:
    I told my wrath, my wrath did end.
    I was angry with my foe:
    I told it not, my wrath did grow.

—WILLIAM BLAKE, A Poison Tree

9. Say, wouldst thou guard thy son,
    That sorrow he may shun?
    Begin at the beginning
    And let him keep from sinning.

    Wouldst guard thy house? One door
    Make to it, and no more.
    Wouldst guard thine orchard wall?
    Be free of fruit to all.

—FRANCESCO DA BABERINO, Of Caution
(Translated by Dante Gabriel Rossetti)

10. Full fathom five thy father lies;
         Of his bones are coral made;
     Those are pearls that were his eyes;
         Nothing of him that doth fade
     But doth suffer a sea-change
         Into something rich and strange.

—WILLIAM SHAKESPEARE, The Tempest

11. I am tired of tears and laughter,
         And men that laugh and weep;
     Of what may come hereafter
         For men that sow to reap:
     I am weary of days and hours,
     Blown buds of barren flowers,
     Desires and dreams and powers,
         And everything but sleep.

—ALGERNON CHARLES SWINBURNE, The Garden of Proserpine

12. When I am dead, my dearest,
    Sing no sad song for me;
Plant thou no roses at my head,
    Nor shady cypress tree:
Be the green grass above me
    With showers and dewdrops wet;
And if thou wilt, remember,
    And if thou wilt, forget.

—CHRISTINA ROSSETTI, *Song*

CHAPTER 8

Duration

Changes in duration, in the time given to the production of speech sounds and the time intervals between phrases, permit us to express feelings and to emphasize and subordinate meanings. On the emotional side, a markedly slow rate of utterance is associated with solemnity, depressed moods, and sadness and sorrow. A marked increase of rate is associated with happier states, with gaiety, and heightened feelings. The heightened feelings, however, need not always be pleasant. Anger is also expressed through an increased rate of utterance.

Changes in rate are associated with our physiological states and resultant muscular activity. We behave more slowly when depressed and quickly when elated; we behave relatively slowly when our thoughts are solemn and more quickly when our mood is gay or when we are excited. The muscles of our vocal and articulatory mechanism normally reflect these changes in our vocal tones and in our articulatory activity.

Changes in rate are, of course, correlated with changes in pitch and force. Heightened feelings are accompanied by increases in pitch level and force; depressed feelings by reduction in pitch level as well as by decreased force.

Changes in duration, as indicated earlier, are achieved through either variation in rate of articulation or the use of pauses between groups of articulated sounds, or both. In general, content that is articulated slowly is considered more important—intellectually more significant—than rapidly articulated content. If we listen to what is spoken slowly and are able to maintain attention while listening, we assume that what we have heard is more important than more quickly evoked content.

Some speech sounds—vowels and vowellike consonants—lend themselves to a varied and controlled rate of articulation. Words such as *alone, rarely, home, gone, away,* and *always* contain these sounds. They can be uttered quickly or slowly according to the will of the speaker. On the other hand, words such as *tip, stop, quick,* and *put* are necessarily articulated rapidly. In lyric prose and poetry dominant moods can be established through language which incorporates "slow" sounds and "rapid" sounds. Compare, for example, Coleridge's

> Alone, alone, all, all alone,
> Alone on a wide, wide sea!

with Milton's

> Come, and trip it as you go
> On the light fantastic toe

and the difference in mood becomes immediately apparent. The first couplet lends itself to a slow rate of articulation. But the lines from Milton's *L'Allegro* have to be articulated quickly, or the result would be absurd.

RATE AND MEANING

We must, of course, appreciate that when the rate of utterance is appreciably changed to be either relatively rapid or relatively slow, the most significant word within the phrase, or the most significant phrase within the sentence, is usually spoken more slowly than the rest of the phrase or sentence. Any sustained, unvarying rate may become monotonous. Nothing of any considerable content that we say or read aloud should be uttered at the same rate, regardless of the feeling or mood.

The *use of pause* as a technique for varying rate is perhaps the best single indication of control and sophistication in speech. Both Winston Churchill and Franklin D. Roosevelt made considerable use of lengthened and intentional pauses to create dramatic effects and to emphasize ideas. When a speaker pauses after a pause, the listener waits. While waiting, he tends to fill in the time gaps with the last bit of content he heard. The inner listener repetition of what the speaker has last said reinforces this content. A pause before and after a word or a phrase sets either off from the rest of the content and so becomes a technique for the vocal underlining of an idea or a unit of thought.

A pause may also be used to indicate transition of thought in a larger context. This is the case when a speaker pauses after the evident completion of a thought. A short pause may separate sentences, a moderate pause may separate paragraphs, and a longer pause may prepare the listeners for a new line of thought.

Dramatic effects may be achieved by combining a pause with a rising inflection. If the phrase before the pause ends with an upward inflection, the result is the "suspension" of a thought. The thought is then completed in the content that follows. A similar effect may be achieved by pausing before and after a presented idea.

The speaker is obligated, when he uses an intentional pause, to satisfy the expectations of his listeners. If what comes after a pause is of no more significance than what some of our announcers of radio commercials present, the speaker has failed to meet his obligation and the listeners are likely to become distrusting.

We all use pauses to separate or group our phrases. In conversational speech such word groupings come naturally with the flow of thought. When our thoughts do not flow as freely as we might like, when we search for words to communicate our thoughts, we reveal it in our *unintentional pauses*. Under pressure of a large or formal audience, we may become fearful and anxious about pausing, and fill in the gaps with *uh uh*'s or their equivalent in nonverbal sounds. The speaker who is poised enough to wait, who pauses with intent and without fear, is one we tend to respect if what he has to say is worthy of our waiting and our listening. With these points in mind, the reader should find the exercises that follow of help in the practice of some of the uses of duration for vocal variety and as a technique for revealing feeling and communicating thought.

Exercises for Practice of Controlled Rate

1.   Read the following sentences so that full value is given to the italicized words. The sentences as a whole are to be spoken slowly, and the italicized words more slowly than the others.

   a.   *Innocence* is *inconsistent* with the *acquisition* of *riches.*
   b.   The *air* was *still,* the sea was *calm.*
   c.   *All* rivers *find* their *way* to the *sea.*
   d.   In *solitude* we may be *least alone.*
   e.   *Life* is what the *living makes* it.
   f.   The *snow* fell and *silently* concealed the *earth.*
   g.   *Freedom* can *survive* only when it is *shared.*
   h.   *Tomorrow* will *come* and pass into *yesterday.*
   i.   Man's *inhumanity* to *man* makes *countless* thousands *mourn.*
   j.   Through *memory* we can *recreate* a *yesterday,* and project a *tomorrow.*
   k.   *Are* we *now* at a *time* when *knowledge* has *outrun wisdom?*

2.   The next group of sentences should be spoken at a moderate rate, but the italicized words somewhat more slowly for emphasis.

   a.   *Mark Twain* held that *cauliflower* was *nothing* but *cabbage* with an *education.*
   b.   It is *rare* for a man to be a *husband and hero* to his *own* wife.
   c.   *Lawyers* soon *learn* that their *opinions* assume *value only* when they *exact* a fee.
   d.   A *good listener* often achieves a *reputation* for being a good *conversationalist.*
   e.   President *Coolidge* held that *one with* the *law* constituted a *majority.*
   f.   *Cynics* hold that a *majority* is *almost always wrong.*
   g.   To *study mankind* we must study *individual* man.
   h.   It might be said of *Thoreau* that he loved not *man* the *less* but *nature* the *more.*
   i.   *Muscles,* like *iron,* wear out *faster* with *disuse* than with *use.*

j.   If we are *fortunate* we *understand* in our *mature years*
     what we *thought we learned* in our *youth.*

k.   James *Monroe* held that *national honor* is national *prop-
     erty* of the *highest* order.

l.   In his *Meditations* Marcus Aurelius observed, "This *Being*
     of mine, whatever it *really* is, consists of a *little flesh*, a
     little *breath*, and the *part* which *governs.*"

m.   *Centuries* ago *Plato* remarked that *man* is a very *incon-
     stant creature.*

n.   In his *Epistles, Seneca* noted, "It is *not* the *man* who has
     too little, but the man who *craves* more, that is *poor.*"

o.   In *The Magic Mountain*, Thomas Mann wrote, "*Human
     reason* needs only to *will* more *strongly* than *fate*, and she
     is fate.*"

3.   Read the following excerpts at appropriate basic rates but
with variation to emphasize the key words and so the essential
ideas. The more serious or solemn the content, the slower the basic
rate.

a.   The childhood shows the man
     As morning shows the day.

                              —JOHN MILTON, *Paradise Lost*

b.   For truth is precious and divine,—
     Too rich a pearl for carnal swine.

                              —SAMUEL BUTLER, *Hudibras*

c.   Words are wise men's counters—they do but reckon by
     them; but they are the money of fools.

                              —THOMAS HOBBES, *Leviathan*

d.   Man is his own star; and that soul that can
     Be honest is the only perfect man.

                              —JOHN FLETCHER, *Upon an Honest Man's Fortune*

e.   Good thoughts his only friends,
         His wealth a well-spent age,
     The earth his sober inn
         And quiet pilgrimage.

                              —THOMAS CAMPION, *Integer Vitae*

f.   Follow a shadow, it still flies you;
         Seem to fly it, it will pursue:

> So court a mistress, she denies you;
> Let her alone, she will court you.
>
> —BEN JONSON, *Follow a Shadow*

4. Read the following passages, using intentional pauses to set off the significant thought groups. Punctuation may help, but occasionally it may be misleading. Determine the units of thought, and pause whether or not the material is punctuated. Indicate pauses by inserting the sign ‖ at the end of thought units at which you intend to pause. Underline the words that carry the essential meanings in each selection.

 a. The vagabond, when rich, is called a tourist.

> —PAUL RICHARD, *The Scourge of Christ*

 b. A man lives not only his personal life, as an individual, but also, consciously or unconsciously, the life of his epoch and his contemporaries.

> —THOMAS MANN, *The Magic Mountain*

 c. . . . they shall beat their swords into plowshares, and their spears into pruning-hooks; nation shall not lift up sword against nation, neither shall they learn war any more.

> —Isaiah 2:4

 d. I live in the crowd of jollity, not so much to enjoy company as to shun myself.

> —SAMUEL JOHNSON, *Rasselas*

 e. 'Tis known by the name of perseverance in a good cause— and of obstinacy in a bad one.

> —LAWRENCE STERNE, *Tristram Shandy*

 f. There is no cure for birth and death save to enjoy the interval.

> —GEORGE SANTAYANA, *Soliloquies in England*

 g. There is nothing more tragic in life than the utter impossibility of changing what you have done.

> —JOHN GALSWORTHY, *Justice*

5. The passages that follow call for more deliberate pauses to achieve emotional impact or to heighten dramatic meaning. In many instances these effects may be attained by pauses before as well as after the significant words or phrases.

a. To be honest, to be kind—to earn a little and spend a little
    less, to make upon the whole a family happier for his
    presence, to renounce when that shall be necessary and
    not to be embittered, to keep a few friends, but these with-
    out capitulation—above all, on the same grim conditions,
    to keep friends with himself—here is a task for all that a
    man has of fortitude and delicacy.

    —ROBERT LOUIS STEVENSON, *A Christmas Sermon*

b. The deepest thing in our nature is this dumb region of the
    heart in which we dwell alone with our willingnesses and
    our unwillingnesses, our faiths and our fears.

    —WILLIAM JAMES, *The Will to Believe*

c. Men grind and grind in the mill of a truism, and nothing
    comes out but what was put in. But the moment they
    desert the tradition for a spontaneous thought, then
    poetry, wit, hope, virtue, learning, anecdote, all flock to
    their aid.

    —RALPH WALDO EMERSON, *Literary Ethics*

d. Inferiors revolt in order that they may be equal, and
    equals that they may be superior. Such is the state of
    mind which creates revolutions.

    —ARISTOTLE, *Politics*

e. Then darkness enveloped the whole American armada.
    Not a pinpoint of light showed from those hundreds of
    ships as they surged on through the night toward their
    destiny, carrying across the ageless and indifferent sea
    tens of thousands of young men, fighting for . . . for . . .
    well, at least for each other.

    —ERNIE PYLE, *Brave Men*

f. I have learned silence from the talkative, toleration from
    the intolerant, and kindness from the unkind; yet strange,
    I am ungrateful to these teachers.

    —KAHLIL GIBRAN, *Sand and Foam*

g. If we open a quarrel between the past and the present, we
    shall find that we have lost the future.

    —WINSTON CHURCHILL, Speech, House of Commons, 1940

h. There be three things which are too wonderful for me, yea four, which I know not: the way of an eagle in the air; the way of a serpent upon a rock; the way of a ship in the midst of the sea; and the way of a man with a maid.

—Proverbs 30:18–19

CHAPTER 9

Vocal Variety in Speaking and Reading

Although this chapter is specifically entitled "Vocal Variety," we have been anticipating and considering aspects and implications of this subject in several of the immediately preceding chapters. When we discussed *loudness*, we considered first the fundamental need for the speaker to be heard if his intentions to communicate were to be fruitful. Beyond this we also considered the use of vocal force as related to word meanings, sentence meanings, and overall communicative efforts. *Pitch* was likewise considered as a basic attribute of voice that could be used to enhance vocalization *per se*. Pitch was also discussed in relationship to linguistic melody, to word and phrase meaning, and to the expression of states of feeling. Similarly, the vocal attribute *duration* was viewed in relationship to the speaker's physiological state, to feeling, and to semantic implications.

The present chapter is in one sense a review and reconsideration of some aspects of vocal variety previously discussed. It will also provide us with an opportunity to emphasize some aspects briefly touched on in the previous chapters that deal separately with individual attributes of voice.

Through the attributes of voice—pitch, quality, loudness, and duration—we tend to reveal our thoughts and feelings. The less inhibited we are, the more the element of feeling is expressed and conveyed through voice. When we were very young and not yet aware of and influenced by cultural pressures, our voices reflexively expressed our changes in feelings and moods. As we grew older, cultural pressures exerted increasing control and we learned, almost always without awareness, of *how* we show feeling through voice. Even the manner of laughter was related to how people around us laughed. Our pitch ranges narrowed and began to conform to a pattern and to the linguistic code of our culture. The result was that by the time we were of school age, most of us spoke both the sounds and the melody (intonation) of the language or languages of our culture. We learned also that American-English speech has syllable stress within a word and word stress within a phrase. So we became able to emphasize ideas as we spoke. Our tendencies to talk at changing rates according to mood, to talk more rapidly under heightened feelings, more slowly in the absence of heightened feelings, and quite slowly when sad or depressed, also became modified by cultural influences. Although these cultural modifications direct us toward norms of behavior most of us still maintain and express our individualities. Sometimes we kick over the traces, and our voices minimize the influences and effects of environmental training and pressures. But usually we manage to conform to a sufficient degree to sound considerably like the people around us while still sounding like our identifiable selves.

Igor Stravinsky, the noted composer, with considerably more sophistication and a much better than average ear for vocal nuances, listened carefully to how people talked. In one of his books [1] Stravinsky presented graphic as well as verbal descriptions of the vocal characteristics of several of his friends. Stravinsky described one friend as a "virtuoso talker who *likes* to talk, just as Rubinstein *likes* to play the piano." A second friend is described as "fast and funny." A third "talks in spurts like a ticker tape." Another "fishes ... profoundly between words." Still another (Aldous Huxley) is "too serenely high in tessitura and in volume too suavely soft."

[1] Igor Stravinsky and Robert Craft, *Dialogues and a Diary* (Garden City, N.Y.: Doubleday, 1963).

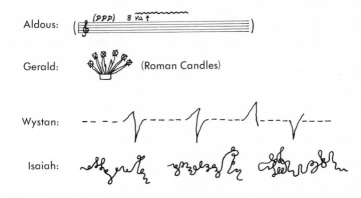

FIGURE 9-1. "Four Friends. Gerald [Heard] is a virtuoso talker, the most brilliant I have ever heard, and he *likes* to talk, just as Arthur Rubinstein *likes* to play the piano. Isaiah Berlin is even faster and funnier—an ironical gaiety underlies everything he says—but Isaiah tends to speak in spurts, like a ticker tape. Wystan Auden, by comparison, fishes, though profoundly, between words, and Aldous [Huxley] is too serenely high in tessitura, and in volume too suavely soft." (From *Dialogues and a Diary* by Igor Stravinsky and Robert Craft. Copyright © 1961, 1962, 1963 by Igor Stravinsky. Reprinted by permission of Doubleday & Company, Inc., and Faber and Faber, Ltd.

IMPLICATIONS OF VOCAL ATTRIBUTES

With the possible exception of quality, each vocal attribute is capable of revealing thought as well as feeling. Within a phrase, the important word is likely to be spoken more loudly, more slowly, and at a different pitch from the other words.[2] These changes are paralleled for the phrase-sentence relationships, as well as for the sentence-paragraph, and so forth.

Through the use of vocal variety we are also able to capture attention and maintain listener interest. In brief, through voice we are able to reveal thought and feeling, to emphasize ideas, and to keep listeners attentive to our communicative efforts.

Quality

In our earlier discussions of quality we considered its relationship to resonance and to the avoidance of undesirable vocal aspects such

---

[2]See M. D. Steer and J. Tiffin, "An Experimental Analysis of Emphasis," *Speech Monographs,* 1937, pp. 69–74, for basic research on this point.

as excessive nasality and breathiness. At this time we shall consider quality as it is related to feelings and moods and as an aspect of vocal variety.

Although modifications in vocal quality take place as a result of inherent characteristics of our resonating cavities, except for those of us who tend to be either nasal or denasal, there is little that we normally should do consciously to bring about these changes. Normal changes in quality are related to feelings and moods, to the emotional rather than the intellectual aspects of our behavior. Unless we are dealing with a greatly inhibited individual, the feeling tone will be reflected and expressed in his vocal efforts. Usually, we have more difficulty in concealing our feelings than in revealing them. The speaker who does not strive to conceal his inner feelings, and yet does not make a point of putting them on display, will have no difficulty with quality changes. The normally responsive speaker who initiates tone properly and who uses an appropriate and flexible pitch range will do best with the quality which emerges reflexively and naturally.

Reading Aloud

When a speaker chooses to read material written by another person, he has the dual responsibilities of "translating" and transmitting thoughts and feelings that did not originate with him in the specific verbal formulations with which he must deal. The reader who is about to speak another's words, another's thoughts and feelings, must of course determine what these are. The reader-speaker must be certain not only that he knows the denotative or literal meaning of each word, but the *intentions* of the words—the verbal formulations—and their connotations and implications. He must be aware that the written material he is about to translate and transmit represents the feelings as well as the thoughts of another and that a reader, in expressing these feelings and thoughts, has an implicit ethical obligation to be faithful to them. With such awareness of responsibility, and with such an appreciation of the task, the reader-speaker will set about to determine the dominant mood and nuances of feeling of each selection to be read aloud, as well as the underlying theme and specific thoughts to be communicated. Even the most proficient of professional actors—who are essentially readers because they are dealing with the verbal formulations of others—accept the need to study their lines carefully before they read them aloud. Such study is, of course, recommended to our student-readers.

When, as a reader, you are able to understand the mood, feelings, and thoughts inherent in the selections studied-to-be-read-aloud, you should begin to do your reading aloud. If at all possible, record and play back your efforts. Listen objectively and determine whether what you thought you thought, and felt you felt, is being expressed in your speaking of and with another person's words. Remember, you must have an overall appreciation of intention, mood, meaning, and meanings in dealing with another person's words just as you generally know how you think and feel or feel and think about what you are about to say in your own words before you start. With such preparation and appreciation, appropriate initial vocal qualities to establish the dominant mood, and changes in quality to suggest the particular feelings associated with particular ideas should take place "almost as spontaneously as if the words and feelings were initially your own." But because they are not your own, you will just have to work a bit harder to be effective in your role as a translator and transmitter of someone else's words.

Exercises for Vocal Quality: Establishing Mood

1.   During the whole of a dull, dark, and resoundless day in the autumn of the year, when the clouds hung oppressively low in the heavens, I had been passing alone, on horseback, through a singularly dreary track of country, and at length found myself, as the shades of evening drew on, within view of the melancholy House of Usher. I know not how it was—but, with the first glimpse of the building, a sense of insufferable gloom pervaded my spirit.

—EDGAR ALLAN POE, *The Fall of the House of Usher*

2.   Come, dear children, let us away;
     Down and away below.
     Now my brothers call from the bay;
     Now the great winds shorewards blow;
     Now the salt tides seawards flow;
     Now the wild white horses play,
     Champ and chafe and toss in the spray.

—MATTHEW ARNOLD, *The Forsaken Merman*

3. I am tired of tears and laughter,
    And men that laugh and weep;
Of what may come hereafter
    For men that sow to reap:

I am weary of days and hours,
Blown buds of barren flowers,
Desires and dreams and powers,
    And everything but sleep.
                —ALGERNON CHARLES SWINBURNE, *The Garden of Proserpine*

4. She left the web, she left the loom,
She made three paces thro' the room,
She saw the water lily bloom,
She saw the helmet and the plume,
    She look'd down to Camelot.
                —ALFRED, LORD TENNYSON, *The Lady of Shalott*

5. The centipede was happy quite
    Until a toad in fun
Said, "Pray, which leg goes after which?"
That worked her mind to such a pitch,
She lay distracted in a ditch
    Considering how to run.
                —MRS. EDWARD CRASTER, *Pinafore Poems*

6. Shall I, wasting in despair,
Die because a woman's fair?
Or make pale my cheeks with care
'Cause another's rosy are?
Be she fairer than the day
Or the flowery meads in May,
    If she be not so to me,
    What care I how fair she be?
                —GEORGE WITHER, *Shall I, Wasting in Despair*

7. A flock of sheep that leisurely pass by,
One after one; the sound of rain, and bees
Murmuring; the fall of rivers, winds, and seas,
Smooth fields, white sheets of water, and pure sky;
I have thought of all by turns, and yet do lie
Sleepless! and soon the small birds' melodies

Must hear, first uttered from my orchard trees;
And the first cuckoo's melancholy cry.

—WILLIAM WORDSWORTH, *To Sleep*

8. It is better to lose health like a spendthrift than to waste it like a miser. It is better to live and be done with it, than to die daily in the sickroom. By all means begin your folio; even if the doctor does not give you a year, even if he hesitates about a month, make one brave push and see what can be accomplished in a week. It is not only in finished undertakings that we ought to honour useful labour. A spirit goes out of the man who means execution, which outlives the most untimely ending. All who have meant good work with their whole hearts, have done good work, although they may die before they have the time to sign it. Every heart that has beat strong and cheerfully has left a hopeful impulse behind it in the world, and bettered the tradition of mankind.

—ROBERT LOUIS STEVENSON, *Aes Triplex*

9. No longer mourn for me when I am dead
    Than you shall hear the surly sullen bell
    Give warning to the world that I am fled
    From this vile world, with vilest worms to dwell:
    Nay, if you read this line, remember not
    The hand that writ it; for I love you so,
    That I in your sweet thoughts would be forgot,
    If thinking on me then should make you woe.
    O, if I say, you look upon this verse
    When I perhaps compounded am with clay,
    Do not so much as my poor name rehearse,
    But let your love even with my life decay;
    Lest the wise world should look into your moan,
    And mock you with me after I am gone.

—WILLIAM SHAKESPEARE, *Sonnet 71*

The materials that follow will afford opportunities, some in depth, to employ knowledge and skill in the use of vocal variety. Be sure that you first read and understand the entire selection, and note the underlying, fundamental thought and mood as well as the nuances in feeling and thought. Experiment, using different techniques of emphasis—e.g., basic pitch change, force, or duration—and decide which of these is most appropriate to express the dominant meaning of each selection.

Review Selections for Vocal Variety

1.   Language is not an abstract construction of the learned, or of dictionary makers, but is something arising out of work, needs, ties, joys, affections, tastes, of long generations of humanity, and has its bases broad and low, close to the ground.

—WALT WHITMAN, *Slang in America*

2.   As long as war is regarded as wicked, it will always have its fascination. When it is looked upon as vulgar, it will cease to be popular.

—OSCAR WILDE, *The Critic as Artist*

3.   O, who rides by night thro' the woodland so wild?
It is the fond father embracing his child;
And close the boy nestles within his loved arm,
To hold himself fast and to keep himself warm.

"O father, my father, see yonder," he says;
"My boy, upon what dost thou fearfully gaze?"
"O, 'tis the Erl-King with his crown and his shroud."
"No, my son, it is but a dark wreath of the cloud."

"O, come and go with me, thou loveliest child;
By many a gay sport shall thy time be beguiled;
My mother keeps for thee full many a fair toy,
And many a fine flower shall she pluck for my boy."

"O, father, my father, and did you not hear
The Erl-King whisper so low in my ear?"
"Be still, my heart's darling—my child, be at ease;
It was but the wild blast as it sung thro' the trees."

"O, wilt thou go with me, thou loveliest boy?
My daughter shall tend thee with care and with joy;
She shall bear thee so lightly thro' wet and thro' wild,
And press thee, and kiss thee and sing to my child."

"O father, my father, and saw you not plain,
The Erl-King's pale daughter glide past through the rain?"
"O yes, my loved treasure, I knew it full soon;
It was the gray willow that danced to the moon."

"O, come and go with me, no longer delay,
Or else, silly child, I will drag thee away."
"O father! O father! now, now keep your hold,
The Erl-King has seized me—his grasp is so cold!"

Sore trembled the father; he spurred thro' the wild,
Clasping close to his bosom his shuddering child;
He reaches his dwelling in doubt and in dread,
But, clasped to his bosom, the infant was dead!

—SIR WALTER SCOTT, *The Erl King* (translation)

4. Home they brought her warrior dead;
    She nor swoon'd, nor utter'd cry:
  All her maidens, watching, said,
    "She must weep or she will die."

  Then they praised him, soft and low,
    Call'd him worthy to be loved,
  Truest friend and noblest foe;
    Yet she neither spoke nor moved.

  Stole a maiden from her place,
    Lightly to the warrior stept,
  Took the face-cloth from the face;
    Yet she neither moved nor wept.

  Rose a nurse of ninety years,
    Set his child upon her knee—
  Like summer tempest came her tears—
    "Sweet my child, I live for thee."

—ALFRED, LORD TENNYSON, *Home They Brought Her Warrior Dead*

5. How doth the little crocodile
    Improve his shining tail,
  And pour the waters of the Nile
    On every shining scale!

  How cheerfully he seems to grin,
    How neatly spreads his claws,
  And welcomes little fishes in
    With gently smiling jaws.

—LEWIS CARROLL, *The Crocodile*

6. Mycilla dyes her locks, 'tis said,
    But 'tis a foul aspersion;

She buys them black, they therefore need
    No subsequent immersion.

          —LUCILIUS, *On an Old Woman*
          (Translated by William Cowper)

7.   They call thee rich; I deem thee poor;
     Since, if thou darest not use thy store,
     But savest only for thine heirs,
     The treasure is not thine, but theirs.

          —LUCILIUS, *Treasure*
          (Translated by William Cowper)

8.   When all the world is young, lad,
      And all the trees are green;
    And every goose a swan, lad,
      And every lass a queen;
    Then hey for boot and horse, lad,
      And round the world away;
    Young blood must have its course, lad,
      And every dog his day.

    When all the world is old, lad,
      And all the trees are brown;
    And all the sport is stale, lad,
      And all the wheels run down:
    Creep home, and take your place there,
      The spent and maimed among:
    God grant you find one face there,
      You loved when all was young.

          —CHARLES KINGSLEY, *Water Babies*

9.   Remember me when I am gone away,
     Gone far away into the silent land;
     When you can no more hold me by the hand,
     Nor I half turn to go, yet turning stay.
     Remember me when no more, day by day,
     You tell me of our future that you planned;
     Only remember me; you understand
     It will be too late to counsel then or pray.
     Yet if you should forget me for a while
     And afterwards remember, do not grieve:
     For if the darkness and corruption leave
     A vestige of the thoughts that once I had,

Better by far you should forget and smile
Than that you should remember and be sad.

—CHRISTINA ROSSETTI, *Remember*

10. In the following excerpts from the speeches and writings of John F. Kennedy, essential ideas are brought out by balancing of phrases and by verbal contrasts resulting from positions of words within phrases. Often the same words occur in contexts which are *almost but not quite the same.* Be certain that in your study of the selections you anticipate and prepare to bring out the related yet contrasting thoughts and the subtleties and nuances in feeling as well as in thought by appropriate vocal changes.

a.   . . . democracy means much more than popular government and majority rule, much more than a system of political techniques to flatter or deceive powerful blocs of voters . . . the true democracy, living and growing and inspiring, puts its faith in the people—faith that the people will not simply elect men who will represent their views ably and faithfully, but also elect men who will exercise their conscientious judgment—faith that the people will not condone those whose devotion to principle leads them to unpopular causes, but will reward courage, respect honor and ultimately recognize right.

—JOHN F. KENNEDY, *Profiles in Courage*

b.   And ·thus, in the days ahead, only the very courageous will be able to take the hard and unpopular decisions necessary for our survival in the struggle with a powerful enemy—an enemy with leaders who need give little thought to the popularity of their course, who need pay little tribute to the public opinion they themselves manipulate, and who may force, without fear of retaliation at the polls, their citizens to sacrifice present laughter for future glory. And only the very courageous will be able to keep alive the spirit of individualism and dissent which gave birth to this nation, nourished it as an infant and carried it through its severest tests upon the attainment of its majority.

—JOHN F. KENNEDY, *Profiles in Courage*

c.   I want to be a President who responds to a problem not by hoping his subordinates will act, but by directing them to act.

When things are very quiet and beautifully organized I think it's time to be concerned.

—JOHN F. KENNEDY, Speech, 1960

d. So let us begin anew—remembering on both sides that civility is not a sign of weakness, and sincerity is always subject to proof. Let us never negotiate out of fear. But let us never fear to negotiate.

Let both sides explore what problems unite us instead of belaboring those problems which divide us.

Let both sides, for the first time, formulate serious and precise proposals for the inspection and control of arms —and bring the absolute power to destroy other nations under the absolute control of all nations.

—JOHN F. KENNEDY, Inaugural Address

11. To every thing there is a season, and a time to every purpose under the heaven: a time to be born, and a time to die; a time to plant, and a time to pluck up that which is planted; a time to kill, and a time to heal; a time to break down, and a time to build up; a time to weep, and a time to laugh; a time to mourn, and a time to dance; a time to cast away stones, and a time to gather stones together; a time to embrace, and a time to refrain from embracing; a time to seek, and a time to lose; a time to keep, and a time to cast away; a time to rend, and a time to sew; a time to keep silence, and a time to speak; a time to love, and a time to hate; a time for war, and a time for peace.

—Ecclesiastes 3:1–8

SUMMARY

Vocal variety may be used to express feelings, to communicate meanings, to hold attention, and to make speaking and listening interesting. Any of the attributes of voice—pitch, quality, loudness, or duration—may be used toward these ends. Rarely is a single attribute used alone. Changes in pitch and force are frequently made together. Usually words spoken slowly are also spoken with increased force. The effective speaker achieves his effects by a combination of vocal factors, but is able to control the factors according to the nature of what he has to say. The effective speaker is able to use a widened pitch range, appropriate inflection, modifications in vocal intensity, and changes in the tempo of his speech to indicate how he feels about his thoughts as he talks. Furthermore, he can use vocal variety as a means of pointing up essential ideas and subordinating less important ones.

PART

DICTION

CHAPTER 10

Our Changing Speech Patterns

Two of our leading textbooks on the phonetics of our language make it clear in their titles that their authors are careful to limit their considerations to American English rather than to English in general. Thus, Bronstein's text is called *The Pronunciation of American English*[1] and Thomas' text is called *An Introduction to the Phonetics of American English*.[2] The fact that Americans, persons who are identified as citizens of one of the fifty of the United States, speak a variety of English at all, deserves some special consideration. We shall therefore begin this chapter with a brief historical review of the factors and forces that enabled the complex of linguistic habits we call English to be established as our basic system of utterance.

ENGLISH HISTORICAL BACKGROUNDS

From the time of ancient Romans until the eleventh century, the land masses known as the British Isles were successively conquered and occupied by peoples of many nations. Each of the conquering

[1] A. J. Bronstein, *The Pronunciation of American English* (New York: Appleton-Century-Crofts, 1960).

[2] C. K. Thomas, *An Introduction to the Phonetics of American English* (2nd ed.; New York: Ronald Press, 1958).

peoples left traces of influence on a language whose basic forms and structure were not to be determined until the sixteenth century.

The Romans under Caesar came to Britain in 55 B.C. and did not finally leave until about A.D. 400. The inhabitants who remained behind, other than the Romans, spoke a Celtic dialect but retained the use of Roman names for roads and many geographic locations (place names).

In the middle of the fifth century Angles, Saxons, and Jutes began to invade Britain and drove the Celts westward into Wales and Cornwall and northward toward what is now Scotland. The term *English* is used for the Germanic speech of these groups of invaders and their descendants. It is important to appreciate, however, that the earlier inhabitants of Britain did not suddenly change their speech habits, and those who stayed behind and were not pushed to the west or to the north continued to speak a language much as they had spoken, except that new linguistic forms—those of their conquerors—were incorporated and modified into their previous linguistic habits. Essentially, despite military conquests, the language of the conquered assimilated that of the conquerors.

Christianity came to Saxon England during the first half of the seventh century. With Christianity, Latin was introduced as the spoken and written language for religious and learned purposes. This influence on the common man, however, was not significantly reflected in his everyday speech.

Between the eighth and eleventh centuries, Scandinavians in increasing numbers came to Britain, and with it Scandinavian influences on what was to become English. The Scandinavians, for the most part Danes, also invaded and conquered the northeastern parts of France and ultimately became the ruling aristocracy of Normandy. During this period of achievement, the Scandinavians assumed Gallic ways, including French as a language, and their own Germanic speech was lost.

In the historically critical year 1066, the descendants of the Scandinavians, who now were Normans and who had become essentially French in culture and in their linguistic habits, invaded England under William the Conqueror, and became the established power in England. Though French then became the language of the ruling class in England, the masses continued to speak a Germanic language. In time the language of the Norman conquerors was reduced in influence, and all but disappeared, at least as far as the speech of the common man was concerned.

The English most people in England speak today, and the American English most Americans speak, are both derived from the speech of the inhabitants of the London area from the time of William the Conqueror through the Elizabethan period. But England throughout its history has never been free of divergent dialects. The Germanic groups—the Angles, Saxons, and Jutes—came from different parts of the continental lowlands. The groups spoke different dialects, settled in different parts of England, and left their linguistic influences where they settled. One important result is that the dialectical differences among the inhabitants of England today are greater and more divergent than are the regional-dialect differences in the United States.

It does not require an expert ear to discern differences between American and British speech, even assuming that the comparison is made between an educated Englishman who has lived most of his life in or near London and an educated American who has lived most of his life in or around Boston and is a Harvard graduate. These representative speakers are selected because, though the differences between American English and upper class London English are comparatively few, yet differences exist. They exist in idiom and in specific words to denote situations and events as well as in word pronunciation and stress and in manner of articulation. Differences are also found in speech melody. The Londoner and the Bostonian are not likely to express their enthusiasms or their irritations with the same choice of words or the same manner of vocal melody. *A bloody American mess* has different connotations from *a bloody English mess*. The Bostonian gets about in streetcars or subway trains while his London cousin gets about in trams and by way of the underground. The Bostonian who does not own his own home lives in an apartment; his London counterpart lives in a flat. The Bostonian leaves his car in a ga*rage* rather than in a *gara*ge. He watches *TV* rather than "*telly.*" The Bostonian law enforcer is a *policeman,* or a *cop,* rather than a *bobby;* the Bostonian is entertained at the *movies* rather than at the *cinema*. The melody pattern of the Londoner, whether his utterance is intellectual or emotional, is likely to be characterized by wider inflectional changes than is that of the Bostonian. Articulatory differences may also be heard. The sound *t* in an unstressed syllable, as in *pity,* is likely to be more clearly and more lightly articulated by our English representative than it is by the American. Neither speaker is likely to pronounce an *r* when it is in a final position in a word, as in *dear* or *hear,* but the *r* would be articulated differently in words such as *very.* Our English representative pronounces the word *very* in a manner which phoneticians describe as a single flapped sound. Americans may think of it as approximating the pronunciation *veddy* as in "veddy nice," which of course it is not, except possibly to the prejudiced and motivated ear of an American comic strip artist trying to get across a notion of English pronunciation to an American comic strip reader.

STANDARD ENGLISH SPEECH?

If an American living in the first quarter of this century were to judge English speech by what he heard from Englishmen who were visiting in the United States, he might well have concluded that Englishmen speak pretty much alike. Had he read Shaw's *Pygmalion,* he would have been puzzled by Professor Higgins' complaints. Yet both the American's and Professor Higgins' observations were correct. It is likely that the American, unless he happened to have traveled widely in England, would have been exposed only to the speech of British stage personalities, British political personages, members of the royal family, and well-to-do and well-educated Englishmen with public (really private) secondary school and Oxford or Cambridge backgrounds. Their speech is almost standard.

The speech of these groups is characterized by English phoneticians as *Received Pronunciation;* by *received* is meant "accepted in approved circles." This speech is described by the English phonetician Daniel Jones in his *An Outline of English Phonetics.*[3] Individual recommended pronunciations may be found in Jones' *Pronunciation of English.*[4]

Though "Received speech" was the one that Professor Higgins spoke as a matter of course and that Eliza Doolittle learned to speak after much rigorous training, but which broke down under emotional stress, it is not the standard for the speech of all English-

[3]Daniel Jones, *An Outline of English Phonetics* (8th ed.; Cambridge, England: W. Hefner and Sons, 1956).
[4]Daniel Jones, *The Pronunciation of English* (3rd ed.; Cambridge, England: W. Hefner and Sons, 1950).

men—not even for those with moderate amounts of education who live in or near the City of London. Members of the English Parliament, including those who represent the Conservatives, are today more likely to speak with the accents and pronunciations of the British Broadcasting Company than those identified with Eton and Oxford. A Labor member of Parliament is not likely to assume Tory accents, or even a Tory vocabulary, when he is aware that he may be on the air and his words heard by his constituents in the evening news broadcast. In brief, the forces of democracy in England, as well as the forces of the mass media of communicating, have worked in directions away from Received Pronunciation. Despite Professor Higgins, the English will go on being themselves and listening, so that they can appreciate British Broadcasting Company diction, American movies, and American television programs.

It should be of interest to us that Received Pronunciation—mostly as represented by British actors and by American actors trained, at least as far as diction is concerned, in the British tradition—was recommended as a model if not a standard for American speakers. Margaret P. McLean's *Good American Speech*[5] was essentially a book describing "good" British stage diction. This text influenced several American teachers of voice and diction—for the most part those living in the Eastern Atlantic and New England states—in their own speech practices and in their teachings. Their influence, however, competed with nationwide radio, moving pictures, and later with television. Though some American stage actors and a few American screen actresses reflected this influence in their own speech, the "accents" were considered too self-conscious, too affected, and too imitative for most Americans exposed to the advocates or practitioners of a British standard for Americans. Thus, neither in Britain nor in the United States was British Standard (Received Pronunciation) accepted by a sufficient number of speakers to make a lasting or significant difference for most citizens of either of the English-speaking nations.

AMERICAN BEGINNINGS

When, may we say, did American speech become sufficiently different from the English to give us the beginning of American

[5]Margaret P. McLean, *Good American Speech* (New York: Dutton, 1928).

English? What were the influences that produced and nurtured these differences? In what ways were they peculiarly a result of a new culture and new forces related to this culture? What forces, regardless of culture, continue to exert their effects on our ever-changing speech patterns?

At the opening of the nineteenth century, the United States had its critics and deplorers who raised the hue and cry, "What is happening to our language?" They were referring to English, and were warning Americans about the need to keep their language pure and free from new vulgarisms. John Witherspoon, a Scottish clergyman who came to the United States to become the president of Princeton, suffered considerable anguish at the thought of the development of an American language. Mencken, in *The American Language*, cites Witherspoon as being pained by what he heard in "public and solemn discourses." Said Witherspoon:[6]

I have heard in this country, in the senate, at the bar, and from the pulpit, and see daily in dissertations from the press, errors in grammar, improprieties and vulgarisms which hardly any person of the same class in point of rank and literature would have fallen into in Great Britain.

But persons such as Witherspoon, however great their prestige, were opposed by such Americans as John Adams and Thomas Jefferson. Perhaps more realistically, as Mencken notes on the same page, Jefferson declared:

The new circumstances under which we are placed call for new words, new phrases, and for the transfer of old words to new objects. An American dialect will therefore be formed.

While the dispute between Americans for English English and those for American English was going on, Noah Webster was busily at work on his *Grammatical Institute of the English Language* and, perhaps more importantly, on his *American Dictionary of the English Language*. Certainly, with the publication of the latter in 1828, American English achieved status and recognition, and became established as a major variant of the English language.

Even a cursory review of the forces that established American English as an independent variant of the English language would reveal the following: The American geography and physiography

[6]H. L. Mencken, *The American Language* (New York: Knopf, 1946), p. 5.

presented new features, new creatures, new ways of working for a livelihood, and with them the need for new words. Many of the words came from the Indians and had no competition from the mother tongue. Thus, words such as *skunk, hickory, moose, opossum, persimmon,* and *squash* came into our language. Place names, Mencken points out,[7] also came from the Indians. So did such names for articles of clothing and frequently used objects as *tomahawk, wigwam, toboggan,* and *mackinaw.*

It would, however, be erroneous to conclude that the spirit of rebellion and the influence of the Indians were the only forces that shaped American English. The early colonists, from the very outset, had linguistic influences as a result of accretions from the languages of other colonizations. From the French came words such as *cache, portage,* and *voyageur,* as well as *prairie, bureau,* and *gopher.* From the Dutch in New Amsterdam, Mencken tells us, came such words as *cruller, cole-slaw, cookey, scow, patroon,* as well as *boss* and *Santa Claus.*[8] Many place names in the Hudson area containing *dorp, kill,* and *hook* are also directly from the Dutch. The word *Yankee,* according to Mencken (p. 110), is possibly the most notable of all contributions of Knickerbocker Dutch to the American language.

Spanish influences came later, mostly following the Louisiana Purchase, when American English had become fairly well established and had taken form and direction as a variant of English speech.

The American colonists were ready borrowers of words from other languages, but they were also ready creators of words and phrases that were "coined in English metal" (Mencken, p. 113). Some of these words were a product of the new circumstances and conditions in which the colonists found themselves, but others reveal an underlying way people—any uninhibited and resourceful people—have with words. For a variety of reasons, words were invented. One of the reasons is that inventing words is fun. It is a kind of pleasure in which we indulged ourselves as very young children and again as adolescents. Word-inventing can be a sheer delight, and our American colonists needed to be delighted. Mencken reminds us that "the American, even in the seventeenth century, already showed many of the characteristics that were to set him off from the Eng-

[7]H. L. Mencken, *op. cit.,* p. 105.
[8]H. L. Mencken, *op. cit.,* p. 108.

lishman later on—his bold and somewhat grotesque imagination, his contempt for dignified authority, his lack of aesthetic sensitiveness, his extravagant humor" (pp. 113–114). Not restrained by grammatical awareness or a knowledge of the structure of their language, and largely illiterate, our uncouth and headstrong early colonists added words as the needs of the occasions demanded. So nouns such as *cowhide* and *logroll,* and adjectives and adverbs such as *no-account, no-how,* and *lickity-split* became terms to reckon with and by in the utterances of our seventeenth century Americans. These speakers also introduced such compound words as *bullfrog, hogwallow,* and *hoecake.* All of these are useful terms for persons who are busy working with or against the creatures and forces of nature in a new environment.

A living language often shows the effects of a busy people. Americans were always a busy people, and literally made short of many words and phrases. Leisurely parliamentarians may "lay a matter on the table" for future discussion; busier ones merely decide to "table the matter." We shall later consider, in some detail, other examples of abbreviatory processes that have us riding in *autos* or *cars* rather than in *automobiles,* or watching *TV* rather than *television.* Early in our history the word *cent,* a verbal invention of Governeur Morris, was substituted for the two-syllable English word *penny. Dime* was a Jeffersonian invention derived from the French word *dixième.*

ONGOING FORCES FOR CHANGE

Thus far we have traced the influences that created an American English and some of the differences in linguistic forms between British English and American English. Now we shall consider some of the forces that make any living language a changing language, constantly though slowly yielding to human inclinations and to changing verbal habits. To begin with, we should appreciate the effects of our contemporary ability for speed of movement and our general mobility as a nation of people on wheels or on wings. Washington and Julius Caesar traveled on state occasions in much the same kind of vehicles. Except for slight differences in styling and the addition of springs, similar vehicles were used by our Presidents up to McKinley, though out of choice rather than of necessity, to ride to their inaugurations. Recent Presidents are no longer earthbound; they may move about with the speed of sound. What influence future Presidents will have on American speech, or on English speech throughout the English-speaking world, is a matter of conjecture.

Despite the efforts, reviewed earlier, of some of our early twentieth-century teachers of elocution and diction, and despite the hard work and recommendation of those advocates of "American stage diction," which is or was remarkably like British "stage diction," as the standard for all American diction, the people in the United States are not on a single standard of pronunciation or even of favored idioms for expressing common ideas. According to C. K. Thomas[9] we have ten regional dialects in the United States. By *dialect* we mean a variety of language with a sufficient number of characteristic features to distinguish it from other varieties of the same language. Distinguishing features, for the most part reflected more in the pronunciation of vowels than of consonants, enable C. K. Thomas to distinguish the following regional dialects in the United States: Eastern New England, New York City, Middle Atlantic, the South, Southern Mountain States, the North Central Area, the Central Midland, the Northwest, the Southwest Coastal Area, and Western Pennsylvania.

Regional Differences

In continental United States, differences in pronunciation are most striking along the Atlantic Coast. As we move inland and westward, the differences, C. K. Thomas observes, ". . . become blurred. Over large areas, from the Connecticut valley to the Oregon Coast, for instance, differences are so slight that casual listeners rarely notice them at all." Although differences are greatest along the Atlantic Coast, the merchant from Maine has no anxiety that he will not be readily understood if he speaks by telephone to a merchant from New York, or Maryland, or Florida.

Most students of American dialects agree with Thomas that "the most striking differences between the various regional pronunciations, and the difference around which the most lively, though

[9]C. K. Thomas, *An Introduction to the Phonetics of American English* (2nd ed.; New York: Ronald Press, 1958), p. 232.

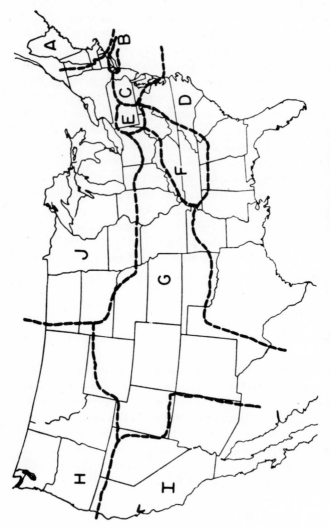

FIGURE 10–1. Map showing the major regional speech areas: A: Eastern New England; B: New York City; C: Middle Atlantic; D: Southern; E: Western Pennsylvania; F: Southern Mountain; G: Central Midland; H: Northwest; I: Southwest; J: North Central. (From Charles Kenneth Thomas, An Introduction to the Phonetics of American English, Second Edition. Copyright © 1958 The Ronald Press Company.)

inconclusive, arguments have revolved, is the nature of the sounds which correspond to the letter *r*."[10]

Who Determines Standards of Usage?

At this point we might, by way of review, ask, "Who determines our pronunciations, and who determines when new words become respectable, and old words acceptable in their emerging forms?" We have no equivalent of a French Academy whose members meet at a common time and place to make such decisions for all Americans. Our dictionary editors are usually insistent that they record what is established and current, and are reluctant to accept the responsibility for establishing standards by virtue of printed and widely distributed publications. Harrison Platt, Jr., presents what we consider a fair view of the degree of responsibility and authority the editors of a respected dictionary cannot avoid. In an Appendix to *The American College Dictionary*,[11] Platt says:

What . . . is the rôle of a dictionary in settling questions of pronunciation or meaning or grammar? It is not a legislating authority on good English. It attempts to record what usage at any time actually is. Insofar as possible, it points out divided usage. It indicates regional variations of pronunciation or meaning wherever practical. It points out meanings and uses peculiar to a trade, profession, or special activity. It suggests the levels on which certain words or usages are appropriate. A dictionary . . . based on a realistic sampling of usage, furnishes the information necessary for a sound judgment of what is good English in a given situation. To this extent the dictionary is an authority, and beyond this authority should not go.

In the light of the above, we may reassess the significance of the entry on *ain't* in *Webster's Third New International Dictionary*. *Ain't*, according to the entry on page 45, is a contraction of *are not, is not, am not,* or *have not*. Further, we are told, *ain't* ". . . though disapproved by many, and more common in less educated speech [is] used orally in most parts of the U.S. by many cultivated speakers esp. in the phrase *ain't I*." Some critics of this dictionary have point-

---

[10]C. K. Thomas, *op. cit.* See pages 172–175 of the present text for a discussion of this and other regional variants.

[11]Harrison Platt, Jr., "Appendix," *The American College Dictionary* (New York: Random House, 1964), p. 1425.

edly asked what is meant by "less educated speech" and imply that somewhere and somehow a comparison seems to be missing. On page 209, we learn that the entry *between* is no longer limited to an implication of two but may be used to suggest division or participation by two or more. The entry cites such usage by *Time Magazine* and by eminent scholars, including a linguist from Harvard University.

One of the supporters of the changes accepted, and so presumably given authority in the Webster's Third Edition, is Bergen Evans, recognized as a lexicographer, a language specialist, as well as the coauthor of *A Dictionary of Contemporary American Usage.* Professor Evans, in an informative and amusing article,[12] opens with the suggestion to "Mind your language, friend: words are changing their meaning all the time, some moving up the ladder of social acceptability and others down." In response to critics who accuse dictionary editors of condoning corruption and "low usage," Evans says: "Alas, the tendencies they deplore have been evident for as long as we have any record of language and are as indifferent to indignation or approval as the tides." As examples of changes in word meaning, Evans points out that the word *resentment* once could mean "gratitude"; in Samuel Johnson's time, it came to mean "a species of revenge" and now means "indignation." The word *censure* once meant simply "to pass judgment"; *censure* now implies "a judgment with negative criticism." The word *uncouth* once meant "unknown" (*couth* itself meant "known") without any contemporary implications of "a lack of polish or 'good' (approved) manners." Few of us are aware that *wench* could once (as late as 1200) be used to refer to "a child of either sex" or that *counterfeit* once had no implication of illegal reproduction but meant "to imitate" or "to model," even after a worthy ideal.

Sumner Ives, in an article reviewing as well as anticipating the controversy that followed the publication of *Webster's Third New International Dictionary,*[13] makes a number of points relative to diction and grammatical usage that are decidedly worthy of our consideration. We shall summarize several of these points:

[12]Bergen Evans, "Couth to Uncouth and Vice Versa," *New York Times Magazine,* November 10, 1963), pp. 22ff.
[13]Sumner Ives, "*A Review of Webster's Third New International Dictionary,*" *Word Study* (December, 1961).

1.   English has changed more during the past fifty years than during any similar period in the past.

2.   Language, any language, is a system of human conventions rather than a system of natural laws: ". . . there is no such thing as grammar apart from the individual grammars of individual languages."

3.   A dictionary is reliable only insofar as it comprehensively and accurately describes current practices in a language, including community opinion as to the social and regional associations of each practice described.

4.   ". . . 'good' English is that which most effectively accomplishes the purpose of the author (or speaker) without drawing irrelevant attention from the purpose to the words or constructions by which this purpose is accomplished. Thus, for ordinary purposes, 'good' English is that which is customary and familiar in a given context and in the pursuit of a given objective."

5.   Words may have more than one pronunciation. "Standards" of pronunciation must make allowances for regional variations and for differences related to specific contexts. *Webster's Third New International Dictionary* represents ". . . the normal pronunciation of English as it is spoken by cultured persons in each major section of the country—the 'language of well-bred ease,' culturally determined."

How Speech "Styles" Are Set

The setting of speech style is rarely a conscious process, except by some of our rebellious, anticonformist adolescents. It sometimes takes generations for a new word to be accepted, or for a pronunciation to be changed so that it is recognized as widespread by dictionary editors. But some words come to life as the result of usage by a single, forceful personality. General Hugh Johnson, Franklin D. Roosevelt's adviser and administrator, gave a new meaning to the word *chisel*. Johnson used *chisel* to mean to evade compliance to the law by concealment or stealth (Mencken, p. 567). The term *beatnik* is attributed to Herb Caen, a popular columnist for the *San Francisco Chronicle*. Walter Winchell through his staccato manner of speech has introduced numerous neologisms and linguistic truncations into our language. Perhaps fortunately for most speakers, and for our language, few of us enjoy being made to feel as nervous as Winchell's manner of speaking tends to do, so his influence may not be pervasive.

Our social scientists, too, have their influence on our language. Brooks Atkinson, in his *Critic at Large* column,[14] deplored the tendency in so-called scientific writing to dehumanize our language. Atkinson complained of the current tendency to ". . . remove English prose from the arena of human beings and pass it through the laboratory, where knowledge can be sterilized." In this process of dehumanization, such verbal products as the following emerge: " 'Our treatment of culture and its evolution rests upon nine heuristic concepts which constitute a mixture of hypothetical postulates and real but tentative observations.' "[15] Brooks Atkinson much prefers more prosaic Anglo-Saxon terminology such as the one he cites from Pogo, who had to tell his friend the alligator, "Albert, you is took leave of your brain bone."

But perhaps Atkinson is overconcerned with what may be a passing phase in verbal habits. We can count on our Walt Kellys today, as we were able to count on Mark Twain early in the century, to use language directly and forcefully and still think, write, and talk impressively. We can also count on our adolescents and their needs for expression to tell one another that they are *lame-brained*, or *squares*, or *jerks*, or *weird*. We perhaps should also be grateful for the references of our adolescents to things or situations that are *super*, or *smooth*, or *drooly*, or simply *way out*. Perhaps it is no accident that many of these terms of affect, the near poetry of slang, are basically Anglo-Saxon. Whatever else these terms may be, they are certainly not dehumanized. Though yesterday's *boob* or *dope* may be today's *creep* or *goof*, the terms are short and some of them may have sufficient lasting power, so that perhaps they may be included in a *fourth* edition of *Webster's New International Dictionary*.

Psychological Determinants

In concluding our discussion of changing speech patterns, we shall review a few psychological factors that determine choice of

---

[14]*New York Times* (September 1, 1961).
[15]Cited by Atkinson from J. H. Steward and D. B. Shimkin, "Some Mechanisms of Sociocultural Evolution," *Daedalus,* **90**, 3 (1961), 479–497.

words and the effects of such choice on our patterns of verbal behavior. By and large the words we use are selected according to our
needs as speakers. The words we select to be impressive depend
upon the situation and the person or persons we wish to impress.
Not infrequently, this person may be the speaker himself rather
than the listener. As speakers, we may have occasional need for a
large mouthful of sounds and so speak polysyllabically and at length
in a manner which would make Freudian listeners click their
tongues and nod their heads with weighty surmises. More frequently, however, other factors determine the words we select. One
such factor is *ease of pronunciation.* With few exceptions, short
words are easier to pronounce than long words, and so, other things
being equal, short words are likely to be chosen over long ones if
they can be used effectively in communicating our thoughts and
feelings. It is no accident that the most frequently used words in our
language are shorter than the words less frequently used. About
twenty-five years ago, the psycholinguist George K. Zipf demonstrated that frequency of word usage is related to length (shortness)
of words and that *words become shorter as spoken words* with increased frequency of usage. Zipf wrote, "There are copious examples
of a decrease in magnitude of a word which results so far as one
can judge solely from an increase in the relative frequence of its
occurrence, as estimated either from the speech of an individual, in
which the shortening may occur, or in the language of a minor
group, or of the major speech group."[16]

We shorten words by processes of *assimilation,* by *truncation,*
and by *abbreviatory substitution.* All three processes, incidentally,
also result in ease of pronunciation. As examples of assimilation,
we have dropped *p* from *cupboard* and most of us drop the *d* from
handkerchief. Even short phrases are made shorter. For example,
the modification of *goodbye* to *gdby,* or just *gby.*

Truncation can be exemplified by the change from *amperes* to
amps, elevator to *el, telephone* to *phone* either as a verb or a noun,
and *automobile* to *auto.* In the San Francisco area the Municipal
Transportation System is briefly referred to as the *Muni. TV* for
television is an example of truncation by abbreviation.

Abbreviatory substitutions are exemplified by *car* for *automobile,*
juice for *electric current,* and *prexy* for *president.* The last two terms,
to be sure, are usages within special groups, but the groups are large

[16]*Psycho-Biology of Language* (Boston: Houghton Mifflin, 1935), p. 29.

and influential. The word *cop* for *policeman* exemplifies the processes of truncation and abbreviation: from *copper* to *cop* as truncation, and *cop* for *policeman* as abbreviatory substitution.

There are, however, counterforces which exert influence in preventing overfrequent use of the same words and with it the process of word shortening. The most potent of these forces is the human drive for variety of experience, including our experience with the words at our command. To avoid monotony, we use synonyms which may be less precise in meaning than would be successive uses of the same word. Early in our school careers our teachers encouraged us to avoid the repeated use of a word merely because repetition is considered undesirable. Partly because of the authority of our teachers and partly because of our drive for variety, we go out of our way to use several different words to communicate an idea that might well be semantically more precise had a previously used word been used (employed).

Taboos and superstitions are two cultural forces which work against the use of some words—frequently short ones of Anglo-Saxon origin—for others which have better social status. Thus, some children are born *out of wedlock,* or *illegitimately,* so that the speaker may avoid a two-syllable term which he tends to use only when he does not really mean what the word denotes. Of late, there is less difference in the productive or functional vocabularies used between men and women in polite social circles, but some of our older (senior) citizens still indicate that they are alarmed when they hear their daughters or granddaughters saying what their sons or grandsons might say with impunity. Thus, we learn euphemisms and employ circumlocutions and say at length in an approximate way what we could say precisely in a brief way if manners and customs and morals were not factors influencing the choice of word usage.

These, briefly, are some of the forces and counterforces that have molded our language, influenced our verbal habits, and continue to modify our slow but ever-changing speech patterns. A living language is a growing language and one that changes forms, adds words and drops others, and modifies pronunciations. Some of the forces are global; others are rather peculiarly American.

CHAPTER 11

Introduction to Study of American-English Sounds

This part of the book has two related purposes. The first is to provide the reader with some fundamentals involved in the production of American-English speech sounds. The second is to provide specific information about the sounds of our language and practice materials for each of the sounds. Both purposes are intended to help the reader in his basic objective of becoming an effective speaker.

IMPROVEMENT OF DICTION

No attempt will be made to be prescriptive or to impose any one standard of diction as better or more desirable than another. We shall, however, work on the basic assumption that any manner or product of speech that attracts attention to itself rather than to the content of speech needs modification.

The sounds of speech, occasionally singly but usually in combination, constitute a symbol code which we use for oral and audible communication. We employ about forty-four distinctive sounds or *phonemes* in the symbol code of American-English speech. There are some variants in this code in different parts of this country. Major variants will be pointed out, but they are relatively few and almost never so great as to prevent ready communication between good speakers from widely separated parts of our country. Poor speakers may have difficulty in communicating in their own areas; their difficulties tend to increase as they try to make themselves understood when they travel at distances from home. For the most part, however, the good speaker from New Orleans, Louisiana, may need a little time to "tune in" to the speech of the Bostonian, the New Yorker, or the citizen from Chicago, but after a brief period all these citizens should be able to understand one another despite some regional differences in diction.

THE SOUNDS OF AMERICAN ENGLISH

Sound Representation

There are two ways of representing the sounds of our language: through spelling (orthographic representation) and through a system in which there is greater consistency between the visible symbol and the sound. It is obvious that a spoken language which has only twenty-six letter symbols and more than forty different sounds cannot have sufficient consistency between letter and sound to provide a reliable guide for articulation and pronunciation. Most of our dictionaries therefore employ a system of diacritical markings and symbols to help the reader appreciate how a word should be pronounced because of or despite its spelling. Unfortunately, even the use of diacritical markings fails to provide a clear one-to-one relationship between sound and symbol. Still another system, more consistent than either of the others, employs selected symbols of the International Phonetic Alphabet (IPA). In the IPA system one symbol is used for each distinctively different sound. Our approach will emphasize the use of the last system of representation. We shall, however, indicate the Webster-Merriam[1] dictionary equivalents of the IPA symbols. Through this approach, we hope that it will become possible for the reader (1) to become aware of the sounds (phonemes) of our language, (2) to make distinctions according to the characteristics of the different sounds, and (3) to

[1] Our reference is to *Webster's New International Dictionary* (2nd ed.; Springfield, Mass.: G. & C. Merriam Co., 1934).

establish a visible basis to cue him on the manner of production for the individual sound, or for a series of sounds, in the contextual flow of speech.

The different sounds of American-English speech and their phonetic symbol and dictionary symbol representations are shown in Tables 11-1 and 11-2.

The Phoneme

Our study of the sounds of American-English speech will be approached through a consideration of the basic unit or sound family —the *phoneme.* Phonemes are distinctive phonetic (sound) elements of words. The phonetic elements are distinctive in that they constitute sound differences which enable us to distinguish between spoken words. For example, the word *sad* has three phonemes. If we change the first, we can distinguish between *sad* and *mad;* if we change the second, we can distinguish between *sad* and *sod;* if we change the last, we can distinguish between *sad* and *sap.*

A second aspect of the phoneme concept is variation. Speech sounds vary in production according to context. The [t] in *tell* is somewhat different from the [t] in *its* and *plate.* Despite the variations, however, they are essentially more alike than different, and we respond to all of these words as containing a [t]. These sound variations which do not affect our understanding of what we hear constitute the members of the phoneme or sound family. The individual variants are called *allophones.*

If our pronunciations and articulatory efforts do not show regard for possible phonemic differences, our listeners may become confused. If the vowel of *bad* begins to approximate the vowel of *bed* we may be misunderstood if we utter a sentence such as *This will be bad for you.* Similarly, if an [s] is produced so that it begins to suggest an [ʃ] (sh), we may not know whether something is for *sipping* or *shipping.*

Some of the difficulty foreign-born persons have in learning to speak English may be attributed to the fact that the phonemes in their native language are not always directly equivalent to ours. For example, we make a significant distinction between the vowels of words such as *heel* and *hill* and *seen* and *sin.* By way of television, radio, or movies, if not by direct experience, most of us know that many of our Mexican neighbors *think* with the vowel of *seen.* They

Table 11-1. THE COMMON PHONEMES OF AMERICAN ENGLISH (CONSONANTS)

KEY WORD	DICTIONARY SYMBOL	IPA SYMBOL
1. *p*at	p	[p]
2. *b*ee	b	[b]
3. *t*in	t	[t]
4. *d*en	d	[d]
5. *c*ook	k	[k]
6. *g*et	g	[g]
7. *f*ast	f	[f]
8. *v*an	v	[v]
9. *th*in	th	[θ]
10. *th*is	t̶h̶	[ð]
11. *s*ea	s	[s]
12. *z*oo	z	[z]
13. *sh*e	sh	[ʃ]
14. trea*s*ure	zh	[ʒ]
15. *ch*ick	ch	[tʃ]
16. *j*ump	j	[dʒ]
17. *m*e	m	[m]
18. *n*o	n	[n]
19. si*ng*	ng	[ŋ]
20. *l*et	l	[l]
21. *r*un	r	[r]
22. *y*ell	y	[j]
23. *h*at	h	[h]
24. *w*on	w	[w]
25. *wh*at	hw	[ʍ] or [hw]

Table 11-2. THE COMMON PHONEMES OF AMERICAN ENGLISH (VOWELS)

KEY WORD	DICTIONARY SYMBOL	IPA SYMBOL
26. fee	ē	[i]
27. sit	ĭ	[ɪ]
28. take	ā	[e]
29. met	ĕ	[ɛ]
30. cat	ă	[æ]
31. task	ă or à	[æ] or [a] depending upon regional or individual variations
32. calm	ä	[ɑ]
33. hot	ŏ or ä	[ɒ] or [ɑ] depending upon regional or individual variations
34. saw	ô	[ɔ]
35. vote	ō	[o] or [ou]
36. bull	ŏŏ	[ʊ]
37. too	ōō	[u]
38. hut	ŭ	[ʌ]
39. about	ă,ĕ,ĭ,ŏ,ŭ,à,ē	[ə]
40. upper	ẽr	[ɚ] by most Americans and [ə] by many others
41. bird	ûr	[ɝ] by most Americans and [ɜ] by many others

Phonemic Diphthongs

42. ice	[ī]	[aɪ]
43. now	[ou]	[au] or [ɑʊ]
44. boy	[oi]	[ɔɪ]

may also have difficulty with the distinctions we make between *hail* and *hell*. We, of course, are not immune from these errors when we learn a foreign language. When speaking another language, we often produce vowels and some consonants of our closest equivalents and so manage to sound like a foreigner.

CLASSIFICATION OF SOUNDS

The sounds of our language may be classified in three large groups: consonants, vowels, and diphthongs. All are produced as a result of some modification of the outgoing breath by the organs of articulation.

Consonants are speech sounds which are produced by either a complete or partial obstruction or modification of the breath channel by the organs of articulation. Aside from voice, the sound character- istics of each consonant result from the manner of vibration of the breath stream. This is determined by the way in which the breath stream is (1) modified by the closures produced by articulatory activity, (2) released by the activity of the opening of the closure, or (3) modified but not completely obstructed (stopped) by the narrowing of the breath channel.

Vowels are produced by articulatory movements of the speech organs without obstruction or interference of the vibrating breath stream in its passage through the breath channel. We determine the characteristic features of the vowels of our language by modifying the size and shape of the mouth cavity and by changing the position of the tongue within the mouth.

Diphthongs are voiced glides which are uttered in a single breath impulse. Some diphthongs are blends of two vowels. Most, however, represent an instability or "breakdown" of what at one time in the history of our language was one vowel. Regardless of historical development, a diphthong may be defined as ". . . a syllabic ele- ment, which begins with one sound and shifts to another, and we understand this to exclude consideration of those brief building-up and dying-out stages which characterize every speech sound."[2]

[2]R-M. S. Heffner, *General Phonetics* (Madison, Wisc.: University of Wiscon- sin Press, 1949), p. 112.

A diphthong may also be defined as a syllabic in which two vowel resonances are clearly identified, but with a *change of resonance* as an essential charac-

Voice

All vowels and diphthongs, unless intentionally whispered, are produced with vocalization accompanying the articulatory activity. Consonants, however, may be produced with or without accompanying vocalization. Those which are produced with vocalization are known as *voiced* consonants, those produced without vocalization are referred to as *voiceless*.

Manner and Place of Articulation

In the individual descriptions of the consonant sounds which will be presented later, the manner and place of articulation will be considered for each sound. Some consonants will be described as *plosives*, others as either *fricatives, glides,* or *nasals*. We shall anticipate some of the descriptions by defining a few terms at the present time.

Plosive, or stop, sounds are produced by a stopping of the breath stream. The plosive sounds are [p], [b], [t], [d], [k], and [g].

Fricatives are produced by a partial closure of the articulators. This action results in the creation of a constricted passage through which the stream of air must be forced. The partial closures may take place as a result of the grooving of the tongue or of having other organs of articulation come close together. The distinctively fricative sounds are [f], [v], [θ] (th), [ð] (th), [s], [z], [ʃ] (sh). and [ʒ] (zh). The sound [h] is produced with laryngeal constriction.

Nasal sounds are reinforced and emitted nasally. The three nasals are [m], [n], and [ŋ] (ng).

Glides are sounds which are produced with continuous rather than fixed articulatory positions. The glide consonants are [hw] or [ʌ], [w], [j] (y), and most varieties of [r].

Affricates are blends of two sounds, one a plosive and the other a fricative. There are two affricates, [tʃ] (ch) as in *chum* and [dʒ] (dzh) as in *jam*.

The sound [l] is a *lateral* consonant. It is produced by the emis-

---

teristic. See J. Carrell and W. R. Tiffany, *Phonetics* (New York: McGraw-Hill Book Co., 1960), p. 121.

sion of vocalized breath at both sides of the tongue while the tip of
the tongue is in contact with the gum ridge.

SOUNDS IN CONTEXT

Although our approach to the improvement of diction will begin
with a descriptive analysis of the individual sounds of our language,
speech does not consist of a series of individual sounds. Speech is a
sequence or context of sounds. In context, individual sounds may be
modified and produced differently from what they would be in isolation. If one were to speak as though our linguistic symbols were
a series of sounds, he would be uttering phonetic nonsense. In context, differences in force and duration to emphasize meanings,
differences according to the formality or informality of the speech
situation, and differences according to the size of the listening group,
all make for modifications of individual sounds in the flow of speech.
Some of these differences will be considered briefly.

ASSIMILATION

If asked for the pronunciation of the words *education, mature,*
and *income,* many persons would carefully pronounce these words
differently from their pronunciations in contextual speech. The
word *education* may regularly be pronounced [ɛdjukeʃən] (ĕdūkā-
shən) by some persons, but most of us are likely to say [ɛdʒəkeʃən]
(ĕjəkāshən) in talking about "the education of our children" or in
asserting that "education means—." When we change from the careful but less usual pronunciation of words such as *educate, income,
handkerchief* or phrases such as *don't you* and *meet you* to the
easier and more usual ones we are yielding to and demonstrating
the effects of *assimilation in connected speech.*

Assimilation refers to the phonetic changes that take place when
one sound is modified as the result of a neighboring sound or sounds
in connected speech. Some of these changes become relatively fixed
and so regularly influence the pronunciations of many words. Other
assimilations depend upon particular verbal contexts and so influence
the articulation and pronunciation of words only in these contexts.
Examples of each will be given in our brief discussions of some types
of assimilative modifications.

Anticipatory Changes

Most assimilations reflect the influences of anticipatory changes. That is, the organs of articulation, in anticipation of a sound to follow, modify a preceding sound. The change tends to simplify or facilitate articulation. For example, in the word *congress*, the letter *n* is sounded as an [ŋ] (ng) in anticipation of the sound [g] that follows. It is easier to articulate [ŋg] than [n + g] simply because both the [ŋ] and the [g] are produced with the same parts of the tongue and the palate. For the same reason *income* is pronounced with an [ŋ] rather than an [n] followed by a [k]. Similarly, it is easier to say *this shoe* with a lengthened [ʃ] (sh) than with an [s] followed by an [ʃ]. The pronunciation of *this shoe*, incidentally, is an example of contextual, temporary assimilation.

Voicing

Changes produced in voicing by assimilation are perhaps best exemplified in words that end with a final *s* or *d*. In the words *liked, heaped, rasped, guessed* and *ropes, takes,* and *plates* the next to the last produced sound is a voiceless consonant. (The letter *e*, in each case, is silent.) As a result, the final *d* is pronounced as a [t] rather than [d] and the final *s* as an [s] rather than [z].

In words such as *passes, hedges, riches,* and *roses* the final *s* is produced as [z] because the next to the last sound is a vowel and is vocalized. Similarly, *grounded, breaded,* and *heeded* are each pronounced with a final [d]. In the words *begs, seems, togs,* and *roams* the final sound is voiced because of the influence of the preceding voiced consonant.

Other Assimilations

In some cases assimilations may result in the complete loss of one or more sounds which are replaced by a third sound. This happens in the assimilated pronunciation of *picture, nature,* and *feature,* where the sound [tʃ] (ch) is heard in the second syllable of each of the words.

STYLES OF SPEECH

In both manner and content, speech is appropriate or inappropriate, correct or incorrect, according to circumstances and occasion. Despite possible differences in education, profession, and speaking ability, an individual's manner of communicating will or should vary according to the time, the place, and the speaking situation. The minister who feels the need to deliver a sermon to his family should do so differently from the way he would speak to his congregation in church. The minister should certainly not converse at home, with members of his family or with visiting members of his congregation, as he would talk to them from his pulpit. The lecturer speaking to a large audience on a formal occasion is likely to use more elevated language than the same speaker at his club, on a picnic, with friends, or at a home social gathering.

Informal speech employs many contractions. We use more *he*'s, *dont*'s, and *I'm*'s when speaking informally and intimately than when speaking formally. We do not, however, usually employ contracted forms when emphasis is intended. Public addresses, with the exception of the humorous afterdinner speech, are generally delivered formally unless, for special purposes (usually political), the speaker wants his listeners to feel that he is "one of the boys."

SPEECH STANDARDS

Pronunciation Variants

In going over the list of consonants and vowel sounds some observations may be made relative to minor differences in pronunciation among Americans.

Many of us do not distinguish between the [hw] in *what* and the [w] of *watt* but pronounce both the way we do the first sound of *will*.

There is considerable variation as to the pronunciation of the vowel of the word *ask*. Most Americans use the same vowel in the words *ask* and *hat*; others broaden the vowel in *ask* to that of the [ɑ] of *calm;* a smaller number of Americans use the vowel [a] which is phonetically between [æ] and [ɑ].

Most Americans use the same vowel in *hot* as they do in *calm*. A few, however, use a vowel intermediate between the vowel of *call* and the vowel of *calm*.

There is considerable variation in the production of the vowel of words such as *bird* and *heard*. Some use the vowel [ɝ] which has *r* coloring. Others include a clear-cut *r* preceded by a vowel much like the one in the word *bud*.

Paralleling the variations in the vowel of words such as *bird, heard, surf,* and *mirth* are those for the final sound of the words such as *after, supper,* and *thunder*. Most of us use the vowel [ɚ] which is much like the first sound of the word *above* with the addition of *r* coloring. Others add a clear-cut [r] sound after the same vowel, and a smaller number make no distinction between the first sound of the word *above* and the last sound of *after* and use [ə] for both.

To this short list of variants in American pronunciation, we might add another relative to the articulation of the [r] sound in words in which the spelling includes the letter *r*. We are in common agreement that an [r] sound is produced whenever a word contains an initial *r* in its spelling, as in *rug, rice, rain,* and *runs* and in words in which the *r* is preceded by a consonant and followed by a vowel as in *tree, grease,* and *prize*. The [r] is also pronounced in medial positions when it is followed by a vowel as in *forest* and *touring*. Practice differs, however, in words in which the *r* is medial in spelling and followed by a consonant as in *farm, card,* and *sharp* or final in the spelling as in *car, far,* and *soar*. These differences will be considered again in our more detailed consideration of the [r] phoneme.

Assimilations and Speech Standards

Most of the examples of assimilation given earlier are considered acceptable and in good standing by all except the most pedantic people. Some persons may prefer the unassimilated pronunciations of words such as *congress* and *income* and tax themselves to maintain the [n] rather than yield to economy in articulation and produce an [ŋ]. Not all assimilations, however, are acceptable even to our liberal dictionary editors. For example, the word *open,* despite temptation and frequent pronunciation by small children, should still be produced with a final [n] rather than an [m].[3] The word *gas* is still better pronounced with a final [s] than with a [z], though the second pronunciation is frequently given by persons not habitually careless in their speech.

Criteria for Speech Standards

Speech in general and pronunciation in particular are appropriate if they are consistent with the objectives of the speaker in his role of communicator of ideas. The listeners, the occasion, and the speaker as a personality are some of the factors which determine appropriateness. What is appropriate may be accepted as standard. Speech becomes substandard if the pronunciations are such that they violate the judgments and tastes of the listeners. We are likely to sense such violations if an official in high government office speaks to us as members of a large audience as he might to some of his intimate friends on a fishing trip. We might also sense some violation if a college president talking on the topic "The Need for a Liberal Arts Education" were to do so in the manner of a sports announcer.

Speech becomes distinctly substandard if it employs pronunciations that are not currently used by any persons whose backgrounds as speakers make their judgments as regards linguistic usage worthy of respect. Even a liberal attitude toward pronunciation would not now justify the pronunciation of *asked* as [æst] (ăst) or of *something* as [sʌmpɪm] (sŭmpĭm).

Pronunciations that reveal foreign language influence, such as the substitution of a sound which approximates the appropriate one in English, would also constitute substandard speech. The substitution of a [v] for a [w] in words such as *wife* and *went* or an [f] for a [v] in words such as *give* and *leave* are examples of substandard pronunciations frequently resulting from foreign language influence. Occasionally, they may reflect persistent foreign language influences in dialectal speech within this country.

The speaker who wishes to improve his speech, his articulation, and his pronunciation as well as his word usage, must be a good

[3]A. J. Bronstein in his *The Pronunciation of American English* (New York: Appleton-Century-Crofts, 1960), p. 212, recognizes that an *m* may be heard in the phrase "open the door" in assimilated colloquial educated speech.

listener. He must listen with discrimination for what is best and current in the community in which he lives. He must listen to the educated and respected members of the community and use them as models but not imitate them slavishly. Above all, he should avoid trying to sound like somebody else, thus seeming to deny his individuality and his place of origin. This does not mean that he should maintain what may have been substandard in his background. It does mean that the man from New York should not consciously try to sound as though he were from Atlanta, Georgia, and that the speaker from Houston, Texas, should not try to sound like the Harvard-educated Bostonian. In time, if any of these speakers live long enough in an area, some of the flavor of the area's speech will naturally begin to appear. Careful listening is likely to translate itself into unconscious imitation of the speech of the immediate environment unless the speaker is negatively motivated toward the persons to whom he is listening.

CHAPTER 12

Individual Study of American-English Sounds: The Vowels

In our study of the sounds of American-English speech we shall maintain our objective of the improvement of diction. Some sounds have been found to be more troublesome—more frequently produced in a faulty manner—than others. These sounds will receive our major emphasis. They will be treated in more detail and a larger amount of practice-exercise material will be provided for them than for the sounds which cause little difficulty for the vast majority of speakers of American English.

We shall begin our study with an analysis of the vowel sounds. Although differences in practice relative to the pronunciation of vowels are fairly wide in different parts of the country, most vowel sounds, because of their intensity and "open" manner of production, are comparatively easy to imitate. Pronunciation habits based upon regional practice may, however, result in the persistent use of one vowel in some words when most Americans use another. For example, there is considerable variation in the pronunciation of the vowel in the words *had, have, candy, bad,* and *sad,* depending upon regional custom. There is also a fair amount of regional variation in the pronunciation of the vowels in words such as *word, bird, heard, dearth, earth, curdle,* and *merge.* There is also some variation in the choice of vowel for words such as *path, ask,* and *dance.* Some of the variations in practice in different parts of the country will be considered when the individual vowel sounds are discussed.

VOWEL PRODUCTION

All vowels share several characteristics: (1) They are all voiced sounds; (2) all are articulated in essentially the same manner in that they are continuant sounds without interruption and without restriction of the stream of breath; and (3) though lip activity is involved, the activity of the tongue makes the essential difference in the production of the different vowel sounds.

Vowel Classification

Vowels may be conveniently classified according to the part of the tongue most actively involved in the production of the sound. If you concentrate on the vowel sounds of the words *me* and *moo,* you should be able to note that the blade of the tongue moves forward toward the hard palate for *me.* For *moo,* the back of the tongue moves toward the soft palate. Similar activity may be noted if you compare the vowels of *pet* and *paw.* For *pet,* the front of the tongue is most active. And for *paw* the back of the tongue is most active. For neither of the vowels, however, does the tongue move as high as for the vowels of *me* and *moo.* Comparable activity may be observed for all the other *front vowels* (those produced with the front or blade of the tongue most active) compared with the corresponding *back vowels* (those produced with the back of the tongue most active).

The approximate differences in tongue position for the front and back vowels are illustrated in Figures 12–1 and 12–2 on the facing page.

Figure 12–3 illustrates the position of the tongue for the central vowels, or mid-vowels (those produced with the middle of the tongue most active).

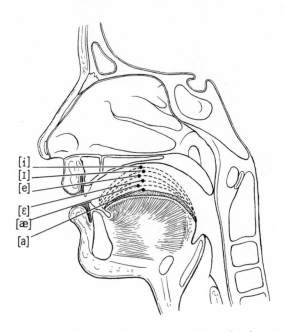

[i]
[ɪ]
[e]
[ɛ]
[æ]
[a]

FIGURE 12–1.   Representative tongue positions for front vowels.

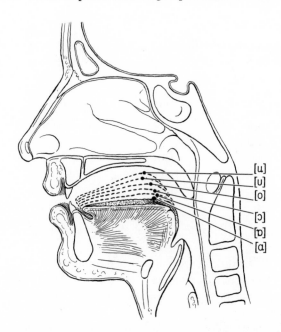

[u]
[ʊ]
[o]
[ɔ]
[ɒ]
[ɑ]

FIGURE 12–2.   Representative tongue positions for back vowels.

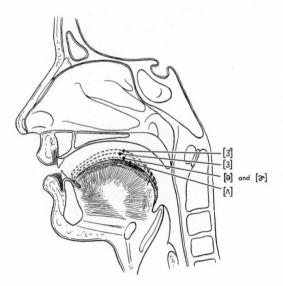

FIGURE 12–3. Representative tongue positions for the central vowels, or mid-vowels.

You may test these representative tongue positions with your own articulatory behavior relative to these vowels by incorporating them in the following key words.

Front	*Central*	*Back*
me		boot
mit		book
made	mirth	boat
met	*a*bove, upp*er*	bought
mat	mud	box
mask		balm

On the basis of the production of the key vowels, a twofold basis for classification becomes possible.

First, vowels differ in production according to *place of articulation*—and so may be classified as *front, mid-,* or *back* vowels according to the part of the tongue that is most actively involved in their production.

Second, vowels differ as to *height-of-tongue* position. The vowel of *me* is a high front vowel; the vowel of *moon* is a high back vowel.

Table 12-1. VOWELS OF AMERICAN–ENGLISH SPEECH

Front Vowels

	PHONETIC SYMBOL	DICTIONARY SYMBOL
meet	[i]	ē
milk	[ɪ]	ĭ
may	[e]	ā
men	[ε]	ĕ
mat	[æ]	ǎ
ask*	[a]	à

Central Vowels

	PHONETIC SYMBOL	DICTIONARY SYMBOL
mirth	[ɜ] or [ɝ]	ûr
about	[ə]	ā, ē, ĭ, ŏ / ŭ, à, ē
upper	[ɚ]	ẽr
mud	[ʌ]	ŭ

Back Vowels

	PHONETIC SYMBOL	DICTIONARY SYMBOL
boon	[u]	ōō
book	[ʊ]	ŏŏ
boat	[o]	ō
ball	[ɔ]	ô
bog	[ɒ]	ǒ
balm	[a]	ä

*When the speaker compromises between the vowels of *mat* and of *balm*. This vowel is intermediate in placement as well as in sound between [æ] and [ɑ].

181

The vowel of *mask* is a low front vowel; that of *balm* is a low back vowel.

A *third basis* for the classification of vowels is *muscle tension*. If we compare the vowel of *peek* with that of *pick*, we should feel that the tongue is more tense for the vowel of *peek* than it is for the one in *pick*. Similarly, the vowel of *boat* is produced with the tongue somewhat more tense than in the production of the vowel of *book*. Tension may also be felt in the muscles behind the chin.

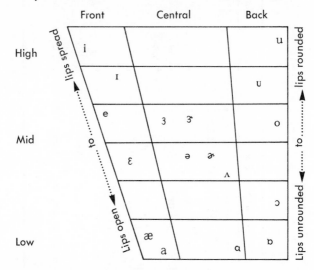

FIGURE 12–4. Tongue and lip positions of the American-English vowels. (From: *The Pronunciation of American English* by Arthur J. Bronstein. Copyright © 1960, Appleton-Century-Crofts, Inc. Reprinted by permission of Appleton-Century-Crofts.)

Before we go into our more detailed discussion of the individual sounds of our language, we might review briefly some features of vowel production. All vowels, unless intentionally whispered, are voiced, continuant sounds. When produced as isolated sounds, the tongue tip is usually placed behind the lower gum ridge. The vowel sounds are differentiated as a result of activity of the blade, the middle or the back of the tongue elevated to different positions (heights) within the mouth cavity. Some vowels are produced with muscle tension as an additional characteristic. The articulatory aspects which characterize the production of each of the vowels will now be considered.

THE FRONT VOWELS

[i] (ē) As in *See*

The vowel [i] is a high front vowel.

An examination of the front-vowel diagram (Figure 12–1) will reveal that [i] is produced with the blade of the tongue arched high in the front of the mouth. It is produced with a considerable degree of tongue tension and a lesser degree of lip tension. When [i] is produced as an isolated sound, the lip position approximates a tight-lipped grin. Tension should also be present in the muscle bulge behind the chin.

Muscle tension is necessary to produce a clear [i] and to distinguish it from the vowel [ɪ] (ĭ) which is a more relaxed sound.

The sound [i] has many different English spellings. The most frequent include *e, ee, ea, ei, i,* and *ie* as in *be, see, each, receipt, ski,* and *believe.*

Practice Materials

Initial

each	easy	eke	eerie
even	eager	equal	ego
ether	eel	eaves	Easter
east	eat	ease	edict

Medial

beach	beast	appease	frieze
breathe	feast	conceive	machine
breed	meat	please	crease
cheese	sweet	breeze	team
heat	yield	intrigue	achieve
beet	steel	sneeze	tease

Final

agree	pea	tree	sea
glee	flee	ski	spree
esprit	key	bee	lea
tee	she	we	knee
fee	dee	free	quay

Phrases

sweets to the sweet	flee the bees
breathe easily	tease and sneeze
team achievement	gleeful sprees
seasonal trees	eerie and not dreary
beat the heat	breed of beast

Sentences

1. Eastern breezes frequently bring teeming rain.
2. Beans and peas grow in green pods.
3. Steve was eager to eat the eels.
4. Eve's tempter lived in a tree in the Garden of Eden.
5. Machines seem to be able to think, but have not yet achieved an ability for intrigue.
6. Rita, who was frequently as sweet and pleasing as she could be, sometimes went on a teasing spree.
7. Steele complained that it was either a feast or a famine at mealtime.
8. McFee watched his golf ball speed down the sixteeenth green.
9. Lee believed that the Greeks have a unique place in history.
10. Browning believed that a man's reach should exceed his grasp.

[ɪ] (ĭ) As in *Bit*

[ɪ] is also a high, front vowel. [ɪ] differs from [i] in two respects; [ɪ] is produced with a tongue position somewhat lower than is [i] and *without articulatory tension.*

The lip position for [ɪ] is approximately a relaxed smile in contrast with the tight-lipped grin for [i]. The difference in tension and lip may be observed by placing your hand behind your chin and looking in the mirror as you change from the word *heat* to *hit.*

The most frequent spelling for [ɪ] is the letter *i* as in *sit, wit, fit,* and *lit;* other spellings include *u, ui,* and *e* as in *busy, build,* and *English.*

Some speakers use the vowel [ɪ] for the final *y* in words such as *busy, city, petty.* Other speakers are likely to use a vowel somewhere between [i] and [ɪ]. Still others may use a vowel closer to [i] than to [ɪ].

Determine your own practice by testing yourself with the following lists of words. The words are to be read across the page.

seat	city	sit
peat	pity	pit
key	kitty	kit
meat	meaty	mit
cheese	cheesy	chit
we	weedy	wit

Practice Materials

Initial

ilk	its	ingot	infer
imp	is	Italy	intake
ink	itch	indicate	ignore
Indian	inch	inn	insert
into	imply	ignorant	image
imbue	ingrate	impale	impact

Medial

mist	list	fist	grip
business	tryst	strip	flick
differ	women	shrimp	whisk
fill	wishes	shrill	hymn
quick	drip	grill	quilt
wilt	mince	lick	think
eclipse	instill	bib	admit
addict	crib	simple	spin
frantic	abyss	aphid	antic

Sentences

1. Simpson was a businessman with strong ethical principles.
2. Kimball made a quick trip to an inland city.
3. Rivers, big and little, join to form the Mississippi.
4. Wilson was an industrious physicist.
5. William was an intrepid investigator.
6. A man convinced against his will is of the same opinion still.

7. Dixon predicted the moon's eclipse.
8. Jill's dinner included six Indian dishes.
9. Bill's system of thinking made an indelible impression on Jim.
10. The wind whistled through the kitchen window.

Selection

The moving finger writes, and having writ,
Moves on. Nor all your piety nor wit
   Shall lure it back to cancel half a line,
Nor all your tears wash out a word of it.
      —*The Rubaiyat of Omar Khayyám* (Translated by Edward Fitzgerald)

For persons who have difficulty in distinguishing between the tense vowel [i] and the relaxed [ɪ] the following material should be of help. Place your hand behind your chin and feel the tension for the vowel in the first word of each pair. The second word, in contrast, should have a relaxed chin.

seat	sit	leak	lick
beat	bit	sheep	ship
meat	mit	sleep	slip
heat	hit	peach	pitch
greet	grit	leap	lip
cheap	chip	green	grin
peep	pip	heap	hip
fleet	flit	peak	pick
reed	rid	greed	grid
feel	fill	heel	hill

In the following sentences the first italicized word has the tense vowel [i]; the second has the relaxed vowel [ɪ].

1. They climbed to *reach* the *rich* mine.
2. The *beans* were stored in *bins*.
3. Much *steel* is *still* imported.
4. The *team* counted on *Tim*.
5. Ten *sheep* were sent by *ship*.
6. A rod and *reel* were lost in the *rill*.
7. The *deed* he *did* took courage.
8. At *least* ten items were on the *list*.

[ɪ] in Unstressed Syllables

The vowel [ɪ] occurs rather frequently in the unstressed syllables of many polysyllabic words as in add*ed*, frett*ed*, tep*i*d, *i*nept, *i*nstead, and *i*mply. In some instances the speaker may use the vowel [ə] rather than [ɪ] in the unstressed syllable. The following word lists will provide practice with the [ɪ] in unstressed positions.

practice	wedded	impart	plosive
merit	sterile	instead	corrosive
encrusted	junket	inept	listed
frosting	rusted	immerse	watches
bursting	tempted	intend	matches

In the following lists, the [ɪ] occurs in both the stressed and unstressed syllable or syllables.

implement	respective	imprinting	imagine
impending	politics	finicky	statistics
implicit	primitive	instinctive	simplify
intended	impinge	misgiving	activity
intuitive	kindling	consistent	indicate

[e] (ā) As in *Mate*

[e] is a mid-high, front vowel. Most Americans are more likely to produce the vowel [e] as part of the diphthong [eɪ] than as a pure vowel. Whether produced as part of a diphthong or as a pure sound [e] is a tense, front, mid-high vowel (see front-vowel diagram, Figure 12–1).

Some speakers use the diphthongal form more or less regularly in a stressed syllable and the pure vowel form in an unstressed syllable. There are, however, no words in our language which would be distinguished in meaning from one another on the basis of the use of a pure vowel [e] or the diphthongal form [eɪ]. We do not recommend the cultivation of either form for the sake of consistency. We do, however, recommend that excessive prolongation of the diphthrong to a triphthong [eɪə] be avoided.

The vowel [e] or the diphthong [eɪ] is most frequently represented in spelling by the letter *a* as in *date, mate,* and *hate;* other frequent spellings include *ay, ai, ey,* and *ei* as in *say, mail, they,* and *vein.*

Practice Materials

Initial

ace	angel	eight	ate
ail	April	ape	ache
age	aim	aviator	aid

Medial

bait	crate	chaotic	fateful
bail	place	grate	station
deign	plate	lace	caged
date	rate	chaste	strafe
sake	flake	awake	failure

Final

dray	repay	dismay	relay
shay	delay	bay	ray
pay	hay	neigh	portray
day	may	betray	fray
way	they	play	display

Note whether you distinguish between the vowel and diphthong forms in the following sentences. Careful listening may help you to decide that sentence context may make a difference.

Sentences

1. Though changed, radio is still a medium of entertainment.
2. Clayton saved paperweights.
3. May has thirty-one days.
4. Nathan was fond of angel cake or anything else that Jane would bake for him.
5. Casco Bay is in the State of Maine.
6. Dale won the relay race on Saturday.
7. Crane saw strange shapes riding in the gray mist.
8. Raymond gazed in dismay at stagestruck Rachel.
9. Grace watched the plane fly off into space.
10. Jayson was fond of cakes and ale.

Selections

1. Ill fares the land, to hastening ills a prey,
   Where wealth accumulates, and men decay;
   Princes and lords may flourish or may fade;
   A breath can make them, as a breath has made.
   —OLIVER GOLDSMITH, *The Deserted Village*

2. He left the name at which the world grew pale,
   To point a moral, or adorn a tale.
   —SAMUEL JOHNSON, *The Vanity of Human Wishes*

[ɛ] (ĕ) As in *Help*

[ɛ] is a mid-front vowel. The vowel [ɛ] differs from [e] in that the former is produced with a slightly lower front tongue position and *without articulatory tension*.

The most frequent spelling for the vowel [ɛ] is the single letter *e*; other spellings include *a* as in *any, ay* as in *says, ai* as in *said,* and *ea* as in *bread.*

Practice Materials

In the lists of words for initial and medial [ɛ] avoid any tendency to prolong the vowel into the diphthong [ɛə].

Initial

effort	emblem	enzyme	enterprise
ebb	empty	enter	engine
end	any	energy	exit
echo	elf	elk	elder
egg	elbow	edge	effort
etch	edible	entry	extra

Medial

reckon	restless	festive	gender
beckon	said	jest	center
lend	gem	wren	theft
guess	thread	deaf	health
pleasant	meant	check	pensive
self	tent	ready	settler

Phrases

elfin jests	tense elders
edible eggs	pensive Frenchmen
ready guests	gentle echoes
enter and exit	thefts of gems
pleasant self	beckon the deaf

Sentences

1. Edward spent ten cents for a lead pencil.
2. The red hen laid an egg every day.
3. Ned avoided ever getting into debt.
4. Men most deaf are those who will not attend.
5. Ethel kept her friends because she was sensitive and dependable.
6. Ben was energetic and often restless.
7. The ebb tide kept the ship from setting sail.
8. The empty room still held the scent of Beth's perfume.
9. The terrier was adept at picking up a scent.
10. Ted developed his method by careful measurements.

Selection

And Marlowe, Webster, Fletcher, Ben,
Whose fire-hearts sowed our furrows when
The world was worthy of such men.

—ELIZABETH BARRETT BROWNING, *A Vision of Poets*

Make certain that clear distinctions are made for the vowels in the italicized words in the sentences that follow.

1. The *pen* was placed next to the *pin.*
2. *Ed* called for *aid.*
3. *Fred* was seldom *afraid.*
4. *Ben,* where have you *been?*

[æ] (ă) As in *Bat*

[æ] is a low front vowel. It is almost always produced with a lax tongue; occasionally some contexts call for a slightly tense tongue but emphatic tension should be avoided. The tongue is lower in position and the mouth wider open for [æ] than it is for [ɛ] (see front-vowel diagram, Figure 12–1).

The letter *a* as in *mash, pack, rack,* and *sack* is the most frequent spelling representation for the vowel [æ].

In some parts of the United States the vowel blend [ɛə] tends to be substituted for the vowel [æ]. In much of the United States a vowel closer to [ɛ] than to [æ] is heard in words in which the vowel is followed by the sound [r] as in *marry, parry,* and *Harry.*

Practice Materials

Determine your own practice for the following words in which the vowel [æ] is an acceptable pronunciation. Doubts, if they exist, should be determined by usage of respected speakers in your community.

map	match	jam	grab
cap	shall	had	bag
can	carry	fact	trapped
cast	parrot	fancy	plant
back	drank	ham	sham

Initial

at	ant	and	answer
angle	antler	act	add
apple	anchor	alkaline	aster
atom	agonize	ample	Alice
angry	abduct	annual	Alps

Medial

crab	wrap	trapper	crash
crack	lacking	jagged	hack
stack	slapped	ragged	wax
mash	flax	flagging	hatched
pack	bagged	wrapped	satin

Phrases

candy and jam	ham sandwich
crack back	animal crackers
ragged and jagged crags	flags wagging
pack the bags	agonizing answer
apple mash	stand fast

Sentences

1. Andrew carried his bride from the carriage into the house.
2. Frank planted three rows of asters.
3. Jack's pack had ample room for a dozen apples.
4. The Swiss Alps have many jagged peaks and crags.
5. Jam and pancakes make a snack for a boy and a meal for a man.
6. Tad fancied himself a man of unflagging action.
7. Alan went to California to enhance his acting career.
8. A good match is preceded by a good catch.
9. The cab's wheels sank deep into the sand.
10. Hatless and ragged, Calvin's spirits never flagged.
11. A hammer rather than an ax should be used for banging a tack.
12. Hank's jam sandwiches were wrapped in wax sacks.

In the following sentences be careful to avoid excessive tension or nasality for the vowels of the italicized words. Keep your jaw and tongue relaxed.

1. *"Can Hank manage* the task?" asked *Nathaniel.*
2. The *ban* on *canned ham* was dropped.
3. *Dan* and *Sam* ran a fast race.
4. Alfred had *random* thoughts when he *cat*napped.
5. *Frank planned* to raise *Angus* cattle.
6. *Andrew* enjoyed *active* sports.

Selection

Clara planned a man to marry,
* A Sam, a Dan, perhaps a Harry,
She asked, she prayed he would not tarry
And that her plan would not miscarry.

[a] (ȧ)

[a] is a low, front, lax vowel.

We are intentionally excluding a key word for the vowel [a] because most Americans do not use this sound as a pure vowel, but use it only as the first element of the diphthong [aɪ] as in *I, my,* and *ice.* The pure vowel [a] is used by a minority of American speakers, most of whom probably reside in the New England area. These speakers would use the vowel in words such as *ask, grass,* and *mask.*

In regard to tongue position the vowel [a] is a compromise between the front vowel [æ] and the low back vowel [ɑ] (ä), as in *calm.*

There is, of course, no objection to cultivating the vowel [a] if there is some cultural reason for doing so. We would suggest, however, that the cultivation of this vowel be accompanied by some degree of consistency and that the speaker avoid fluctuating between [a] in *dance, craft,* and *mask* and [æ] for *France, laugh* and *ask.*

Practice Materials

Determine your pactice in the use of the vowel [æ] or [a] for the following materials. Consistency of vowel pronunciation is recommended but not prescribed.

half	class	last	mast
ask	task	advance	dance
grass	calf	craft	demand
mask	laugh	France	bath

Sentences

1. The birds took their bath in the moist grass.
2. We attended a dance wearing masks.
3. The craft took off for France.
4. The cowboy's task was to rope the calf.
5. Cass attended his last class at Harvard.

THE BACK VOWELS

[ɑ] (ä) As in *Calm*

[ɑ] is a low, back, lax vowel. The back vowels, we recall, are those which are produced with the back of the tongue most active (see Figure 12–2). In changing from the low front vowel [æ] to the back vowel [ɑ] the tongue arching is moved from the front to the back of the tongue.

The vowel [ɑ] is produced with the tongue in about as low a position as it is likely to assume without applying direct external pressure to the flat of the tongue. The mouth is open wide and the lips are unrounded.

In spelling, the [ɑ] is most frequently represented by the letters *a* and *o*. In words such as *ah, alms, charm, psalm,* and *balm*, the sound [ɑ] is consistently heard throughout the United States. In the words *hot, cot, cog, ox* and *stock*, there is less consistency in pronunciation. Many speakers will use the [ɑ] vowel, but others will use a variant with lip rounding [ɒ] which is absent for [ɑ].

Practice Materials

Initial

ah	argue	arbor	ardent
alms	arch	army	Arthur
armor	artful	ark	archives

Medial

alarm	lark	harm	father
calm	hearten	qualify	balmy
cargo	guard	sergeant	carved

Phrases

calm harbor	smart partner
scarred farthing	stark farmer
arctic stars	charms of palms

Sentences

1. Arthur set to sea when the night was calm and the air was balmy.

2. The ship's cargo was thrown into the harbor.
3. Noah's ark had a varied cargo.
4. The recruit's awkardness jarred the drill sergeant.
5. Fathers do not always behave like guardian angels.
6. The shah enjoyed his sparse bazaar.

Most speakers use the vowel [ɑ] for the following words with *o* spellings. Others modify the sound by some lip rounding and so produce a sound which is or approximates [ɒ] (ŏ).

Determine your tendency by looking at your mouth in a mirror as you practice with the following materials.

bog	odd	nod	pod
cod	option	cot	otter
olive	cog	job	fodder
occupy	frog	rob	locket
ox	hot	hod	respond
got	golf	pocket	stop

Sentences

1. Olive had to exercise her odd option to buy the stock.
2. An ox may fear a frog.
3. Tom used a hod to carry the bricks aloft.
4. The otter did not enjoy the hot weather.
5. Rockwell was too shocked to respond after he was robbed.
6. A stopwatch cannot take much shock.
7. Bob's job was to supply fodder to the stock.
8. Jock, a Scotsman, was fond of chocolate.

Selection

Camelot, a dot
Of space in time,
Begot
By need of man
To spot and plot
A dream
Of what
Man hopes of man:
Of Launcelot
Tried by Guinivere,
Of Arthur

Tried by love and fear
And knowing
More than he could know.
Camelot, a dot
Of time that was, to be
A spot to plot
And prophetically, to see.

—J. E., Suggested by T. H. White's *The Once and Future King*

[ɒ] (ŏ)

[ɒ] is a low, back, lax, rounded vowel.

As we noted earlier, the vowel [ɒ] is used by some Americans in words in which the vowel [ɑ] is used by others. The vowel [ɑ] is also used as a variant for the vowel [ɔ] (ô) as in *dog* and *cough*.

In manner of production and in acoustic impression, [ɒ] is somewhere between [ɔ] and [ɑ]. The vowel [ɒ] is low and lax and is produced with slight rounding of the lips.

No list can be given of words for which the vowel [ɒ] is consistently used throughout the United States, or even in any major area within the United States. Though not confined to eastern New England, the sound [ɒ] is more likely to be heard there than elsewhere.

The vowel [ɒ] may be heard in words in which the spelling includes the letter *o* followed by the consonants [f], [θ] (th), or [s]. It is not, however, limited to these spellings.

Practice Materials

In the practice materials which follow determine what your pronunciation is for the key words and compare your pronunciation with that of the respected members of your community. First, however, you may wish to review the word list and sentences for the vowels [ɑ] or [ɒ] previously considered.

choral	floral	wrong	moral
cough	aloft	across	broth
loss	coffee	moss	soft
office	froth	costly	scoff
glossy	tossed	offer	frost

frothy broth	lost dog
wrong crossing	odd stock
costly offer	office job
soft cloth	sorry song
hot coffee	mossy forest

Sentences

1. The frosty weather made Ross cough.
2. Hot coffee has become a costly drink.
3. A moth is not likely to scoff at the flame.
4. Does the boss determine costs in your office?
5. Bob preferred a clear broth to a soft drink with froth.

Additional opportunity for practice will be furnished after our consideration of the vowel [ɔ] (ô).

[ɔ] (ô) As in *Author*

[ɔ] is a low, back vowel produced with definite lip rounding. The tongue is slightly higher for [ɔ] than it is for [ɑ] and [ɒ] (see back-vowel diagram, Figure 12–2).

The most frequent spellings for [ɔ] include *a* as in *ball,* *aw* as in *lawful,* *au* as in *taught,* *ou* as in *bought,* and the letter *o* as in *horse.*

In many words, including some of those used as examples in the previous paragraph, the vowel [ɑ], and less frequently [ɒ], may be heard instead of [ɔ]. Some of the variations are more or less uniform according to geographic regions; others seem to be more individualized according to speaker choice.

Practice Materials

If you are not certain of your own pronunciation habits, practice before a mirror will help to distinguish the [ɔ] from the [ɑ] pronunciations. If you wish to establish a clear distinction make certain that your lips are rounded for [ɔ]; for [ɑ] the lips are unrounded and the tongue is lax.

In the list that follows, the words of the first two columns are most likely to be pronounced with the vowel [ɔ]; the words of the other columns are likely to be pronounced with [ɑ] or [ɒ]. The vowel [ɔ] may, however, be used for any of the words.

hall	hawk	song	frog
ball	sawing	wrong	torrid
fought	call	soft	orange
taught	flawless	lost	foreign
wall	chalk	off	porridge
August	awesome	cost	forest
auto	claws	coffin	horrible

The words in the following list are most likely to be pronounced with the vowel [ɔ] rather than either of the other back vowels we have studied.

author	calked	orphan	stall
awkward	yawn	north	organ
tall	falter	halt	thorn
nought	ordeal	shawl	horse
horn	fourth	reform	snort
corn	born	morbid	scorned
fortune	mourning	normal	storm

tall horse	awkward author
August storm	law and order
normally warm	orphan of the storm
corn stalk	born to yawn
pause for nought	calked yawl

Sentences

1. Dawson did not falter on his journey to the north.
2. The yawl was calked to prevent leaking.
3. Because he did not know his parents, the orphan felt morbid.
4. It is normal for an adolescent to be awkward.
5. The author's autobiography told how his novel thoughts were born.
6. Paul's widow wore a black shawl to show all that she was in mourning.
7. Autoists ought to sound their automobile horns only as a warning.
8. A tall man may feel forlorn in a country of dwarfs.
9. Norman's jaw became set and taut when he heard his wife's hoarse warning cough.
10. Paul caught a long fly ball in the hot August sun.

[o] (ō) As in *Mode*

[o] is a mid-high, rounded back vowel. (See back-vowel diagram, Figure 12–2). The tongue position is higher for [o] than for the vowel [ɔ]. The vowel [o] is only infrequently used as a pure sound. In most contexts, this sound is likely to be lengthened into the diphthong [ou].

The most frequent spellings of the vowel [o] or the diphthong [ou] are the letters *o, oe, oa,* and *ow* as in *no, foe, boat,* and *grow*.

There is no special value in working to maintain a distinction between the vowel [o] and the diphthong variant [ou]. Phonetic context will generally determine whether the vowel or diphthong will be used. There is value in avoiding excessive prolongation so that a triphthong ending with a weak vowel [ə] is produced and a word such as *hold* [hold] becomes [houəld].

Practice Materials

Initial

ohm	obey	odor	Oklahoma
opa	old	ocean	only
oat	oaf	own	overt
ode	opaque	Ohio	open

Medial

bold	hold	gross	most
boast	scold	frozen	flowing
boat	grope	moaned	choked
bones	coma	slowly	stone
loan	folder	soldier	whole
poker	mode	joker	gloat
hope	vote	note	scope

Final

blow	mellow	grow	tomato
woe	low	dough	Joe
foe	snow	bureau	hoe
stow	borrow	know	crow
flow	yellow	tow	below

Sentences

1. Joe was full of woe because he was so poor a beau.
2. The old boat sailed slowly down the flowing river.
3. Broken bones followed the poker game.
4. O'Brien gave his love a yellow gold choker.
5. "So long" may be words of hope or of sorrow.
6. The joker is a good card to hold in the game of poker.
7. Winter snow falls in Iowa, Ohio, and Oklahoma.
8. Jones broke his toe with a hoe.
9. Poe's poetry often showed that he borrowed the sorrows of tomorrow for his odes of today.
10. Homer could blow the oboe only to make woeful sounds.

Selections

1. Rattle his bones over the stones!
   He's only a pauper, whom nobody owns!

   —THOMAS NOEL, *The Pauper's Drive*

2. Hope tells a flattering tale,
   Delusive, vain, and hollow.
   Ah! let not hope prevail
   Lest disappointment follow.

   —MISS WROTHER, *The Universal Songster*

[ʊ] (o͝o) As in *Book* and [u] (o͞o) As in *Pool*

[ʊ] is a high, back, lip-rounded vowel. The tongue is lax and in a higher position than for the vowel [o].

The spellings for [ʊ] include *u* as in *pull, full,* and *put, oo* as in *book* and *cook, ou* as in *could* and *would,* and *o* as in *wolf.*

In many words of native English origin, especially those spelled with *oo,* practice varies as to the use of [ʊ] or the vowel [u] (o͞o). For comparative purposes, therefore, we shall need to describe the vowel [u].

[u] (o͞o) is characterized by more lip rounding than any of the other vowels in American-English speech. [u] is the highest of the back vowels (see back-vowel diagram, Figure 12–2, and compare [ʊ] and [u]. The tongue is tense in contrast with the lax tongue for [ʊ].

The most frequent spellings for [u] are *oo* as in *school, fool, ooze,* and *choose; o* as in *do; u* as in *dupe;* and *ou* as in *coup* and *soup.*

The distinction between [ʊ] and [u] may be brought out by comparing the pronunciation of the following pairs of words.

[u]	[ʊ]	[u]	[ʊ]
pool	pull	tool	took
shoe	should	shoot	shook
boot	book	wooed	would
fool	full	cooed	could
rude	roof	sue	forsook

Determine your pronunciation of the words below. If your tongue is tense and your lips rounded, you are using the vowel phoneme [u]; if your tongue feels relaxed and your lips not so distinctively rounded, then you are probably using the vowel phoneme [ʊ]. Do not be surprised that you are not entirely consistent in vowel usage for the words that follow. Many Americans vary according to the individual word. Make certain, however, that your pronunciation is distinctly either [u] or [ʊ].

roof	hoop
room	hooves
broom	root

Practice Materials

The material which follows immediately is for practice with the vowel [ʊ]. Note its regular occurrence as a medial sound.

bush	cook	crooked	mistook
could	wolf	pudding	neighborhood
hood	should	wooden	pulpit
good	bull	woolen	sugar
put	bosom	Brooklyn	understood
stood	bushel	would	pullet
rook	bulletin	forsook	cookies

push and pull	hooded crook
bushels of pudding	good looks
sugar cookies	forsook the pulpit
took the books	woman butcher
wooded nooks	poor wolf

Sentences

1. Goodson did what he could for his bosom buddy.
2. Woodworth was a bookish man.
3. Brooks read the bulletin from the pulpit.
4. The cook could not prepare the pudding without sugar.
5. The neighborhood children ate cookies by the bushel.
6. The bull calf cooled himself in the bushes.
7. Cookson considered himself a misunderstood man.
8. Joe Hood was good at the shot put.
9. Bob was fond of his woolen pullover sweater.
10. The wolf came out of the woods and stole a pullet, which he ate as fast as he could.

The material below is for practice with the vowel [u].

boost	rude	truant	gruesome
tomb	loon	druid	boom
ooze	brood	blooming	recluse
food	whose	toothless	shrew
group	choose	accrue	threw
true	through	ado	goose
swoon	spoon	brew	lute
troops	tool	zoom	rue
move	rumor	buffoon	blue
booth	luminate	soup	plume

spooky moor	rumor of boom
grew moody	goose stew
moving troops	June's lute
toothless shrew	too soon
gloomy fool	blue buffoon

Sentences

1. The new zoo was proud of its moose and mongoose.
2. Lucy enoyed making soup for her groom.
3. None knew who started the rumor.
4. In the depths of the tomb, the shoeless, toothless witch stewed an evil brew.
5. We cannot be sure that a movement, even though started by a buffoon, is doomed to fail.

6. According to superstition, lunatics became foolish, as a result of lunar influences.

7. Lou was a man of many moods.

8. Loose thoughts produce much ado about nothing.

9. Ruth liked long walks in the cool of the afternoon.

10. Truths applied by rule may become ruthless.

Many [u] words are preceded by the sound [j] (y) as in *you, youth, use,* and *hue.* In some of these words, the spelling *y* suggests the sound [j], but in others the spelling is not a guide to the pronunciation. The following list contains some of the more frequent [ju] words.

fuse	useful	feud	hew
you	utilize	cue	accuse
youth	mule	mute	huge
usury	hue	imbue	humor
unique	pupil	review	pew
eulogy	amuse	few	humid

Sentences

1. Few youths enjoy humid weather.

2. Our usury laws need review.

3. The mute mule carried a huge load.

4. Eulogies are not intended to be amusing nor unduly platitudinous.

5. The unique feud began over a ewe and was resumed every Tuesday.

There is considerable regional and individual variation as to the use of [ju] or [u] for some words. Tendencies exist on historical bases and may influence local and individual pronunciations. In general, our advice is to follow the pronunciations of persons in your community whose speech is deserving of respect. Do not strain for consistency for groups of words. Instead, work for consistency in the acceptable pronunciation of individual words.

Additional Practice Materials

Sentences

1. The prudent butcher was accused of having crooked scales.

2. A few groups of everblooming bushes grew in the garden.

3. Some who pretend to be buffoons are too shrewd to be truly fools.

4. Tuesday we will say our adieus and leave for the kangaroo country.

5. Though the Sioux Indian knew that something was askew, he was not sure what he should do.

6. Too few brides choose pewter for their trousseaus.

7. Few students review enough to be imbued with or lucid about what they are taught.

8. Sue looked as if she could ride either a broom or a mule.

9. The blue goose plume belonged to Lucy.

10. Matthew blew the tuba better than he could the flute.

Selections

1.   My only books
                 Were women's looks.
          And folly's all they've taught me.

—THOMAS MOORE, *The Time I've Lost in Wooing*

2. Yet let not each gay turn thy rapture move,
   For fools admire, but men of sense approve.

—ALEXANDER POPE, *An Essay on Criticism*

CENTRAL VOWELS

The *central vowels* are those which are made with the middle of the tongue arched toward the palate. The central vowels include [ɝ] (ûr), [ɜ] (ûr), [ɚ] (ər), [ə] (ə), and [ʌ] (ŭ) (see central-vowel diagram, Figure 12–3).

[ɝ] (ûr) or [ɜ] As in *Bird*, *Curl*, and *World*

Most Americans use the vowel [ɝ] in the key words indicated above and in the accented syllable of words such as *avert, guerdon, journal,* and *unfurl.* Some phoneticians consider the [ɝ] to be essentially a variety of the [r] sound and suggest that the articulation of the sound can best be acquired by lengthening the initial [r] of words such as *rose, red,* and *rim.* Such an [r] might be produced with the tongue as a whole slightly retracted and the middle of the tongue raised toward the soft palate. We may think of the sound [ɝ] as a vowel blended with the vowelized consonant [r]. The lips are unrounded for the production of [ɝ].

Speakers who generally do not use the [r] sound except when the letter *r* is immediately followed by a vowel are likely also to use [ɜ] rather than [ɝ] in the key words given in the preceding paragraph. The sound [ɜ] is produced with a slightly lower tongue position, with lips unrounded, and without the [r] coloring of [ɝ].

The use of [ɝ] or [ɜ] is largely a matter of regional practice. In the list of words which follows, most Americans would use [ɝ]. Many speakers in New England, New York City, and in the southern coastal states, however, use [ɜ]. Individual speakers who have been influenced by British speech or who were trained for the stage with eastern or British "standard" diction might also use [ɜ] regardless of where they live.

We may note that the spelling of words in which [ɝ] or [ɜ] is used usually includes the letters *ur, or, ir,* or *ear.* The word *colonel* is one of the few exceptions in which the spelling does not include the letter *r.*

Some speakers substitute the diphthongal blend [ɜɪ] for the vowel [ɜ]. The word *bird* may then become [bɜɪd] and *girl* may become [gɜɪl]. This diphthongal variant seems acceptable to many speakers in the South.

Practice Materials

Initial

earth	urchin	ermine	irksome
earn	irked	earnest	erg
err	urban	earl	urn
early	erstwhile	urge	Ernest

Medial

certain	sermon	determine	preserve
curl	terse	concern	rehearse
first	dirt	swirl	spurn
guerdon	third	excursion	curd
hurt	bird	person	unfurl
mirth	word	avert	burden
skirt	curve	heard	shirk
swerve	surface	lurk	adjourn

Final

fir	purr	aver	sir
her	fur	occur	cur
err	stir	refer	demur
blur	infer	defer	burr
deter	were	spur	inter

Phrases

terse sermon	earnest urging
affirm and aver	unfurl with a swirl
irksome urchin	avert being hurt
determined person	swerving skirts
shirk the burden	certain purpose
worried personnel	worthy circles

Sentences

1. The customers were terse but the merchant far from taciturn.
2. Bertha needed little urging to marry Earl.
3. A bird in the hand is worth a good deal on earth.
4. Shirley did not bestir herself to avert the falling urn.

5. The colonel's third lady looked well preserved in ermine.
6. The curtain fell and the rehearsal was adjourned.
7. Ernest was disturbingly discursive throughout the journey.
8. Few girls need to be urged to burden themselves with ermine.

[ɚ] [ər] or (ẽr) and [ə] As in Unstressed Syllables of *Ever* and *Other*

The vowel [ɚ] is the unstressed "equivalent" of [ɝ]. In words such as *earner* and *murmur* the first syllable vowels are stressed and so are pronounced as [ɝ] by most American speakers. The second, unstressed, syllable is pronounced [ɚ] by the same speakers—the majority of Americans who habitually pronounce medial or final *r*'s whenever the letter occurs in the spelling of the word.

[ɚ] is a lax, unrounded, mid-vowel. It has a lower tongue position than [ɝ]. Because of its occurrence in the unstressed position, [ɚ] is less intense and shorter in duration than its stresed counterpart.

[ə] is a mid-vowel produced with a lax tongue and unrounded lips in a position slightly lower than [ɜ].

[ə] is probably the most frequently used vowel in our language. This is so for the following reasons:

1. It is the most frequently used vowel in unstressed syllables regardless of the spelling of the vowel. Some examples of the varied spellings are indicated in the italicized letters of the following: *a*lone, sof*a*, foc*u*s, lab*e*l, prec*iou*s.

2. In addition to its occurrence in unstressed syllables of polysyllabic words, [ə] is also the most frequently used vowel when prepositions, articles, conjunctions, and auxiliary verbs are unstressed in sentence context. For example, in the sentence, "I of*ten* find it difficult *to* believe *the* man," each italicized word or syllable may appropriately be pronounced with the vowel [ə].

3. The vowel [ə] also replaces [r] in words such as *hear, dare,* and *cure* for those speakers who do not pronounce final *r*'s or *r*'s in general unless they are immediately followed by vowels. These, of course, are the same speakers from New England, New York City, and parts of the South who use [ɜ] rather than [ɝ] in stressed syllables.

Practice Materials

Check the pronunciation in your community and decide whether you prefer [ɚ] or [ə] for the unstressed syllables of the following words.

answer	center	after	dollar
baker	either	better	alter
copper	treasure	other	feather
drummer	brother	humor	weather
driver	poster	mirror	murmur
wander	yonder	squander	hinder
greater	later	crater	labor

ever after	surprised together
brother and sister	proper neighbor
further away	modern doctors
another answer	summer flowers
November weather	mother and father

Sentences

1. After November comes December.
2. Baker's brother was rather a good drummer.
3. Mother taught her daughter to cook a proper dinner.
4. Major Robert's brother was a junior officer.
5. Esther enjoyed seeing herself in the mirror or in a newspaper.
6. Arthur treasured a good dinner.

Note the occurrence of the "weak" vowel [ə] in the unstressed syllables of the words in the list and in the sentences that follow.

above	annoy	tuba	American
about	agree	soda	urban
allow	anoint	data	surgeon
appoint	Texas	Canada	precious
avoid	assist	circus	stirrup

Sentences

1. The American spoke with a typical Texas drawl.
2. A tuba may be annoying to hear alone.
3. Canada is north or above the United States of America.
4. Vienna is the capital city of Austria.

5. Ella was fond of azaleas and petunias.
6. Bacon and eggs make a good breakfast.
7. Are you aware of how often the vowel [ə] is used in American speech?
8. Eva and Ella had vanilla sodas.
9. The Russian avoided the open forum.
10. Johanna was gracious in her expressions.
11. Mica is a hydrous, disilicate mineral.
12. It is best not to annoy a sleeping gorilla.

[ʌ] (ŭ) As in *Cup*

[ʌ] is produced with a relatively relaxed tongue arched a little bit toward the middle or back of the palate. If it is produced with middle of the tongue arching, it is a mid-vowel. Many persons, however, produce the sound with back tongue arching as a back vowel rather than a mid-vowel. Either way, the mouth is open fairly wide *without* lip rounding. The tongue should be arched higher for [ʌ] than for [ɑ] so that a clear distinction is made between these vowels and between words such as *sup* and *sop*, *suck* and *sock*, and *nut* and *not*.

The vowel [ʌ] is represented by several letters in spelling, including *u* as in *cup*, *ou* as in *double*, and *o* as in *done*.

Except for the tendency of some speakers to produce an [ɑ] instead of a [ʌ], the vowel causes little difficulty. For those persons who may be inclined to make the [ɑ] substitution, it might be of help to know that [ʌ] is the vowel the American Indian is alleged to make when he grunts "Ugh."

Practice Materials

The first set of exercises should help to establish the distinction between [ʌ] and [ɑ]. Be certain to raise your tongue slightly higher for [ʌ] than for [ɑ]. The mouth is somewhat more open for [ɑ] than for [ʌ]. Note that [ʌ] appears only in stressed syllables.

[ʌ]	[ɑ]	[ʌ]	[ɑ]
come	calm	gut	got
done	don	color	collar
sup	sop	chuck	chock

[ʌ]	[ɑ]		[ʌ]	[ɑ]
suck	sock		wonder	wander
nut	not		bubble	bobble
duck	dock		putt	pot
pup	pop		cluck	clock

In the sentences that follow the first italicized word contains the vowel [ʌ], the second the vowel [ɑ].

1. Do *come* and *calm* down.
2. A job well *done* is what *Don* liked.
3. The *pup* was frightened by the loud *pop*.
4. It was poor *luck* to lose the key to the *lock*.
5. The bear *cub* was fond of corn on the *cob*.
6. The *duck* hunter fired from the *dock*.
7. The *hut* was exposed to the *hot* sun.

Additional Practice Materials

Initial

up	other	udder	upward
under	onion	utter	ulcer
us	ugly	uncle	Ulster
upper	usher	oven	ultimate

Medial

blood	lunge	asunder	mud
blunder	mumble	assumption	much
brother	mutton	begun	rugged
bud	once	benumb	stuck
cub	rubber	instruct	tuck
club	supper	lump	won
done	punish	hungry	thunder
cuff	rough	enough	thumb
love	monkey	honey	funny
buck	bubble	trouble	rubble

Phrases

hungry brother	month of Sundays
supper club	country cousin
double trouble	something for mother

begun and done	subject for study
blood and thunder	fund of money

Sentences

1.   The night is done; get up and greet the new day's sun.
2.   Thunder tore the bridge asunder.
3.   Twins have been defined as double trouble.
4.   Customs get some of us in a rut.
5.   Young Brother had too much for supper.
6.   From Monday through Sunday, Bud shunned jobs that needed to be done.
7.   Hunter enjoyed the company of his club brothers.
8.   Husbands must not forget that love has a fund of honeyed words.
9.   Assumptions should be tested by judgments before they are made public.
10.   Duncan's income came from a trust fund.

Selections

1.   Not a face below the sun
    But is precious—unto one!

    —SIR EDWIN ARNOLD, *Facies non Omnibus Una*

2.   Double, double, toil and trouble;
    Fire burn and cauldron bubble.

    —WILLIAM SHAKESPEARE, *Macbeth*

CHAPTER 13

Diphthongs

Diphthongs are vocalic glides that are uttered in a single breath impulse within a single syllable. A superficial analysis of a diphthong, as well as a literal interpretation of the term, suggests that a diphthong is a combination of two sounds. Actually, a diphthong is a continuous change of sound from the first element to the second. The first phonetic symbol of a diphthong really represents the approximate initial sound, and the second element represents the approximate final sound. Thus, the diphthong [ɔɪ] (oi) is initiated with the sound [ɔ]. The organs of articulation are then modified to produce a continuous change of sound until the diphthong is completed with what approximates the vowel [ɪ].

We shall consider first three American-English phonemic diphthongs. Each represents a distinctive sound unit and each serves as a basis by which we distinguish between spoken words without depending upon context. The phonemic diphthongs are [aɪ] (ī) as in *I* and *my;* [ɔɪ] (oi) as in *boy* and *toy;* and [ɑʊ] (ou) as in *house* and *out.*

Earlier, in our study of the individual vowel sounds, nonphonemic variants of the vowels [e] and [o] were considered. Another group of sounds which might be considered diphthongal variants are the sound combinations of persons who do not pronounce final *r*'s. This group of sounds include [ɪə], [ʊə], [ɔə], and [ɛə] as pronunciations for words such as *dear, poor, core,* and *care.*

[aɪ] (ī) As in *Ice* and *Nice*

The diphthong [aɪ] is initiated with a raising of the tongue in the front part of the mouth. It ends, as indicated, with the vowel [ɪ].

The most frequent spellings for [aɪ] are *i* at the beginning and middle of words and *y* as the final letter of words as in *ice, spice, entice, my,* and *cry.*

Practice Materials

idea	refine	sign	prize
aisle	ripe	riot	invite
ice	diagram	aspire	remind
item	drive	beguile	requite
idle	height	design	unsightly
eyes	mine	devise	aside
iron	ride	bribe	butterfly
island	thigh	kind	spy
I'll	twice	strive	try
I'm	slide	rhyme	buy
idea	why	time	pie

bright child	sigh and imply
nine miles	trying crime
define and design	behind the divide
ride by night	five Fridays
smile wisely	provide a guide
high ideals	entire environment
right and might	surprising sight
frightened knight	mind's eye

Sentences

1. The bride had a beguiling smile as she walked down the aisle.

2. The spy tried to bribe the designer of the island bridge.

3. The sun is high in the sky in June and July.

4. Michael was reminded by his bright daughter that she was made entirely of sugar and spice and allied things equally nice.

5.   Time and tide reach a height and finally slide away.
6.   Eileen's bright-eyed glances caused mild riots.
7.   No tiger got his stripes by striving for or buying them.
8.   There are always times to try men's lives and test the heights
to which they might aspire.
9.   Knight ran a mile every Friday.
10.   Lila was surprised that her child could be so wise.

Selections

1.   My object all sublime
     I shall achieve in time—
     To let the punishment fit the crime,
     The punishment fit the crime.

                    —w. s. GILBERT, *The Mikado*

2.   When I was five
     My father was the wisest man alive.
     At ten and five
     I doubted he had wits enough to thrive.
     At five and twenty
     He acquired new brains aplenty.

                    —J. E., *Intellectual Evolution*

3.   She walks in beauty, like the night
         Of cloudless climes and starry skies;
     And all that's best of dark and bright
         Meet in her aspect and her eyes:
     Thus mellow'd to that tender light
         Which heaven to gaudy day denies.

                    —LORD BYRON, *She Walks in Beauty*

4.   There was an old woman who swallowed a fly,
     I don't know why she swallowed a fly.
     Poor old woman, she'll probably die.

                    —*The Old Woman Who Swallowed a Fly*, Ballad

[aʊ] (ou) [ɑʊ] As in *Now* and *How*

Whether the speaker produces the diphthong [aʊ] or [ɑʊ] in the
indicated key word depends phonetically on whether the front or
back of the tongue is elevated in the first part of the blend. It is

likely that his articulatory habit is determined by what he hears in his community. Both pronunciations are used by cultured and educated speakers throughout the United States.

The tendency to substitute the vowel [æ] for the first element of the diphthong is one we recommend avoiding or correcting. We also recommend avoiding or correcting the triple vowel combinations [æaʊ] or [æɑʊ] for either [aʊ] or [ɑʊ].

The most frequent spellings for the diphthong are *ou* as in *out, house,* and *mouse* and *ow* as in *cow, how,* and *brow.*

Practice Materials

ounce	proud	allow	mouth
out	shout	bow	stout
owl	town	brow	tower
count	about	cow	lounge
doubt	announce	how	mount
gown	trounce	now	south
frown	astound	plough	hound
ground	rebound	thou	flower
outline	carouse	impound	shower
our	abound	endow	flout

hourly count	proud to announce
outside sounds	outline the boundary
about a thousand	doubt and flout
crowded house	around the town
plow the ground	frowning brow

Sentences

1. The count dismounted and bounded into the tower.
2. The town dogcatcher had to impound the howling hound.
3. Our farmer friend was proud of his cow because she could frown and look profound.
4. We could not allow the scoundrel his wish to see his hangman in a shroud.
5. For an hour showers wet the ground and freshened the flowers.
6. Our house in town looks over a mound to the south.
7. A place to carouse is often someone else's house.
8. Powers could not account for his endowment.

Selections

1. When clouds appear like rocks and towers,
   The earth's refreshed by frequent showers.

   —Old Weather Rhyme

2. He never sold the truth to serve the hour,
   Nor paltered with Eternal God for power.

   —ALFRED, LORD TENNYSON, *Ode on the Death of the Duke of Wellington*

3. The strongest castle, towers, and town,
   The golden bullet beats it down.

   —WILLIAM SHAKESPEARE, *Sonnets to Sundry Notes of Music*

4. Like leaves on trees the race of man is found,
   Now green in youth, now withering on the ground.

   —ALEXANDER POPE, *The Iliad of Homer*

[ɔɪ] (oi) As in *Boy, Soil,* and *Noise*

The diphthong [ɔɪ] is appropriately produced by beginning with the back, rounded vowel [ɔ] and ending with the front vowel [ɪ]. The most frequent spellings include *oi* and *oy* as in *oil, boil, toy,* and *boy.*

Some speakers tend to substitute [ɜɪ] for [ɔɪ]. This tendency is generally considered substandard and we recommend that it be avoided or corrected. Another tendency to be avoided is the substitution of [oɪ] for [ɔɪ].

Practice Materials

oil	join	employ	anoint
oyster	broil	decoy	rejoice
ointment	toil	enjoy	void
choice	coil	poison	cloy
joy	soil	adjoin	spoils
boy	annoy	foyer	poignant
poise	noise	point	recoil
voice	foil	embroil	foist

poignant choice   employ a decoy
joyous noise   annoying boys

Practice Materials (*Cont.*)

boiled in oil	broiled oysters
avoid the void	recoil from toil
poison ointment	royal coins

Sentences

1. Boyd advised, "Avoid a voice that makes you coy or a manner that seems to cloy."
2. Joyce enjoyed bluepoint oysters.
3. Roy liked to work with the soil.
4. Most coins are metal alloys.
5. Poi is a Hawaiian dish that is improved by soy sauce.
6. Small boys like noise making toys.
7. Ointments are often made with oils.
8. A hoyden is a boisterous tomboy.
9. Doyle joined a company of lawyers.
10. Troy was a piano hoister who took great joy in his toil.

[ɛə] (âə) As in *There*

The nonphonemic diphthong [ɛə] is used instead of the more frequently heard [ɛr] or [ɛɚ] by persons who omit *r*'s in their pronunciations except before vowels. It is heard in such words as *air, their, fair, care, dare, chair,* and *pear.*

[ɛə] is also heard as a not entirely approved substitution for the vowels [æ] and [a] in words such as *ask, last, class,* and *bath.*

Speakers who generally pronounce their *r*'s when they occur in the spelling are likely to use the combination [ɛr] or [ɛɚ] rather than [ɛə] in the words that follow:

Practice Materials

air	lair	compare	repair
bear	fair	declare	unaware
care	their	chair	heirloom
dare	wear	forbear	heiress
flair	affair	prepare	impair
hair	beware	welfare	despair
spare	stare	square	scared

air of care	scarcely aware
square pair	theirs to spare
their share	rare heirloom
daring flair	declare and forbear

Sentences

1. The unwary bear was caught in his own lair.
2. Mary was often to be in despair about things to wear.
3. The heiress would not declare her heirlooms.
4. The mare won a prize at the country fair.
5. The pair would not share the chair.

Selections

1. I could lie down like a tired child,
   And weep away the life of care
   Which I have bourne, and yet must bear.

   —PERCY BYSSHE SHELLEY, *Dejection*

2. There is a time, we know not when,
      A point we know not where,
   That marks the destiny of men,
      For glory or despair.

   —JOSEPH A. ALEXANDER, *The Doomed Man*

[ɔə] and [oə] (ȯə)

The diphthongs [ɔə] and [oə] are used by persons who are inclined to omit the [r] from their pronunciations except before vowels. Practice in regard to [ɔə] and [ɔr] or [oə] and [or] varies along the following lines.[1]

In words such as *horse, lord, accord* and *north* usage is fairly uniform throughout the United States. The pronunciation is [ɔr] for most Americans and [ɔə] in the "r-dropping" sections of the country.

Usage varies between [o] and [ɔ] pronunciations for the words *board, mourning, course,* and *more.* These words are pronounced with either [o] or [or] by most American speakers. In the New York City area these words are pronounced with [ɔ] by "native" speakers. Thus, except for the New York City area, most Americans make distinctions between the words *horse* and *hoarse, for* and *four,* and

[1] The transcriptions [ɔɚ] and [oɚ] are alternatives for [ɔə] and [or].

cord and *cored*. The sound [ɔ] is more likely to be used for the first word of these pairs and the [o] for the second.

Practice Materials

Determine your own practice by comparing the pronunciation of the following pairs of words.

border	boarder
horse	hoarse
morning	mourning
war	wore

Sentences

1. Guns were stored in the fort.
2. Each pull on his oars brought him closer to the shore.
3. Four hours of riding on his horse brought him to the border.
4. The lion roared because he wanted more food.
5. The owner of the resort inn was noted for being in accord with forty different points of view.

Selections

1. Cruel Remorse! where Youth and Pleasure sport,
   And thoughtless Folly keeps her court—

   —ANNA L. BARABAULD, *Ode to Remorse*

2. Come in the evening, or come in the morning,
   Come when you're looked for, or come without warning,
   Kisses and welcome you'll find here before you,
   And the oftener you come here the more I'll adore you.

   —THOMAS O. DAVIS, *The Welcome*

3. He will hold thee, when his passion shall have spent its novel
   force,
   Something better than his dog, a little dearer than his horse.

   —ALFRED, LORD TENNYSON, *Locksley Hall*

4. Three poets, in three distant ages born,
   Greece, Italy, and England did adorn.

   —JOHN DRYDEN, *Under Mr. Milton's Picture*

[ɪə] (ĭə) As in *Dear*

The diphthong [ɪə] (ĭə), as noted earlier, is used by persons who omit medial and final [r] sounds from the pronunciation of such words as *dear, fear, hear, beard, cheerful,* and *earful.* Throughout most of the United States, all of these words are more frequently pronounced with the combinations [ɪr] or [ɪɚ) rather than with the diphthong [ɪə].

Practice Materials

Determine your own pronunciation for the following words and compare them with the pronunciation of respected speakers in your community.

beard	pier	gear	piercing
beer	cheer	queer	seared
dear	arrear	cheerful	fierce
fear	mere	earful	spear
hear	drear	fearful	bier
merely	clear	we're	year

fearfully dear	steer clear
eerie bier	year's arrears
we're here	tearful earful
queer gear	fiercely pierced

Sentences

1. Geary's beard appeared to be seared.
2. The hunter's gear included a fearful-looking spear.
3. The trees looked dreary because of the sere leaves.
4. A fierce fire destroyed the pier.
5. Beardsley was not considered a cheerful person because of his habit of crying in his beer.

Selections

1. But at my back I always hear
   Time's wingèd chariot hurrying near;

   —ANDREW MARVELL, *To His Coy Mistress*

2. Damn with faint praise, assent with civil leer,
    And without sneering, teach the rest to sneer;

—ALEXANDER POPE, *Prologue to Satires*

[ʊə] (ŏŏə) As in *Poor*

The diphthong [ʊə] is likely to be used by speakers who are inclined to pronounce [r] only in contexts in which the letter *r* is immediately followed by a vowel. These speakers would probably use [ʊə] rather than [ʊr] or [ʊɚ] in words such as *poor, sure,* and *tour.*

Practice Materials

Determine your own pronunciation for the words that follow and compare each with what is current in your community.

poor	lured	assure	fury
sure	moor	jury	endure
tour	boor	ensure	alluring

Sentences

1. Be he rich or poor, there is little that is alluring about a boor.
2. What we cannot cure we must learn to endure.
3. If you're surely poor, you can hardly afford to tour among the Moors.
4. The jurymen had to control their fury to ensure a fair and enduring verdict.
5. Though Moore was a poor man, he felt socially secure.
6. The cat's nine lives was no insurance against curiosity.

[eɪ] (ā) As in *Gale*

Earlier we discussed [eɪ] as a nonphonemic variant of the vowel [e] (see page 187). At this point, we shall merely present additional practice materials that include words that may be appropriately pronounced with the diphthong [eɪ].

Practice Materials

brain	train	nature	refrain
braid	afraid	pain	waiver

grade	labor	radio	wane
grain	maybe	Spain	ways
trade	mail	stranger	weight
famous	failure	shady	zany

Sentences

1. Crayton ate his fill of crayfish fresh from Biscayne Bay.
2. Mabel waited on table without waste of patience.
3. Fate, according to Kate, was to be hailed without haste or hate.
4. The trade wind that swept across the bay caught the sails of the ship *Lady May*.
5. Mason prayed that his essay would not be assailed.
6. Grayson, a new farmhand, was grateful to learn that he could pile more hay with a fork than a spade.
7. Daybreak came, and with it the quaint and plaintive calls of the quail.
8. Jayson was little more than a baby when he learned that try as he may he could not stay a moment of any day.
9. Kate, according to Shakespeare, became a tamed shrew; but Shakespeare did not betray whether the taming was for a day or a decade.
10. Wade ran the relay, though dazed by the blazing sun.

Selection

Why so pale and wan, fond lover?
　　Prithee, why so pale?
Will when looking well can't move her,
　　Looking ill prevail?

—JOHN SUCKLING, Song

[oʊ] (ō) As in *Bone*

Earlier we discussed [oʊ] as a nonphonemic variant of the mid-high, rounded back vowel [o] (see page 199). We shall now present some additional practice materials in which [oʊ] may be appropriately used. We should have in mind, however, that words such as *bone, home,* or *grow* do not change in meaning whether they are pronounced with the vowel [o] or the diphthong [oʊ].

Practice Materials

alone	code	moan	enroll
atone	cone	nosy	resole
bonus	control	over	although
broker	hold	older	below
chose	homely	prone	bestow
coal	know	prose	regrow

Sentences

1. Grover was prone to broken bones.
2. Tons of coal were loaded into the ship's hold.
3. Jones chose to speak in prose.
4. Rose preferred older and homely men because they were easier to control.
5. Chicago is likely to be cold most of the winter.
6. No one knew who owned the gold left on the old road.

Selection

I'm growing frugal of my gold;
I'm growing wise; I'm growing—yes—
I'm growing old.

—JOHN GODFREY SAXE, *I'm Growing Old*

CHAPTER 14

Consonants: The Lip (Bilabial) Sounds

Consonants, we recall, are speech sounds produced as a result of modification of the outgoing breath stream by the organs of articulation. The form of modification produces the characteristics peculiar to the various consonants. Unlike vowels, which are all voiced sounds unless the speaker is intentionally whispering, some consonants are appropriately voiced and others are appropriately voiceless.

The description and manner of production of each of the consonant sounds will be considered individually. Precautions to be observed and pitfalls to be avoided will be indicated for those sounds which many American-English speaking adults find difficult.

THE FAVORED ARTICULATORY CONTACT

Many languages seem to have a favored place of articulatory contact. In French, Spanish, and Italian many sounds are produced by contact between the tongue tip and the upper teeth. In German the point of contact is a bit lower. In American English, the favored contact area is the upper gum ridge. At this point, by contact with

225

the tongue tip, the sounds [t], [d], [l], and [n] are articulated. A fraction of an inch behind the gum ridge, articulatory placements are made for the sounds [s], [z], [ʃ] (sh), [ʒ] (zh), [tʃ] (ch), [dʒ] (j), and for one of the varieties of [r].

Because of the proximity of articulatory positions for the American-English sounds and those much like them in Spanish, French, Italian, and German, the tendency to carry over foreign language speech habits is understandable. We should also be able to appreciate the need for special precautions and considerable practice to overcome these foreign language influences. A good beginning in correcting such influences, and in establishing awareness of the favored place of American-English articulation, is to study the diagram of Figure 14–1.

The consonant sounds will be presented approximately according to place of major articulatory activity proceeding from the front to the back of the mouth (see chart, page 227). This order of presentation is not to be interpreted as necessarily the most desirable or

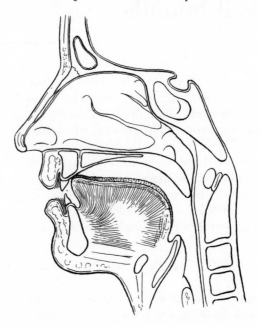

FIGURE 14–1. Diagram indicating the "favored contact area" for American-English consonants. The upper gum ridge is the contact point for [t], [d], and [l]. Essentially the same tongue-tip and gum-ridge contact is made for [n].

Table 14-1. CLASSIFICATION OF CONSONANTS OF AMERICAN–ENGLISH SPEECH

MANNER OF ARTICULATION	LIPS (BILABIAL)	LIP-TEETH (LABIO-DENTAL)	TONGUE-TEETH (LINGUA-DENTAL)	TONGUE-GUM-RIDGE (ALVEOLAR)	TONGUE-HARD PALATE (POST-ALVEOLAR)	TONGUE-BLADE-PALATE (PALATAL)	TONGUE-VELUM (VELAR)	LARYNX (GLOTTAL)
Voiceless stops	p			t			k	ʔ
Voiced stops	b			d			g	
Voiceless fricatives	ʍ (hw)	f	θ (th)	s	ʃ (sh)			h
Voiced fricatives		v	ð (th)	z	ʒ (zh)			
Nasals (voiced)	m			n			ŋ (ng)	
Lateral				l				
Glides (vowel-like consonants)	w				r*	r / j (y)		
Voiceless affricate					tʃ (ch)			
Voiced affricate					dʒ (dzh)			

*In our discussion of the [r] phoneme, the variable characteristics of [r] will be considered.

the prescribed one to be followed. We believe that the specific order of consonant study should be determined by the instructional needs of the students or the philosophy of the teacher. An individual student, aware of his own limitations in diction, or striving for improvement in a given direction, might well begin with the sound, or one of the sounds, requiring attention. An instructor might determine the order of consonant study based on a screening of his group of students. The sound most in need of improvement for the largest number of students in his class may then be selected as the one with which to begin. If the instructor believes that it is better to teach a relatively difficult sound by contrasting it with another easier sound for the student, then this may become the proper initial sound to be studied. An instructor who has many students coming from a given speech region and who, on the basis of his experience, is able to anticipate frequent consonant difficulties, may choose to begin his improvement program in the light of his anticipations. He will soon learn whether the students are living up to his expectations or whether his own program for his particular group of students is in need of modification. Such an approach will afford the individual student and the class as a whole the greatest amount of instructional time and opportunity for work on common problems and for frequent review during the course of a term.

THE BILABIAL SOUNDS

[p] As in *Pea, Soap, Separate,* and *Spy*

[p] and [b] are bilabial, closed lip, stop consonants. These sounds are produced as a result of lip-closing action that momentarily stops the flow of breath. Both of these sounds require a raised soft palate[1] so that after the lip action, the sound produced is emitted orally rather than nasally.

The sound [p] in initial or stressed positions, as in *pea* and *plate,* requires considerable breath pressure. The lips must be tightly compressed to permit the production of a vigorous [p]. The separation of the lips in anticipation of the next sound should be accompanied

---

[1] All but three American-English sounds are normally produced with an elevated soft palate. Except for the three nasal consonants [n], [m], and [ŋ] (ng), the reader should assume that the directions for the production of a sound include the one to *elevate the soft palate.*

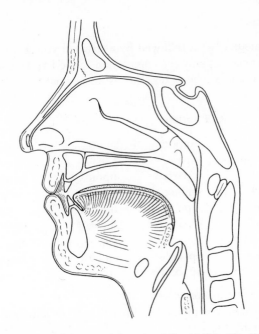

FIGURE 14–2. Articulatory positions for [p] and [b]. The lips are tightly compressed and the soft palate is raised.

by a noticeable puff of breath. In other positions there is considerably less breath pressure and less vigorous lip action. In final positions, [p] may not be exploded. In all positions, [p] is a voiceless sound. In an initial [p] followed by a vowel, a distinct puff of breath should accompany the completion of the sound.

Practice Materials

Initial

pea	pool	person	pound
peat	pull	pert	pout
peel	poor	purse	powder
pill	poke	pun	power
pit	pole	put	peace
paid	paltry	pike	pitch
pay	paw	pile	peg
pen	park	pine	patch
pat	pond	point	pack
path	pot	poise	poem

When a medial [p] is followed by a stressed vowel, a distinct puff of air should accompany the completion of the [p]. In combinations preceded by an [s], however, the aspirate quality is considerably reduced.

Medial (Stressed Positions)

appeal	rapport	apart	rupee
appease	repair	repay	turnpike
repeat	repartee	upon	repugnant
repeal	impact	apology	umpire
unpin	report	deport	suppose
repaid	repatriate	despair	epistle
repent	repose	support	inspire
repel	oppose	superior	inspect
repast	appoint	superb	respite

For a medial [p] in unstressed positions lip activity is less vigorous and there is less accompanying breath puff in anticipation of the sound following the [p].

Medial (Unstressed Positions)

aped	stupor	rapier	napping
happy	sweeping	steeple	chopping
carpet	champion	taper	clapped
typify	grapple	stepping	flippant
tipped	hoping	clipping	wrapper

[pl] *and* [pr] *Blends*

plea	plume	plight	place
please	Pluto	pliant	play
plenty	plot	plow	pleasure
plate	plum	applaud	plural
plain	plug	aplomb	plunder
plan	pluck	plausible	plunge
preen	prune	price	spread
pray	reprove	pride	sprite
prick	proof	proud	sprawl
press	prawn	prow	sprain
prank	prod	praise	spree
prattle	prolix	approve	priz_ed

Sentences

1. Piper was fond of drinking out of pink paper cups.
2. Paul's pride made him aspire to the ping-pong championship.
3. The press publicity produced a probe of the public funds.
4. Some of the Alps are perpetually capped with snow.
5. Polly was pleased with her plain plaid apron.
6. Pearson ate humble pie with a prodigious appetite.
7. Peter was a prodigy at painting and sculpting.
8. A pig with an apple in his mouth is a helping beyond help.
9. The plundering of the ships was blamed on a plot by harpies.
10. Pinkerton preferred maple syrup with pancakes as a pleasant dish for breakfast.
11. Products become worth what their purchasers will pay for them.
12. The poorest persons are those who have not learned how to employ their pennies.

Selection

Now when a doctor's patients are perplexed,
A consultation comes in order next—
You know what that is? In a certain place
Meet certain doctors to discuss a case
And other matters, such as weather, crops,
Potatoes, pumpkins, lager-beer, and hops.

—OLIVER WENDELL HOLMES, *Rip Van Winkle, M.D.*

[b] As in *Bean, Rabid,* and *Robe*

[b] is a voiced, lip-stop consonant produced with less lip and breath pressure than [p]. Lip activity should be precise so that there is a clear-cut stop and release action for the [b] even though it is less vigorous than for the [p].

By way of review, [b] is articulated with (1), a firm closing of the lips, (2) a compression of air behind the lips, and (3) a sudden parting of the lips to release the *vocalized sound*. Final [b] may be articulated without the explosive or release phase.

Practice Materials

Make certain that you show a clear distinction between [p] and [b] in the following words and sentences.

peat	beat	punch	bunch
pin	bin	puck	buck
pail	bail	poor	boor
pelt	belt	pall	ball
pack	back	palm	balm
pan	ban	pie	bye
pounce	bounce	pride	bride

Sentences

1. Pat carried his pack on his back.
2. Peg ate the pie and waved good-bye.
3. A bunch of grapes floated in the punch bowl.
4. The belt was made of leather pelt.
5. The sad tidings caused a pall to fall over the dancers at the ball.

Initial

bean	boon	burn	broom
bill	bull	bud	bruise
bale	boor	breach	brought
beg	boat	bring	brain
back	ball	bread	brine
bask	bog	brass	brown
busy	bulk	bleed	bloom
bunch	burrow	blink	blue
base	bird	black	block
blame	burst	breath	blurt

Medial

about	table	somebody	disturbing
abate	feeble	habit	rubber
abbey	stable	noble	ribbon
abet	number	tumble	tribute
abhor	lumber	fumble	robust

Final

rib	tube	disturb	curb
crab	nub	cube	jibe
web	rub	hob	daub
stab	robe	sob	cob
dab	lobe	rob	mob

Sentences

1. Bill is fond of brown berries and broiled bass.
2. Ben abhorred boasting but liked to be busy.
3. Bacon and beans were a habit with Bess and Bob.
4. Benton played a brass tuba in the Boys Band.
5. Somebody permitted the black horse to break out of the barn.
6. Few buds bloom in February to attract bees.
7. The stable was swept with a bulky brown broom.
8. Lobsters and crabs were brought in on the old flat-bottomed boat.
9. Bricks and boards are basic building materials.
10. Brad hit the ball for a three-base hit.

Selections

1. But far on the deep there are billows
   That never shall break on the beach.

   —A. J. RYAN, *Song of the Mystic*

2. This truth within thy mind rehearse,
   That in a boundless universe
   Is boundless better, boundless worse.

   —ALFRED, LORD TENNYSON, *The Two Voices*

[m] As in *Me, Summer,* and *Plum*

[m] is one of the three nasal, continuant consonants. As such, it is produced with a lowered soft palate, nasal cavity reinforcement, and nasal emission. [m] is articulated with the lips in relaxed contact and the teeth slightly parted. Vocal fold vibration is a necessary accompaniment for the [m] as well as for the other two nasal sounds. As indicated in Figure 14–3, the tongue usually lies at the bottom of the mouth in the production of the [m].

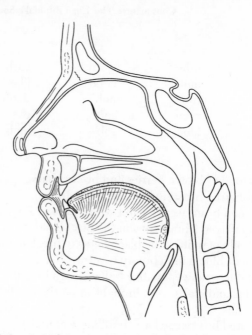

FIGURE 14–3. Articulatory positions for [m]. Note lip-contact and lowered soft palate.

The sound [m] is usually represented by the single letter *m*. Occasionally, the *m* is followed or preceded by a "silent" letter as in *lumb* and *dumb*, *psalm* and *calm*. The sound is found in initial, medial, and final positions. Unless hurried, slurred, or produced with the lips too tight, the [m] is a relatively easy sound to produce. As suggested in our discussion on nasal reinforcement (see pages 87–90), the [m] lends fullness and roundness to the voice. The material and exercises for [m] in the section on voice should now be reviewed.

Practice Materials

Initial

me	main	most	mirth
meek	mend	mode	murky
meal	met	mote	murder
mean	mess	motive	mud
meat	man	motor	moist

middle	map	mourn	mouth
milk	mash	mortar	mount
mist	mask	mauve	mouse
make	mass	mock	my
mate	match	month	might
mail	mood	mob	mine
made	moon	monk	mile

Medial

demean	ember	foaming	human
seemly	emanate	reformed	humor
seamstress	embank	informing	grimy
dreaming	embassy	armor	slimy
remit	embattle	termed	omit
permit	cement	termite	remind
simple	amnesty	terminal	remedy
Amy	remove	grumble	remark
emblem	emote	stumble	almond
empty	bemoan	umbrella	lament

Final

beam	game	groom	worm
seem	gem	tomb	term
team	stem	tome	drum
theme	phlegm	comb	hum
dream	lamb	dome	I'm
dim	ham	home	dime
trim	tam	form	climb
slim	sham	dorm	grime
aim	slam	calm	crime
same	doom	farm	prime
tame	room	alarm	column
blame	broom	bomb	autumn

In final, unstressed position, the final [m] may sometimes have syllabic value. What is your pronunciation for the words that follow?

chasm	schism	spasm	bedlam
bottom	rhythm	theism	bosom
prism	atom	truism	column

In the material below, work for a light, sustained [m]. At first exaggerate the length of the [m] and avoid carrying over nasal quality to proximate nonnasal sounds.

Sentences

1. Moss covered the bottom of the maples in the Maine forest.
2. Miniver mourned for memories that might have been.
3. Termites undermined the dismal mansion.
4. Mamie grumbled because she stumbled over her umbrella.
5. Mason was phlegmatic about matters which made most ill-humored men storm in anger.
6. Mending and making neat seams were Amanda's prime ways of staying calm.
7. The monk remained in good humor as he informed his friends about the grimy tomb.
8. Mortar, a material employed for masonry, is made by mixing lime or cement with sand.
9. Man maintains continuity by making note of his memories.
10. Mary, broom in hand, was in no mood to be stymied by a mouse in either animal or human form.
11. Man is mighty in his ability to transform molehills into mountains by mentation and imagination.
12. Morton dreamed that no mound was too high for him to climb nor chasm too wide for him to jump.
13. Emerson held that each mind has its own method.
14. Men with empires in their minds cannot long remain humble or calm.
15. Many monuments to men in time need their own memorials.
16. The moon may look on many men, but a man has but one moon.
17. Remembrance, and repentance, often come together in the morning.
18. Lamb and ham make fine mincemeat.

Selections

1. In *Moby Dick*, Herman Melville remarked that "to produce a mighty book you must choose a mighty theme."

2. Hawthorne, in his *Mosses from an Old Manse,* observed that

"an unhappy gentleman, resolving to wed nothing short of perfection, keeps his heart and hand till both get so old and withered that no tolerable woman will accept him."

3.   Thackeray advised young men: "Remember it's as easy to marry a rich woman as a poor woman."

4.   "All human wisdom is summed up in two words—wait and hope."

—ALEXANDER DUMAS, *Count of Monte Cristo*

5.   Go! You may call it madness, folly;
  You shall not chase my gloom away!
 There's such a charm in melancholy,
  I would not, if I could, be gay.

—SAMUEL ROGERS, *To——*

6.   In his *Maxims* Nietzsche remarked, "Many a man fails to become a thinker for the sole reason that his memory is too good."

7.   And frame your mind to mirth and merriment,
 Which bars a thousand harms and lengthens life.

—WILLIAM SHAKESPEARE, *The Taming of the Shrew*

8.   The worst part of an eminent man's conversation is, nine times out of ten, to be found in that part which he means to be clever.

—PHILIP H. STANHOPE, *Caxtonia*

9.   We are the music-makers,
  And we are the dreamers of dreams,
 Wandering by lone sea-breakers,
  And sitting by desolate streams;
 World-losers and world-forsakers,
  On whom the pale moon gleams:
 Yet we are the movers and shakers
  Of the world for ever, it seems.

—A. W. E. O'SHAUGHNESSY, *Ode*

10.   He left a Corsair's name to other times,
 Linked with one virtue, and a thousand crimes.

—LORD BYRON, *The Corsair*

The Bilabial Glide Consonants: [ʍ] or [hw] (hw) As in *What* and *When* and [w] As in *Will* and *Wit*

The consonants [ʍ] or [hw] and [w] are *glide sounds*. Such sounds are produced with the organs of articulation in movement from an initial, determinate position to a final position determined by the sound which immediately follows. The sound [ʍ] or [hw] is voiceless; [w] is voiced. Both are initiated with the lips rounded in a close, pursed position as for the vowel [u]. The tongue is raised in back toward the soft palate. Study Figure 14–4 for the initial position

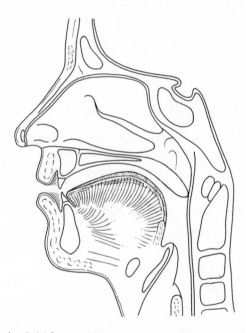

FIGURE 14–4. Initial articulatory position for glide sounds [ʍ] and [w]. Note that the back of the tongue is raised.

for the lip glide sounds. Note that the lips do not touch the teeth, as they necessarily do for the sounds [f] and [v]. The palate is raised for the bilabial glide sounds, and the sounds are emitted orally.

[ʍ] (hw) occurs in words spelled with *wh* initially or medially. Many speakers, however, use the voiced [w] rather than the [ʍ] in words such as *why, what,* and *when.* The [ʍ] also occurs in contexts following a [t], [s], or [k] as in *twine, swim,* and *quit.*

Practice Materials

To determine whether you use a [hw] or [w], place your hand in front of the mouth for the trial words *what* and *where.* The [hw] should begin with a definite stream of unvocalized breath. In contrast, [w] is vocalized and there is no obvious stream of breath. The word pairs which follow should help to make the distinction between the two sounds.

[hw]	[w]	[hw]	[w]
whither	wither	while	wile
where	wear	white	wight
wheel	weal	whether	weather
whet	wet	whacks	wax
what	watt	whirled	world
which	witch	whine	wine
when	wen	Whig	wig
whirred	word	whish	wish
whale	wail	whist	wist
whey	way	whoa	woe

Initial [hw]

wheat	whistle	wharf	whiting
wheedle	whelp	whimper	whittle
wheeze	whence	whimsy	whipsaw
whiff	whirl	whiskey	whang
whim	whistling	whiffle	wheal
whip	whop	whinny	whetstone
whisper	whorl	whisker	whelp

Medial [hw]

pinwheel	somewhat	meanwhile	unwholesome
anywhere	awhile	bobwhite	buckwheat
nowhere	somewhere	freewheeling	erstwhile

Sentences for [hw] and [w] Contrast

1. Do you prefer the song of the bobwhite or the whippoorwill?
2. What was Wilson's whispering about?

3. Where did the whaling ship go when it left the wharf?

4. Despite his wheezing, his appetite was whetted by the sight of the wholesome food.

5. The bewhiskered sailor stood at the wheel of his white ship.

6. Farmer White had a bumper crop of winter wheat.

7. Whitman exercised his whims when playing whist.

8. The cargo was unloaded somewhere on the wide wharf.

9. Whiting and whale meat were served to Will for dinner.

10. Watts whistled and whittled as he worked the mill wheel.

Initial [w]

we	web	woe	wonder
weak	well	won't	wise
weep	went	war	wire
weed	west	warn	wind
wield	wag	wasp	wound
wink	wax	watch	wow
wind	wool	were	worn
wane	wolf	work	worship
waste	woo	worse	wither
wave	womb	won	witness

Medial [w] (*Note That the Spelling May Be* u *and* o *as Well as* w)

biweekly	await	inward	unworthy
unwieldy	reweigh	unwavering	rewed
bewitch	away	awoke	earthworm
unwitting	awake	unworn	reworked
unwary	bewail	rewarned	anyone
unwept	byway	onward	everyone
unwelcome	unwilling	reweave	everyway
unwise	unworldly	reward	inquire
bewilder	unwanted	unwind	liquid
unwell	unwonted	reweb	require

Sentences

1. Wales has many rewarding and wonderful sights.

2. Kingsley wrote that "men must work, and women must weep."

3. Wilton walked west through the quagmire to earn one reward.

4.   The flame waxed and waned and dwindled into nothingness.

5.   On awaking, Watson wanted the market quotations for the stocks over which he often wailed.

6.   William West was fond of walking in the quiet of the evening.

7.   Wanda tripped over a twig and twisted her ankle.

8.   The weary soldiers were in a quandary as to how best to make their way to the winding, willowy fields.

9.   In a twinkling we were deceived by the quick-working, wily magician.

10.   Howard went into the woods which were alive with quail and quacking birds.

Selections

1.   I'll walk where my own nature would be leading—
     It vexes me to choose another guide—
     Where the grey flocks in ferny glens are feeding,
     Where the wild wind blows on the mountain-side.

                              —EMILY BRONTË, *Often Rebuked*

2.   I sigh the lack of many a thing I sought,
     And with old woes new wail my dear time's waste.

                              —WILLIAM SHAKESPEARE, *Sonnet 30*

3.   Wandering between two worlds, one dead,
     The other powerless to be born.

                —MATTHEW ARNOLD, *Stanzas from the Grand Chartreuse*

4.   He was a scholar, and a ripe and good one,
     Exceeding wise, fair-spoken and persuading.

                              —WILLIAM SHAKESPEARE, *King Henry VIII*

5.   For in the time we know not of
                    Did fate begin
     Weaving the web of days that wove
                    Your doom, Faustine.

                    —ALGERNON CHARLES SWINBURNE, *Faustine*

6.   Not from the whole wide world would I choose thee,
     Sweetheart, light of the land and the sea!
     The wide, wide world could not enclose thee,
     For thou art the whole wide world to me.

                              —RICHARD W. GILDER, *Song*

[w] and [v]

Some persons, probably because of foreign language influence, tend to confuse the bilabial [w] with the labiodental (lip-teeth) [v]. The following word pairs should help to establish the distinction between these two sounds. Observe the lip action in a mirror and make certain that there is no contact of the teeth and lips for the [w].

Practice Materials

wane	vein	wend	vend
wary	vary	worse	verse
west	vest	wine	vine
weld	veld	wiper	viper
wiser	visor	wow	vow
went	vent	wile	vile

Sentences

1. It is wise not to get caught in a vise.
2. Wine is made from the fruit of the vine.
3. William West was fond of his velvet vest.
4. As the vain writer grew older, his ability was on the wane and his verse became obviously worse.
5. To vend his various wares he had to wend his weary way and be wary of wily customers along the wayside.
6. The knight looked wiser behind his visor.
7. We were puzzled at the witch's vow never more to use her wiles for vile purposes.

Selection

There is not in the wide world a
    Valley so sweet
As that vale in whose bosom
The bright waters meet.

—THOMAS MOORE, *The Meeting of the Waters*

CHAPTER 15

The Lip-Teeth Sounds

The lip-teeth (labiodental) consonants [f] and [v] present little or no difficulty for native English speakers. Persons for whom Spanish is a first language may carry over a tendency from their native tongue and use the sounds [b] and [v] interchangeably. Another tendency of these speakers is to substitute a sound intermediate between [b] and [v].

Speakers with a Germanic background may confuse [v] and [w] because the letter *w* is pronounced [v] in German. Fortunately, the pronunciation of the letter *v* as [v] is consistent in English so that spelling serves as a reliable guide. Speakers whose first language is German need also to overcome their native inclination to pronounce the letter *f* as [v].

[f] As in *Feel, Fun, Afraid,* and *Enough*

[f] is a voiceless, fricative, lip-teeth (labiodental) consonant. It is made by pressing the lower lip against the upper teeth and forcing a stream of breath between the narrow spaces of the upper teeth or between the lower lip and upper teeth. The soft palate is raised to prevent nasal emission of breath.

In spelling, the sound is most frequently represented by the letter *f*. Other spellings include *ph* as in *phrase* and *gh* as in *rough*. The sound occurs in initial, medial, and final positions.

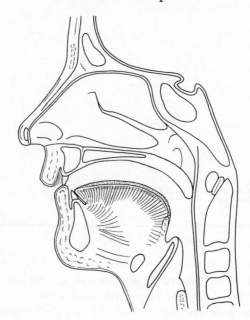

FIGURE 15–1.   Articulatory position for [f] and [v].

Practice Materials

Initial

feed	fad	fob	fire
feel	fan	fog	fowl
fib	food	fox	foible
fin	fool	firm	foil
fit	full	first	foist
fail	phobia	fudge	feud
fame	photo	fuss	fume
fed	falter	fight	fuse
felt	fork	file	future
fence	fought	find	few

Medial

coffee	defect	afford	afar
enfeeble	after	effort	stuffing
effete	aft	soften	rifle
sphere	raft	affirm	trifle
efficient	raffle	refurbish	stifle
sphinx	laughed	unfurl	sapphire
swift	refuse	roughen	refute
chafed	effuse	shuffle	prophet
effect	careful	sofa	reference
defend	barefoot	loafer	breakfast

Final

beef	skiff	chafe	half
chief	cliff	deaf	staff
reef	whiff	chef	graph
belief	stiff	chaff	enough
thief	strafe	laugh	tough
tiff	safe	calf	golf

[fl]

flee	fluke	flirt	flutter
fleet	flute	flourish	flight
flip	flood	flurry	fly
flame	flaw	flub	flounder
flu	floral	flunk	flour
float	Florence	flush	flout

Sentences

1. Despite Phil's rough ways, he was careful not to give offense to his fellows.
2. Fred felt proud to unfurl his fine flag.
3. After the fog lifted, the planes took off for far places.
4. Coffee is a favorite breakfast drink for many of us.
5. Frank and his father are fond of golf and of fishing.
6. "Fair, fat and forty" is fraught with folly for many females.
7. Rudolph went to a physician for his frequent sniffles.

8. The chef served the roast pheasant on a fancy chafing dish.

9. The thief came to grief over the theft of the sapphire.

10. Farnum had a phobia of fire even in a fireplace.

Selections

1. The painful warrior famoused for fight,
   After a thousand victories, once foil'd,
   Is from the books of honor razed quite,
   And all the rest forgot for which he toil'd.

—WILLIAM SHAKESPEARE, *Sonnet 25*

2. Time stoops to no man's lure;
   And love, grown faint and fretful,
   With lips but half regretful
   Sighs, and with eyes forgetful
       Weeps that no loves endure.

—ALGERNON CHARLES SWINBURNE, *The Garden of Prosperine*

3. A faithful friend is a strong defence: and he that hath found such an one hath found a treasure.

—Ecclesiasticus, 6:14

4. Fare thee well! And if forever,
   Still forever, fare thee well.

—LORD BYRON, *Fare Thee Well*

5. When tillage begins, other arts follow. The farmers therefore are the founders of civilization.

—DANIEL WEBSTER, *Remarks on Agriculture*

[v] As in *Vim*, *Evoke*, and *Alive*

[v] is the voiced cognate of [f]. It is, of course, produced like the [f] except that the [v] is voiced and as such requires less breath pressure than the [f].

Except for the *f* of *of*, [v] is spelled as it is sounded.

[v] causes little or no difficulty to American-English speakers. Some foreign-born speakers may have difficulty because they confuse the [v] and [w]. (See page 242.)

Practice Materials

Initial

Venus	valley	vault	visit
veal	van	vaunt	vile
venal	value	varnish	vine
veer	vend	varlet	vital
vigor	very	verse	vulgar
vim	vary	virtue	vulture
victor	voodoo	vernal	volume
vein	vogue	voice	volunteer
vale	vote	void	Volga
vapor	voracious	vice	vowel

Medial

evening	paved	proven	reverse
Eva	shaved	grooved	nervous
even	revel	hooves	convert
believing	event	roving	jovial
given	prevent	clover	revile
livid	having	Dover	trivial
evil	gavel	marvel	avoid
devil	travel	carving	invite
raving	ravel	starving	lover
staved	avid	avert	cover

Final

deceive	delve	mauve	dive
receive	shelve	starve	strive
heave	have	carve	alive
sleeve	salve	nerve	hive
give	move	curve	naive
live	groove	swerve	resolve
gave	prove	glove	revolve
knave	rove	above	twelve
slave	stove	shove	love
stave	strove	dove	trove

Sentences

1.   Victor, for fear of becoming a victim, would not volunteer to test the voodoo.

2.   Eve, an avid traveler, began her voyage from Dover to the Everglades.

3.   The devil, for his evil purposes, can be a scrivener as well as a quoter of scriptures.

4.   It is naive to approach a beehive without a veil for covering.

5.   Jovial conversation accompanied Vera's carving of the turkey.

6.   Some have tried to improve the figure of Venus with drapes, but very few have tried gloves.

7.   Twelve Javanese were found roving through the river valley.

8.   Valentine banged his gavel to put a stop to the verbalizations at the convention.

9.   The thieves found it of value to cultivate a Harvard accent.

10.   Vinson resolved to give up his vain ways and to live a life of value.

Selections

1.   Ever let the Fancy roam,
Pleasure never is at home!

. . . .

Where's the eye, however blue,
Doth not weary? Where's the face
One would meet in every place?
Where's the voice, however soft.
One would hear so very oft?

—JOHN KEATS, *Fancy*

2.   For a man can lose neither the past nor the future; for how can one take from him that which is not his? So remember these two points: first, that each thing is of like form from everlasting and comes round again in its cycle, and that it signifies not whether a man shall look upon the same things for a hundred years or two hundred, or for an infinity of time; second, that the longest lived and the shortest lived man, when they come to die, lose one and the same thing.

—MARCUS AURELIUS, *Meditations*

3.   All is ephemeral—fame and the famous as well.

—MARCUS AURELIUS, *Meditations*

CHAPTER 16

The Tongue-Teeth Sounds

The tongue-teeth consonants [θ] and [ð] present some difficulties for native speakers of English as well as for persons with foreign language backgrounds. The causes of these difficulties and exercises for overcoming them will be presented in the individual considerations of these sounds.

[θ] (th) As in *Thin, Thank, Theory; Anything, Truthful; Faith, Earth*

The [θ] is a voiceless fricative. It is produced by placing the tip of the tongue lightly against the back of the upper teeth or slightly between the teeth. Air is forced through the place of contact to produce the characteristic fricative quality. In spelling, the sound is represented by the letters *th*. [θ] may occur initially, medially, or finally.

[θ] tends to be a somewhat troublesome sound for many speakers. Native-born Americans exposed to substandard speech influences may substitute a [t] for the initial [θ] so that words such as *thin* and *three* are pronounced as though they were *tin* and *tree*. Foreign-born speakers who do not have the [θ] in their native language tend to substitute their nearest approximation for it. Frequent substitutions include a dentalized [s] and a dentalized [t]. A comparison of Figures 16–1 and 17–1 for the [θ] and [t] and practice with the material that immediately follows should help to establish the distinctions between [θ] and [t] and [θ] and [s].

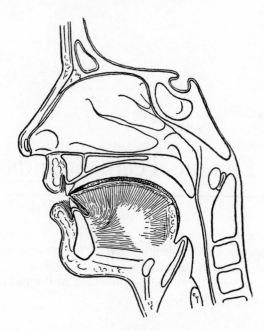

FIGURE 16–1. Representative articulatory positions for [θ] and [ð] as post-dental sounds.

Practice Materials

Distinguish between [θ] and [t]:

thank	tank	theme	team
thin	tin	thought	taught
through	true	deaths	debts
thread	tread	ether	eater
thrill	trill	sheaths	sheets
thick	tick	forth	fort
thrips	trips	bath	bat
thorn	torn	oath	oat

faithful	fateful	ruthless	rootless
myths	mitts	tooth	toot

Distinguish between [θ] and [s]:

theme	seem	thought	sought
think	sink	thumb	sum
thick	sick	thigh	sigh
thing	sing	thin	sin
thank	sank	kith	kiss
thaw	saw	myth	miss
faith	face	moth	moss
truth	truce	bath	bass
mouth	mouse	math	mass
worth	worse	fourth	force

Sentences for [θ], [t], *and* [s] *Contrast*

1. We felt a thrill to hear the trill of the thrush.
2. Theodore was regarded as being a man true blue, all through.
3. The tick was found in the thick woods.
4. Ted, a good student, thought that he had been well taught.
5. Thelma heard the story through and thankfully believed it to be true.
6. Catherine could sing about almost anything.
7. The ache in Matthew's thigh brought forth a deep sigh.
8. The thick, acrid smoke made Thaddeus feel sick.
9. Miss Thornton declared the story to be a myth.
10. Few traces are left of what was once the region of Thrace.

Additional Practice Materials for [θ]

Initial

three	through	thud	thousand
thesis	throe	thunder	thymus
theme	throat	thump	theory
thimble	throne	third	threat
thicken	thrall	Thursday	throttle
theft	thought	thirst	thrust
thalamus	thwart	thirteen	thicket
thank	thaw	thigh	theology

Initial (*Cont.*)

thrash	throb	thyroid	thermostat
Thrace	throng	thrive	Theodore

Medial

ether	pathos	enthusiasm	lengthen
breathy	pathetic	author	strengthen
anything	bathtub	orthodox	earthy
nothing	wrathful	orthopod	forthright
healthy	ruthless	slothful	toothless
wealthy	truthful	mirthful	atheist
stealthy	ethyl	toothache	method
rethread	birthday	mythical	lethargy
deathly	earthquake	synthetic	panther
youthful	hawthorn	arithmetic	Cathay

Final

wreath	booth	month	hearth
beneath	uncouth	mouth	sleuth
myth	both	warmth	troth
pith	oath	south	froth
kith	fourth	growth	length
faith	north	eighth	fifth
death	moth	ninth	breath
zenith	cloth	path	truth
wrath	dearth	mammoth	Ruth
stealth	earth	worth	Beth

Sentences

1. Arithmetic is thought to be the most elementary form of mathematics.

2. *Thank you*'s are better than threats in strengthening associations.

3. Matthew learned how to be thoughtful rather than ruthless in telling the truth.

4. The warmth of the day made Theodore lethargic.

5. Thelma, unlike her brother Thaddeus, enjoyed a bath.

6. The famous author Shaw thought that youth is wasted on the youthful.

7.   Ruth considered the eighth day of the month her thoroughly lucky one.

8.   Beth spotted the panther creeping stealthily through the thicket.

9.   There was no dearth of growth from the fertile soil of the South.

10.   Thursday is the fifth day of the week.

Selections

1.   The youthful Keats was the author of many famous lines. Among the best known are the following from *Endymion* and *Ode on a Grecian Urn:*

A thing of beauty is a joy forever:
Its loveliness increases; it will never
Pass into nothingness.

"Beauty is truth, truth beauty"—that is all
Ye know on earth, and all ye need to know.

2.   In *My Lost Youth* Henry Wadsworth Longfellow, often called the poet of the hearth, wrote:

A boy's will is the wind's will,
And the thoughts of youth are long, long thoughts.

3.   In his *Resignation* Longfellow wrote of death. Perhaps most famous are the lines:

There is no Death! What seems so is transition;
    This life of mortal breath
Is but a suburb of the life elysian,
    Whose portal we call Death.

4.   Thomas Moore is probably best known to us for his tender song themes. He was also the author of the following prophetic and almost wrathful verse taken from his poem *Lalla Rookh:*

And from the lips of Truth one mighty breath
Shall like a whirlwind scatter in its breeze
That whole dark pile of human mockeries—
Then shall the reign of mind commence on earth.
And starting fresh as from a second birth,

Man in the sunshine of the world's new spring
Shall walk transparent like some holy thing!

[ð] As in *That, Those; Either, Weather; Bathe, Breathe*

[ð] is the voiced counterpart of [θ]. It is represented by the letters
th and may occur initially, medially, or finally as in *these, bathing,*
and *wreathe.* The [ð] is produced with light tongue-tip contact
either behind the upper teeth or between the cutting edges of the
teeth. Air is forced through the place of contact while the vocal
folds are in vibration.

There is no certain way of determining whether a particular
word should be pronounced with a [θ] or a [ð]. We may note a
tendency, in initial positions at least, for .words that are stressed
and significant in a sentence, such as nouns, verbs, and adjectives,
to be pronounced with the voiceless [θ]. Pronouns, articles, and conjunctions, which are more likely to be unstressed and weak in sentence context, tend to be pronounced with a [ð]. Because of this
the [ð] tends to occur more often than the [θ] in our speech.

Persons who are inclined to substitute a [t] for a [θ] are also
likely to substitute a [d] for a [ð]. The first set of practice materials
should help to establish a clear distinction between the [d] and [ð].
(See page 265 for description of [d].)

Practice Materials

Distinguish between [ð] and [d]:

thee	dee	their	dare
they	day	thence	dense
then	den	lather	ladder
than	Dan	lathe	laid
though	dough	loathe	load
those	doze	seethe	seed
thy	dye	other	udder
thine	dine	worthy	wordy

Sentences for [ð] *and* [d]

1. Dan was taller than his brother.

2. The laborer loathed his heavy load.
3. "Do not take their dare," warned Ben's mother.
4. They spent the day thinking worthy thoughts.
5. Though they could not bake the dough, they enjoyed the bread.

Additional Practice Materials

Initial

these	than	the	thine
this	those	thus	them
then	though	thy	therefore
they	there	that	therein

Medial

either	weather	although	mother
neither	feather	loathing	bother
heathen	lather	brother	logarithm
leather	rather	father	further

Final

breathe	soothe	scythe	swathe
bathe	scathe	writhe	teethe
wreathe	blithe	tithe	with

Sentences

1. Though he was loathe to speak his mind, father often knew best.
2. Neither mother nor brother enjoyed foggy weather.
3. The word *thine* is the possessive form of *thou*.
4. *This* and *that* are demonstrative pronouns.
5. Mother is fond of feathered creatures.
6. The ghosts gathered among the other blithe spirits.
7. Leather is being replaced by plastic in the making of clothing.
8. The heather withered in the field.
9. The heathen considered it a bother to bathe.
10. Though the birds were of a feather, they preferred not to flock together.

Selections for [θ] *and* [ð]

1. Let us crown ourselves with rosebuds before they be withered.

Wisdom of Solomon, 2:8

2. At the door of life, by the gate of breath,
   There are worse things waiting for men than death.

—ALGERNON CHARLES SWINBURNE, *The Triumph of Time*

CHAPTER 17

The Tongue-Tip to Gum-Ridge and the Postdental Sounds

A glance at the consonant chart will reveal that the tongue-tip to gum-ridge (lingua-alveolar) and the post-alveolar sounds include a third of the American English consonants. The lingua-alveolar and the post-alveolar articulatory positions are distinctive for our language. For this reason the sounds in these groups will be given detailed consideration.

THE TONGUE–TIP TO GUM–RIDGE SOUNDS

We shall begin our study of the tongue-tip to gum-ridge consonants with the [t] as in *tea, ton,* and *too.* It is our belief that if the contact point and manner of articulation for [t] are mastered, the speaker will have an excellent point of reference for the production of other American-English alveolar speech sounds.

[t] As in *Ton, Until,* and *Boat*

To produce the [t] as in *ton* or as an isolated sound, the tongue is raised so that the tongue tip comes into contact with the upper gum ridge (see Figure 17–1). The soft palate is raised to prevent nasal emission of breath. The sides of the tongue near the tip are in contact with the upper molars. The tongue, tense and extended, is held in this position for a fraction of a second. Then, quickly and as completely as possible, the tongue is retracted with a resultant slight "explosion" of air at the tongue tip. This should be felt as a puff of breath if you hold your hand in front of your mouth.

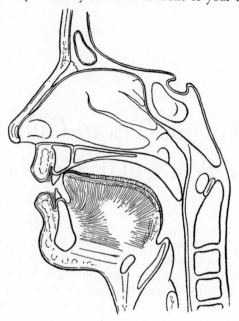

FIGURE 17–1.   Articulatory position for [t] and [d].

The [t] as just described occurs whenever the sound appears in a stressed syllable and is immediately followed by a vowel. The [t] in such contexts is a lingua-alveolar (gum ridge), stop-plosive consonant. In producing this [t] the following cautions should be observed:

1.   Make certain that the tongue tip is in contact with the gum ridge and *not the upper teeth*. The contact, when broken, should be quick and complete.

2.   Do not permit the tongue to slide so that contact is made between the front surface of the tongue and the gum. If this happens, a [ts] blend is likely to be produced.

Practice Materials

Establish the contact position for the stressed [t] by practice with the material that follows. Repeat each of the words of the list at least three times.

Initial

tea	take	too	tole
tee	ten	tube	talk
tip	tell	took	taught
tell	tag	tomb	tog
tape	tap	toe	top
turn	type	town	tone
Turk	time	tower	team
tub	tide	toy	teach
ton	tile	toil	tease
tie	tire	towel	tool

Medial (Followed by a Vowel)

attend	interne	Utopia	partake
atone	iterate	Utah	pitied
attack	deter	intake	rotate
attempt	detect	eternal	entire
attach	until	retool	historical
attain	utensil	retook	intone
entire	intense	return	intend

Phrases

take your time	talk and tell
tip to top	took the tea
ten and ten	ten times ten
twenty and two	turn the tape
tap the top	take a turn
the town tower	tie the tag

Sentences

1. Tom played a tuba to tease Ted.
2. Ted's toe was taped.
3. Tell Tillie the time when it is two P.M.

4. Tea was served privately for the two who wanted to be entirely alone.
5. The tower was attacked and attained.
6. Time and tide are eternal verities.
7. Tuesday was made tag day in town.
8. Utah was named for the Ute Indians.
9. The interne detected a contagious tic.
10. Tom turned detective to test his attainments at detection.

Final[1]

eat	bat	note	cut
it	boot	bought	hut
ate	foot	blot	hurt
might	emit	right	nought
out	flout	might	suit
quoit	incite	sought	root
sight	blight	fort	shoot

Sentences

1. We will eat at eight.
2. Football is a favorite American sport.
3. Nat was hurt by the split bat.
4. Mint and fruit juice make for a pleasant drink.
5. The boat was lost in the mist at night.
6. Nought could induce Chet to emit a sound.
7. Most adolescent boys like to eat things that are sweet.
8. The note was brought by a servant who wore a blue suit.
9. The quoit contest was won by the Ute.
10. A well-fitted boot will not hurt the foot.

[t] As in *Safety*

The sound [t] in an unstressed syllable followed by a vowel is produced in a less vigorous manner than when it occurs in a stressed syllable. The contact between tongue tip and gum ridge is not held as long as for a stressed [t] and there is less breath puff following the breaking of the contact. Avoid assimilating the un-

[1] A final [t] is exploded when it is followed by a vowel in the next word within the same phrase, as in *the cat is here*. Most persons do not explode the final [t] at the end of a sentence as in *I'll come at eight*.

stressed [t] either in the direction of substituting a [d] for it or omitting the sound entirely.

Practice Materials

The words that follow provide practice for the unstressed [t].

city	latter	utter	tempted
plenty	faulty	bitter	twenty
better	mountain	fifty	written
letter	scatter	thirty	litter

Practice in discriminating between the unstressed [t] and [d] in the following pairs of words:

latter	ladder	wetting	wedding
betting	bedding	written	ridden
heated	heeded	butting	budding
bitter	bidder	tenting	tending
rating	raiding	contented	contended
shutter	shudder	writer	rider

The following words provide practice for [t] followed by a vowel and/or in the final position.

tell	waste	fateful	bit	tat
ten	last	inter	flat	tent
till	quite	contain	flute	taste
time	after	rotary	hoot	tight
told	comet	twine	root	taught
tab	lout	twist	tote	toot
tangle	between	twig	wart	tort
toll	return	palliate	what	twist
at	continue	unite	flirt	twit
boat	atone	beet	wheat	tossed

Sentences

1. Ten and ten and two count up to twenty-two if counted right.

2. Tom Tucker will have to be told to wait for tomorrow.

3. Ted, please put the cat and the light out before you take off.

4. The tidings of the times portended that temptation was to be avoided at all cost.

5.   On his trip to Utah, Thomas sat next to a taciturn gentleman from eastern Texas.

6.   The stars twinkled bright in the Oriental sky.

7.   Thomas learned that it was easier to start than to stop a fight.

8.   Thomson could not take being twitted, though he was expert at taunting others not quite his size.

9.   We had to wait for twenty minutes between the acts of the play.

10.   Too few learn in time that it is for them that the bells toll.

Selections

1.   Temptation can be many different things to different men. It has been a time-honored subject for the poet, the moralist, the dramatist, and the timeless philosopher. Some views of temptation will be presented in the quotations that follow.

> a.   "I can resist everything except temptation," Oscar Wilde had one of his characters protest.

> b.   In contrast, the ever optimistic Browning asserts in his *The Ring and the Book:*
>
> Why comes temptation but for man to meet
> And master and make crouch beneath his foot,
> And so be pedestaled in triumph?

> c.   Finally, for the moment at least, we have the terse statement of the British humorist and poet Douglas Jerrold who in his *The Catspaw* contends: Honest bread is very well—it's the butter that makes the temptation.

2.   Take hands and part with laughter;
     Touch lips and part with tears;
Once more and no more after,
     Whatever comes with years.

—ALGERNON CHARLES SWINBURNE, *Rococo*

3.   O, it is excellent
To have a giant's strength; but it is tyrannous
To use it like a giant.

—WILLIAM SHAKESPEARE, *Measure for Measure*

Other Varieties of [t]

As we indicated earlier, the consonant [t] varies somewhat in manner of production and acoustic end result according to speech context. Some of the more frequent variations will be considered.

[t] Followed by [θ] (th) or [ð] (th) As in *Right Things* and *At The*. In combinations such as *at the, hit that, light things,* and *eighth*, the [t] is produced by contact between the tongue tip and the upper teeth rather than at the gum ridge. The dentalized [t] in these combinations is produced as a result of the assimilative influence of the next sound [θ] or [ð] which is articulated dentally.

This variety of [t] is least likely to be produced defectively by persons with foreign language backgrounds. It is the variety most likely to be produced habitually by speakers whose English speech is influenced by French, Spanish, Italian, or German.

Practice Materials

eighth time	sweet thoughts
hit the ball	right thinking
swat the fly	bright theorist
light the lamp	slight theme
stout thump	correct theory

Sentences

1. Bright theories make for right thoughts.
2. Tom struck out the eighth time at bat.
3. Tess could not bear to swat the fly.
4. The poet thought in slight themes.
5. Ted liked to light the lamp.

[t] Followed by [l] or [n] As in *Little* and *Button*. When the [t] sound is immediately followed by an [l] or [n] it is not necessary to remove the tongue tip from the gum ridge to complete the sound. Instead, the sides of the front part of the tongue break contact with the side teeth to permit a *lateral* escape or explosion of breath. When the [t] is followed by [l], as in *little, battle, settle, kettle,* and *mortal,* the breath of the explosion is emitted orally.

In words in which the [t] is followed by [n], as in *written, button,*

cotton, and *rotten,* the tongue position is maintained in going from
the [t] to the [n]. When the velum is lowered for the [n] a nasal
rather than an oral explosion takes place. If you place your hand just
below the nostrils, you should be able to feel a nasally emitted puff
of air.

There is a marked tendency to substitute a throat or glottal (laryngeal) click sound for the [t] when it is followed by [l] or [n]. This
substitution, in American speech, is generally considered substandard. You may check your tendency for glottal substitution by placing
your hand at the larynx while speaking the list of words and sentences that follow. If you feel a click, it is likely that you are using
a glottal (laryngeal) catch sound instead of the [t]. To avoid this
tendency, pay special attention to the prescribed manner of articulation for the [t] in [tl] and [tn] combinations.

Practice Materials

beetle	mortal	bitten	rotten
battle	glottal	button	fountain
metal	bottle	cotton	written
whittle	scuttle	gotten	fatten
settle	rattle	mountain	mutton

Sentences

1. Morton was in fine fettle as he filled the kettle.
2. The mutton chops were too tough to be eaten.
3. The ill-gotten gains were hidden in the mountain.
4. Little by little Benton analyzed the contents of the bottle.
5. The buttons were whittled out of wood.
6. The kitten played with the cotton ball.
7. Skelton hoped to become immortal by well-written words.
8. A metal figure of Triton dominated the fountain.

[t] Followed by [s] and Preceded and Followed by [s] As in *Pets*
and *Posts*. In contexts in which the [t] is immediately followed by
an [s], the tip of the tongue is permitted to slide forward in anticipation of the [s]. Care should be taken not to omit the [t] entirely,
especially in combinations in which the [t] is medial between two
[s] sounds. The fine articulatory movements required for the [sts]
combination increase the tendency for the omission of the [t].

Practice Materials

Practice with the words and sentences that follow should help to focus attention on the precise articulation that is required for [ts] and [sts].

pets	pots	insists	pests
lots	flights	breasts	ghosts
gates	paints	posts	resists
facts	mists	rests	persists
lasts	jests	masts	tests

Sentences

1. The last acts of plays should be the playwright's best.
2. Painted pots were placed next to the fence posts.
3. Gray mists stopped the planes' flights.
4. The hard facts of life may interfere with the attainments of the heart's desires.
5. Birds' nests were found on the masts.

[d] As in *Done, Ado,* and *Glad*

The consonant [d] in *done* is articulated in essentially the same manner as the [t] in *ton* except that the [d] is voiced. The [d], like the [t], is a variable sound. The varieties of [d] parallel those for [t]. Faults in articulation also parallel those for [t], the chief one being the tendency for dental articulation. A second tendency to be avoided is the substitution of a [t] for a [d] in words in which the final [d] should be voiced. This fault may be especially noted in the speech of German-born persons or in the speech of persons for whom German was and perhaps continues to be a strong influence. The probable reason for this is that the final [d] does not occur in German.

Practice Materials

The first set of materials should help to establish a clear distinction between [t] and [d]. Make certain that the [t] is voiceless and the [d] is voiced.

Distinguish between initial [t] and [d]:

tame	dame	tuck	duck
teem	deem	tune	dune
tip	dip	tomb	doom
tail	dale	toe	doe
ten	den	taunt	daunt
tan	Dan	tot	dot
time	dime	town	down
too	do	touch	Dutch

Distinguish between final [t] and [d]:

seat	seed	brute	brood
bit	bid	note	node
ate	aid	nought	gnawed
late	laid	not	nod
mat	mad	coat	code
let	led	writ	rid
bat	bad	cart	card
set	said	stunt	stunned
cat	cad	hurt	heard
beat	bead	curt	curd

Initial

deal	daze	dart	dire
deep	duel	dark	dear
din	dough	dirt	dean
day	dote	dearth	dream
debt	dawn	dub	drip
dance	dock	dike	drain
dew	dog	doubt	draw
dale	damp	dull	does

Phrases

dance till dawn	daily dozen
day by day	duel in the dew
dark and dreary	due date
din at daybreak	dull ditty
dry desert	denizen of the deep
dog at the dock	delicate dough

Medial

admit	fading	bedlam	hinder
ardent	hidden	candor	needed
oddly	eddy	splendor	indoor
edict	adverse	random	odious

Final

add	amid	said	spade
crowd	old	lead	code
rude	bald	heed	abode
hoard	fraud	reed	node
heed	curd	rod	aloud
ode	brood	toad	cloud

Sentences

1. Undaunted by earlier failures, Diane led a dozen determined ladies to begin a ten-day diet.

2. Dan claimed that frequently he could not distinguish between Dick's candor and his rudeness.

3. As the day was dying, a deep-red cloud rested on the mountain top.

4. The dog's barking at dawn warned Daniel and helped him to undo a dastardly plot.

5. Duncan brooded over the fraud that deprived him of his gold and his abode.

6. Daybreak is held to be a good time for undertaking duels.

7. The crowd did not heed the warning to disperse.

8. London is a city of dense fog and bright-minded traders.

9. The drug made Dick's head droop as he dropped off to sleep.

10. Matilda married her admiral who wrote an ode to his bride.

Selections for [t] *and* [d]

1. But when I tell him he hates flatterers,
   He says he does, being then most flattered.

   —WILLIAM SHAKESPEARE, *Julius Caesar*

2. Cowards die many times before their death;
   The valiant never taste of death but once.

   —WILLIAM SHAKESPEARE, *Julius Caesar*

3. My true-love hath my heart, and I have his,
    By just exchange one for the other given;
    I hold his dear, and mine he cannot miss,
    There never was a better bargain driven.

    —PHILLIP SIDNEY, *The Bargain*

4. When Adam was created,
    He dwelt in Eden's shade,
    As Moses has related,
    Before a bride was made;
    Ten thousand times ten thousand
    Things wheelèd all around,
    Before a bride was formed
    Or yet a mate was found.

    —GEORGE PULLEN JACKSON, *Wedlock*

5. The day is done, and the darkness
        Falls from the wings of Night
    As a feather is wafted downward
        From an eagle in his flight.

    . . . .

    And the night shall be filled with music,
        And the cares that infest the day
    Shall fold their tents, like the Arabs
        And as silently steal away.

    —HENRY WADSWORTH LONGFELLOW, *The Day Is Done*

6. No living man can send me to the shades
    Before my time; no man of woman born,
    Coward or brave, can shun his destiny.

    —HOMER, *Iliad*

7. I have long been convinced that institutions purely democratic
    must, sooner or later, destroy liberty or civilization or both. How
    will you cope with seasons of widespread unemployment and dis-
    content, which assail every country? Through such seasons the
    United States will have to pass in the course of the next century, if
    not of this. I heartily wish you good deliverance, but my reason and
    my wishes are at war and I cannot help foreboding the worst. It is
    plain that your government will never be able to restrain a distressed
    and discontented majority. For with you the majority is the govern-
    ment, and it has the rich, who are always the minority, absolutely
    at its mercy. Either some Caesar or Napoleon will seize the reins of

government with a strong hand or your Republic will be as fearfully plundered and laid waste by barbarians in the twentieth century as the Roman Empire was in the fifth. Only the Huns and the Vandals who ravaged the Roman Empire, came from without, and your huns and vandals will have been engendered within your country by your own institutions.

—THOMAS BABINGTON MACAULAY, *From a Letter to a Virginian in 1857*

[s] As in *Sea, Asleep, Icy, Best,* and *Less*

The consonant [s] is a high-frequency, voiceless, tongue-tip fricative which requires careful and precise articulatory action for its production. The adjustments involve the following:

1.   The tongue is raised so that the sides are pressed firmly against the inner surfaces of the upper molars.

2.   The tongue is slightly grooved along the midline. Air is forced down along this groove.

3.   The tip of the tongue is placed about a quarter of an inch behind the upper teeth. The tongue tip is almost in position for a [t]. (Persons not able to attain this adjustment will probably find it easier to place the tongue tip close to the lower gum ridge.)

4.   The teeth are brought in line, with a very narrow space between the rows of teeth.

5.   The breath stream is directed along the groove of the tongue toward the cutting edges of the teeth.

6.   The soft palate is raised to prevent nasal emission of the sound.

Use a mirror to see the articulatory adjustments for the [s]. The recommended articulatory position is represented in Figure 17–2.

In producing the [s], exercise special care to avoid having the tongue tip touch either the upper teeth or the gum ridge. Neither should you permit the tongue tip to slide down so as to protrude between the rows of teeth. The first articulatory error will result in the production of a [ts] blend or in a lateral sound resembling a voiceless [l]. The second fault will result in the production of an infantile lisp resembling a voiceless [θ] (th).

Persons who habitually produce [t] and [d] sounds with dental rather than gum-ridge contacts are likely to lower the tongue tip for the production of [s]. The result, in most instances, is the production of a dull, low-pitched sibilant.

In some instances, the articulatory adjustments just described do not help to produce the desired result of a high-frequency, sibilant sound. Occasionally, the person, possibly because of his unusual mouth structure, must make individual adjustments to arrive at the same acoustic end result. With some articulatory adjustments, a low-pitched sound may be the best that the individual can achieve. Most persons, however, regardless of articulatory mechanism, can learn

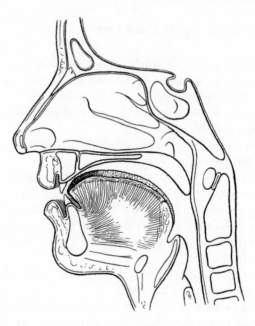

FIGURE 17–2.   Articulatory adjustments for [s] and [z].

to produce an [s] that acoustically resembles the high-pitched frica-tive described above.

Apart from the manner of articulation, the sound [s] in American-English speech may present some difficulty for the foreign-born speaker because of the varied spelling representations for the sound. The most frequent representation is the letter *s*; other representa-tions include the *ss* as in *less*, *sc* as in *scene*, *c* as in *race*, and *x* as in *hoax*. The foreign-born speaker of English may be forgiven his failure to know when to produce the sound [s] if we realize the many ways the letter *s* may be pronounced. In addition to the [s] we have [ʒ] (zh) as in *treasure*, [ʃ] (sh) as in *sure*, and [z] as in *his*. To add to the consternation of the foreign-born speaker, we also have the "silent" *s* as in *island* and *aisle*.

Practice Materials

Because of the frequency of the [s] in American-English speech, we recommend that a considerable amount of attention be given to this sound. Practice first to produce the sound in isolation until a clear, high-frequency sibilant can be articulated at will. Then incorporate the sound in nonsense syllables. The advantage of nonsense syllable practice in the early stages of establishing or correcting a sound lies in the avoidance of habits of articulation that may be faulty. Suggested nonsense syllable combinations precede the word lists.

seef	sif	sef	saf	sek
sah	sof	soo	sook	sawp
sut	sug	sul	sool	sipe

ahsah	ahsaw	eesaw	aysaw
ohso	ohsoo	ooso	oosoo

Initial[2]

see	sew	suck	circuit
seat	soak	seal	cease
say	saw	sale	citric
sane	sought	ceiling	cinch
sin	sog	sigh	scenic
sit	sop	cite	scent
set	song	civil	sceptre
sell	sock	cider	science
sat	sir	cigar	scion
sag	certain	cinder	screen
sue	soil	cipher	screw
soot	sun	circle	scratch

Medial

asleep	boost	essay	tracing
mist	rooster	icy	trousseau

[2]Additional word lists will be provided for [s] blends. Some of the words of the early lists may again be used when the frequent [s] blends are presented.

Medial (*Cont.*)

hasten	boast	pressing	bracer
pest	bossy	blessing	hoist
last	twosome	history	peaceful

Final

crease	loops	choice	loss
leaps	loose	voice	dross
miss	dose	terse	hiss
kiss	horse	verse	hex
pace	Norse	curse	fix
race	bus	fuss	tricks
bets	truss	mouse	cheeks
debts	puss	house	plates
pass	worse	dress	waits
caps	hearse	niece	fleets
farce	entice	boss	keeps

[s] *Preceded and Followed by a Vowel*

deceive	casing	assume	gusset
acetic	assay	twosome	russet
precede	resale	isobar	assign
acid	assemble	isolate	nicety
assimilate	assent	isotype	oscillate
asymmetry	asset	assault	ossify
aseptic	brassy	assort	ascend
essay	glassy	asunder	assail
lacing.	messy	assert	asylum

Sentences

1. Six swift horses started in the historic race.
2. Sue, a suave slim lass, wore a silk dress.
3. Selma Sweet fussed about the small squeaking mouse.
4. Simon insisted that clever verse must be terse.
5. Simson had a steady fondness for sweet cider.
6. The storm tossed sloop sank beneath the spray.
7. Stevenson was a scientist who liked to be certain of his evidence.

8. Stella was enticed by the high ceilings of the house.

9. "Puss in Boots" is a story for small children who like to listen.

10. Some historians say that there is no such thing as a bad peace.

If the [s] sound cannot be mastered directly, it may be of help to begin with a [t] and to work initially for a [ts] blend. This is especially helpful for persons who have no difficulty with the [t] but do have some with the [s]. The words that follow should be useful for this approach.

cleats	meats	fats	kites
heats	mats	yachts	riots
beats	cats	divots	hurts
bits	hoots	blots	nights
gets	notes	ruts	blights
debts	floats	hurts	weights
hits	thoughts	flights	quoits
fights	lights	nuts	rates

[θ] (th) and [s]

Some speakers must exercise caution not to confuse the voiceless [θ] (th) with the [s]. The [θ] is properly produced with the tip of the tongue in contact with the back of the upper teeth or slightly protruded between the teeth. This contact is to be avoided for the [s].

Practice Materials

The following pairs of words should help to establish the difference between articulatory positions and acoustic results.

thin	sin	think	sink
theme	seem	thaw	saw
thick	sick	thuds	suds
thank	sank	thought	sought
thigh	sigh	thong	song
thumb	sum	third	surd
Thane	sane	thunder	sunder

Practice Materials (Cont.)

path	pass	worth	worse
bath	bass	kith	kiss
truth	truce	myth	miss
math	mass	Beth	Bess
faith	face	wraith	race

Make certain that the distinction between the [θ] and the [s] is made clear in the following material.

Sentences

1. In counting the sum, the boy used his fingers and his thumb.
2. The thick smoke made us feel sick.
3. The lightning that tore the sky asunder was followed by thunder.
4. Because the cook did not think, she clogged the sink.
5. No thinking man can win a race with a wraith.
6. Though not a sin, it is a thin faith that is limited to saving face.
7. Although Sam did not catch the bass, he enjoyed a bath in the stream.
8. The path led over the mountain pass.

Frequent [s] Blends and Clusters

Initial [sk]

scheme	scalp	score	sky
skiff	scab	scorch	scare
skin	scan	scorn	scallop
skill	scandal	skirt	scamp
skip	scant	scar	skewer
skit	scatter	Scot	sketch
schedule	school	skull	sceptic
scale	schooner	skunk	squire

Medial [sk]

risking	discount	Alaska	Ruskin
discuss	ensconce	basket	landscape
asking	Muskogee	escape	musket

Final [sk]

brisk	whisk	bask	task
disk	desk	flask	tusk
frisk	musk	mask	rusk

Initial [st]

steam	stay	sterile	stark
steel	stain	stirrup	start
steep	station	stew	starve
steer	stealth	stole	style
stiff	step	stone	store
still	stem	stove	stork
stick	stigma	stack	stock
sting	stool	stamp	stop
stint	stout	stub	storm
steady	stoop	stunt	story

Medial [st]

Easter	roster	wasteful	basting
feasting	mastiff	coaster	toasted
blister	tasty	costly	castor
master	blasted	frosted	castaway
monster	aster	musty	punster

Final [st]

beast	mist	past	host
east	best	roast	cost
least	rest	post	frost
priest	pest	roost	lost
yeast	guest	just	first
fist	cast	rust	nursed
list	last	toast	oust
kissed	mast	most	Faust

Initial [skr]

scream	script	scrap	scrawl
screech	scrutiny	scramble	scrub
screen	scribble	scroll	scribe
scrivener	scrape	scruple	scrabble

Medial [skr]

discredit	miscreant	descry	unscrew
discreet	proscribe	describe	prescribe
discriminate	discretion	enscribe	inscrutable

Initial [str]

streak	strain	straw	strut
stream	strength	strong	stripe
strip	strap	strop	strive
stricken	strew	struck	strident
string	stroke	struggle	striate
stray	stroll	strike	structure

Medial [str]

restrict	instruct	upstream	distrust
construe	restraint	district	distress
constrain	unstrung	destroy	distrophy
constrict	hamstring	distraught	frustrate
construct	enstrange	distract	prostrate

Initial [sm]

smear	smack	smart	smug
smithy	smooth	smolder	smudge
smitten	smote	smother	smile
smell	small	smirk	smite
smelter	smock	Smyrna	smirch

Initial [sw]

Sweden	swing	swoon	swan
sweep	sway	swoop	swamp
sweet	sweat	swollen	swallow
swig	swelter	swarm	swine
swim	swear	swirl	swipe
swivel	swag	swap	swindle

Initial [sn]

sneak	snap	snare	snatch
sneer	snoop	snort	snipe
sniff	snow	snub	snicker
snip	snob	snuff	snug
snail	snarl	snake	snore

Final [ns]

wince	fence	glance	romance
pence	quince	lance	prance
hence	mince	manse	enhance

Medial [ns]

answer	balancing	instead	punster
dancer	instant	install	bouncing
Frances	instill	ensnare	winsome

Initial [sp]

speed	span	spore	spun
speak	sparrow	sparse	spunk
spill	spat	spark	spy
spin	spew	spare	spike
speck	spool	Sparta	spine
spell	spook	spirit	spout
spade	spoof	spur	spoke
Spain	Spode	spurt	spoil
spent	spawn	sponge	spider

Final and Medial [sp]

lisp	crisp	despondent	despoil
asp	grasp	despair	despot
hasp	rasp	desperate	respect
clasp	cusp	aspire	respond
wasp	grasping	despise	respite
wisp	resplendent	bicuspid	perspire

[spl]

split	splendid	splurge	splotch
spleen	splice	splutter	splendor
splay	splint	splash	splat

[spr]

sprain	sprinkle	sprout	sprung
sprig	sprint	spruce	sprocket
spread	sprite	spry	spring

Practice Materials for Blends

  Sentences

1. The sponge is the internal skeleton of a marine animal.
2. A scallop is a bivalve mollusk.
3. Scones are thin cakes made skillfully by the Scots.
4. Skelton swung his ax skillfully to split the stack of logs.
5. The squid is a species of cuttlefish.
6. The northwest coastal area of the United States is warmed by steady moist winds called chinooks.
7. Stewart and six hunters set out to obtain scarce elephant tusks.
8. The swift schooner brought in a catch of sea horses and starfish.
9. Prescott always felt like strutting when he squired his sweet Stella.
10. Scribbled and scrawled manuscripts are likely to receive scanty attention from schoolmasters.
11. The old scow was covered with scale.
12. The sudden squall upset the skiff.
13. Spring rains may come in sprinkles.
14. The sprite was a spry spirit.
15. Smith was smitten by a small girl in a smock.
16. Sperry was smart but not smug.
17. Stacy's voice demonstrated frequent strident tones.
18. Snead was famous, or perhaps infamous, for his stentorious snoring.
19. Struggle, if it is not fruitless, helps to make the struggler strong.
20. The scribe scrutinized his efforts on his manuscript.
21. Swenson was fond of his wife's quince jelly.
22. The boa constrictor was ensnared in a skillfully constructed trap.
23. Lance and Frances aspired to perform in the circus with an expert balancing act.

[sts] *and* [sks]

The combinations [sts] and [sks] are somewhat difficult because of the quick and precise tongue action needed in their production.

Practice Materials

The following word lists and sentences should be useful as practice materials.

beasts	pests	boasts	toasts
feasts	rests	coasts	bursts
fists	casts	posts	firsts
lists	lasts	roasts	jousts
pastes	boosts	ghosts	musts
waists	roosts	hosts	rusts
discs	asks	tasks	whisks
risks	basks	husks	flasks
frisks	masks	tusks	casks

Sentences

1. The insect pests spoiled the outdoor feasts for the guests.
2. Two blasts signaled that the jousts were about to begin as tests for the knights.
3. Ghosts do not bother with boasts.
4. Six gun blasts were fired at the animal pests.
5. Good hosts demonstrate an air of unconcern about costs.
6. Risks must be assumed in many tasks.
7. Large oaken casks were used as tops for desks.

Initial and Final [s]

sauce	source	slips	smacks
sense	seats	slants	streets
since	souse	spots	sinks
saints	sites	spurts	stunts
sweets	saps	speaks	squeaks
swaps	surfs	spouts	scuffs
sass	stoops	smokes	skirts

Additional Practice Materials for [s] *in Various Contexts*

Sentences

1. Genius without a striving for work may be a waste of superior intelligence.
2. Signs on the highways offer sage advice to passing motorists.

3. Satire cannot always be distinguished from farce.

4. The moon cast a silvery light over a serene sea.

5. Some persons scoff at mystics; others seem superstitious about their beliefs.

6. Scrupulous golfers keep honest scores and replace all divots in sight.

7. Ghosts are said to stay in desolate, spooky places.

8. Plates, forks, and spoons constitute table settings.

9. Jurists must listen to and be objective about all aspects of arguments.

10. The silenced sleep their final sleep on a silent hill.

Selections

1. On top of Old Smoky
    All covered in snow,
    I lost my true lover
    By courtin' too slow.

    —*Old Smoky*, American Folk Song

2. Among the many interests of the most versatile of American geniuses, Benjamin Franklin, was spelling reform. Franklin was an astute student of our language and a strong advocate that our spelling be modified. In 1768 the genius Franklin wrote "A Scheme for a New Spelling Alphabet and Reformed Mode of Spelling." It was published in an unfinished state in 1779 as part of his *Political Miscellaneous, and Philosophical Pieces.* Franklin stimulated Noah Webster, who accepted many of his suggestions and recommendations for changing British to American spellings. In a sense, Franklin anticipated the science and study of phonetics. His analysis of sounds was surprisingly accurate. One of the factors that stimulated Franklin in his study of sounds and spelling reform was his observations about the inadequacies of and inconsistencies in English letters as representations of the sounds of our spoken language. Franklin's scheme for spelling reform would have had each sound consistently represented by the same letter. Silent and unnecessary letters were to be dropped. Despite the fact that Franklin did not complete his study and his work, his analysis of the formation of the sounds of our language is still considered to be essentially accurate and phonetically correct.

3. H. L. Mencken, the so-called sage of Baltimore, enjoyed having people think of him as an acidic and outrageous person. He sometimes earned this right by sentences such as: "Philosophy consists very largely of one philosopher arguing that all others are jackasses."

4. How Homo sapiens arrived at speech is lost in prehistory. Speaking man speculates about the onset of speech and through speech conjectures and rationalizes, each according to his needs, present interests, prejudices, and inclinations. The mystery and beginning of speech may be repeated in the cycle of infant development, but the infant forgets how he learned as soon as he becomes a speaking child. Once again, adults speculate about the onset of speech in the child, and about his prelingual stages of development. This is history, fascinating speculative history, with testimony abstracted from those who speak without telling us how or why. The task of learning to speak is immense. The immensity of the task, fortunately, is unconsciously and unwittingly assumed by the child. Before he knows the size or significance of his responsibilities he has assumed, the normal child has accepted and practiced the verbal habits—the ways of speaking—of his special culture and thus himself becomes a transmitter of the verbal habits of those with whom he lives.

[z] As in *Zoo, Cousin, Azalea,* and *Buzz*

Except for accompanying vocalization for the [z], the sound is produced like the [s]. [z] may be described as a lingua-alveolar voiced fricative. Generally it is produced with somewhat less tongue muscle tension than is necessary for the [s].

The spellings for [z] are varied and include *z* as in *zero, s* as in *rose* and *nasal,* and *zz* as in *buzz.*

Persons who have difficulty with the articulation of the [s] are also likely to find the [z] troublesome. Vocalization, however, may conceal some of the acoustic faults that become apparent when an [s] is defectively produced. If your best [s] is articulated with the tongue tip behind the lower teeth rather than behind the upper gum ridge, the same adjustment should be made for the production of [z].

Practice Materials

Initial

zebra	zest	zircon	zeal
zee	zephyr	Zouave	Zeno
Zeeland	Zachary	Zurich	zone
zinc	zoo	zither	zip
zinnia	Zeus	zyme	zoology
zany	zoom	zealous	zounds
zenith	zodiac	Zion	Zoe

Medial

teasing	spasm	designate	design
pleasing	plasma	nozzle	desire
blizzard	music	cousin	enzyme
lazy	using	dozen	raising
daisy	dozing	used	noisy
pleasant	causing	desert	reason
resin	buzzer	deserve	appeasing
hazard	poser	preserve	resign

Final

ease	whose	because	toys
please	choose	repose	annoys
tease	doze	crows	boys
his	woes	yearns	ties
fizz	hose	spurns	replies
raise	grows	burns	dyes
maize	goads	buzz	rhymes
days	claws	eaves	wise
has	flaws	cows	surmise
lads	calls	browse	symbols

Sentences

1. The zoo was open to girls and lads in all seasons.
2. To live zestfully is one of man's objectives.
3. Joe's habit was to doze off when others became aroused by their desires and emotions.
4. Symbols are man's way of communicating and preserving ideas.

5. Zachary was not able to afford diamonds and so presented zircons to his best girls.

6. Snows make the mountains near Zurich ever-pleasant views.

7. The Mormons converted the desert into green pastures.

8. Girls and boys soon learn that some words can tease and others can please.

9. Zinnias bloom late in the summer season, but daisies are early flowers.

10. The blizzard caused the travelers hours of delay in their journeys.

11. Plasma can be preserved for many days.

12. Maize grows in many farms and fields.

[dz]

Persons who have difficulty with the articulatory position for [z] might find it helpful to begin with [d] and to "move" from [d] to [z]. Be sure that you start with a tongue tip to gum ridge contact for the [d] and then retract the tongue tip slightly for the [z]. Practice with the following:

weeds	cads	chords	cards
beads	lads	fords	rods
lids	moods	hoards	brides
bids	foods	birds	chides
maids	toads	herds	tides
raids	loads	builds	grounds

[z] Blends

Many of the words of the practice lists for medial and final [z] contain blends of [z] preceded by an [m], [b], [v], [n], [l], or [d]. The word lists and materials that follow feature these combinations.

Practice Materials

Final [mz]

beams	gems	brooms	alms
creams	frames	combs	calms
reams	names	domes	charms
teams	crams	homes	harms

Final [mz] (*Cont.*)

rims	lambs	storms	qualms
whims	booms	forms	alarms
hems	tombs	norms	farms
stems	chums	climbs	germs
clams	crumbs	chimes	firms
hams	numbs	dimes	terms

Final [bz]

Thebes	webs	dabs	tubes
cribs	ebbs	stabs	absorbs
fibs	jabs	tabs	cobs
nibs	cabs	cubes	nobs
robs	lobes	hubs	disturbs
swabs	jobs	nubs	herbs
squabs	robes	stubs	verbs

Final [vz]

believes	delves	wharves	shoves
deceives	shelves	carves	drives
eaves	elves	starves	hives
thieves	calves	curves	knives
gives	halves	nerves	strives
lives	grooves	serves	thrives
braves	moves	swerves	wives
knaves	proves	doves	leaves
staves	roves	gloves	weaves
waves	stoves	loves	saves

Final [nz]

beans	stains	ruins	darns
screens	remains	fawns	burns
bins	dens	mourns	turns
fins	glens	dawns	spurns
grins	bans	groans	guns
brains	clans	owns	runs
trains	loons	stones	tons
lanes	boons	barns	gowns
refrains	tunes	earns	clowns
mines	signs	coins	joins

Final [lz]

deals	gales	coals	boils
keels	jails	doles	coils
wheels	nails	foals	spoils
hills	bales	moles	tiles
tills	duels	goals	miles
frills	fools	falls	wiles
mills	spools	appalls	jowls
stills	tools	stalls	cowls
gills	pulls	lolls	towels
wills	bulls	hobbles	owls

Final [dz]

beads	heads	goads	birds
bleeds	weds	loads	herds
creeds	cads	frauds	curds
deeds	lads	swords	words
weeds	goods	towards	abides
bids	hoods	hods	hides
rids	foods	nods	chides
aids	moods	pods	abounds
fades	broods	floods	hounds
wades	intrudes	buds	rounds

Sentences

1. Jones had qualms about touching coins because they might be covered with germs.

2. Ben's wife believed that homes are kept clean by new brooms.

3. The ornate picture frames were encrusted with semiprecious gems.

4. Grimes had whims that resulted in his telling many fibs.

5. Hundreds of corncobs were stored in cribs.

6. The thieves wore gloves when they stole the wares from the wharves.

7. Human brains are able to deal with symbols and signs.

8. The young of horses and asses are called foals.

9. Trains still carry goods to and from farms.

10. The storm's fury left many of the town's homes in ruins.

11. Ned's dreams were to write the country's refrains.
12. Ted's moods led him to take long walks down country lanes.

[z] and [s]

Some persons with a foreign language background have difficulty in distinguishing between [z] and the [s]. If the element of voice is not distinctive, then both phonetic and semantic differences may be broken down in word pairs such as *price* and *prize; race* and *raise;* and *zoo* and *sue.*

Practice Materials

Practice with the word pairs and the sentences that follow to make certain that the [z] is clearly voiced and that the [s] is voiceless.

zee	see	lose	loose
zeal	seal	prize	price
zip	sip	doze	dose
zinc	sink	pads	pats
zoo	sue	sends	cents
zone	sown	bids	bits
peas	peace	codes	coats
rays	race	kids	kits
maize	mace	beds	bets
his	hiss	knees	niece

Sentences

1. A seal eats fish with considerable zeal.
2. The bids ran high for the bits of gems.
3. The prize was won at a large price.
4. Selma and Zelda went to see the Zuyder Zee.
5. Zinc was used to line the sink.
6. Cousin Sue enjoyed her trip to the zoo.
7. The lost codes were found in the pockets of the coats.
8. The maize was pounded with a mace.
9. Grace disliked to see her cattle graze in rented fields.
10. The racer was given a razor as a prize.
11. Simpson, though not a psychologist, astutely observed that the things persons say to themselves constitute the basis for de-

ciding what they will say to those who supposedly are listening to
them.

12. When Susan sighed there was little need to explain her sighs
by spoken words.

13. Sylvia was statuesque and stately, and yet blissfully unconscious of these signal attributes.

14. The twins insisted that all the tales to which they listened be
twice-told tales.

15. The American Psychological Association includes a division
called the Sociey for the Psychological Study of Social Issues.

Selections

1. In his *An Unsocial Socialist,* George Bernard Shaw argues
that "a day's work is a day's work, neither more nor less, and the
man who does it needs a day's sustenance, a night's repose, and due
leisure whether he be a painter or ploughman."

2. Speaking of himself in his *Sixteen Self Sketches,* Shaw said,
"I always astonish strangers by my amiability, because, as no human
being could possibly be so disagreeable as they expect me to be, I
have only to be commonly civil to seem quite charming."

3. *Stengelese* is a coined term that refers to inclinations or tendencies in the use and abuse of the English linguistic system. The
term is one that baseball fans should recognize and associate with
Casey Stengel, for many years the successful manager of the New
York Yankees. Some writers say that Casey Stengel's difficulties with
spoken language are pretense. Other writers hold that only a con-
summate thespian could simulate Stengel's linguistic style, which is
characterized by addiction to nonstop sentences, discrete and un-
attachable parts of speech, and sequential non sequiturs. Still other
writers insist that Stengel speaks his thought processes aloud, that
his speech is free associative cerebration. There is obvious disagree-
ment about the backgrounds and forces behind the origins and
onsets of Stengelese. There is however little doubt that even the
baseball scribes, who suspect that Casey can speak more succinctly,
have spoken of him themselves in terms lacking in reverence. For
what it is worth in passing, it happens to be this writer's belief that
Casey Stengel speaks three languages simultaneously: one linguistic
system is addressed to his players, another to the umpires; and the
last is expressive of his innermost thoughts and feelings.

4. There is some soul of goodness in things evil,
    Would men observingly distil it out;
    For our bad neighbor makes us early stirrers,
    Which is both healthful and good husbandry.
    Besides, they are our outward consciences,
    And preachers to us all, admonishing
    That we should dress us fairly for our end.
    Thus may we gather honey from the weed,
    And make a moral of the devil himself.

    —WILLIAM SHAKESPEARE, *Henry V*

5. There is a silence where hath been no sound,
    There is a silence where no sound may be,
    In the cold grave—under the deep, deep sea,
    Or in wide desert where no life is found,
    Which hath been mute, and still must sleep profound;

    —THOMAS HOOD, *Silence*

6. Terms ill defined, and forms misunderstood,
    And customs, where their reasons are unknown,
    Have stirred up many zealous souls
    To fight against imaginary giants.

    —MARTIN F. TUPPER, *Of Tolerance*

7. Good laws lead to the making of better ones; bad ones bring about worse. As soon as any man says of the affairs of the State, "What does it matter to me?" the State may be given up for lost.

    —JEAN JACQUES ROUSSEAU, *The Social Contract*

8. In this best of all possible worlds, the Baron's castle was the most magnificent of castles, and his lady the best of all possible Baronesses.

    —VOLTAIRE, *Candide*

9. It is indeed a desirable thing to be well descended, but the glory belongs to our ancestors.

    —PLUTARCH, *Of the Training of Children*

10. Of all the causes which conspire to blind
    Man's erring judgment, and misguide the mind,
    What the weak head with strongest bias rules,
    Is pride, the never-failing vice of fools.

    —ALEXANDER POPE, *An Essay on Criticism*

THE POST–ALVEOLAR SOUNDS [ʃ] AND [ʒ]

[ʃ] (sh) As in *She, Ashore,* and *Ash*

With the consonant [s] as a basis for comparison, the [ʃ] (sh) should be easy to master. The sound is produced with the entire tongue drawn a little farther back than for the [s]. The tongue surface is broadened and flat so that there is no groove or channel as is

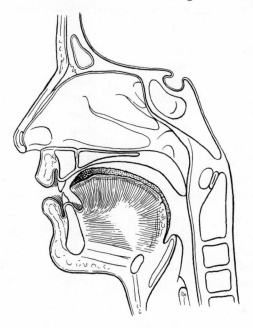

FIGURE 17–3. Articulatory adjustments for [ʃ] and [ʒ].

required for [s]. The stream of breath is forced over the flat tongue surface and emitted between the rows of teeth. [ʃ] is usually produced with slight lip rounding. Acoustically, the principal concentration of acoustic energy is in a lower frequency band than that of [s]. Phonetically, [ʃ] may be described as a voiceless, orally emitted, blade-tongue, post-alveolar fricative sound.

[ʃ] has several spellings. The most frequent is the combination *sh* as in *she*. Other frequent spellings include *ti* as in *nation, si* as in *tension, ci* as in *precious, ch* as in *machine,* and *s* as in *sure*.

For some speakers with a foreign language background and for some who may have a high-frequency hearing loss, the similarities in spelling and in manner of articulation may cause confusion between the [ʃ] and the [s]. Emphasis on lip rounding and on the more retracted and flattened tongue for the [ʃ] should help to contrast it with and distinguish it from the [s].

Practice Materials

Practice before a mirror with the word pairs that follow should be helpful.

she	sea	shoe	sue
sheik	seek	shoot	suit
sheep	seep	show	sew
shield	sealed	shawl	Saul
ship	sip	shore	sore
shin	sin	shop	sop
shay	say	shot	sot
shake	sake	shock	sock
shad	sad	shy	sigh
shall	sal	shed	said
brash	brass	gash	gas
clash	class	plush	plus
mesh	mess	rushed	rust
leash	lease	fashion	fasten
mash	mass	crash	crass

Initial

she	shoe	shirt	shriek
sheen	shoot	shirk	shrimp
ship	should	shut	shred
shin	shook	shun	shrewd
shay	shone	shout	shrub
shame	show	shower	shrine
shell	shawl	shine	shroud
shed	shore	shy	shrank
shall	shop	sugar	shrink
shaggy	shock	shark	shrug

Medial

leashing	lashes	pressure	fission
wishing	passion	quashed	hushing
ashamed	fashion	machine	Flushing
glacier	pushing	pension	national
nation	cushion	delicious	fractious
patient	lotion	conscience	washed
precious	ocean	anxious	crashed
dashes	caution	mission	rushing

Final

leash	hash	hush	Danish
wish	crash	harsh	blemish
fish	bush	marsh	English
dish	push	rush	garnish
mesh	burnish	tarnish	Flemish
flesh	furnish	varnish	brandish
flash	punish	Amish	gnash
cash	blush	vanish	lush

Sentences

1. Ocean fishing furnishes a livelihood for many British fishermen.

2. The shaggy Prussian brandished his tarnished sword.

3. Hamlet had an anxious and disturbed conscience.

4. Shaw was not ashamed to be fractious.

5. The chef earned a pension for his well-garnished dishes.

6. Sheila shrugged her shoulders as she added sugar to her milk shake.

7. The motion of the ship on the ocean made a patient of the man from Flushing.

8. A flash flood transformed the shrubless field into a marsh.

9. Some nations have a passion for peace; others seem to have a passion for aggression.

10. Ship-to-shore communication is available for most of our nation.

11. Do you anticipate a clash among the boys in the class?

12. Sam Sherman shunned the sun.

Selections

1.   Over here, lonely crowds and status seekers and organization men seem to have readily entered the basic vocabulary of cocktail-party English. Electronic computers are common enough to be taken for granted, and can crosstabulate for the professional sociologist prodigious collections of data on anything from consumer habits to consciousness of social class. Such well-established research institutions as the Survey Research Center at Michigan or Columbia's own Bureau of Applied Social Research represent an accumulation of skill, information, and resources far beyond anything which any British university can boast of or even foreseeably aspire to. As a visitor one is of course prone to exaggerate one's impressions; but it all seems a good illustration of Gertrude Stein's remark that America is the oldest country in the world because the first to enter the twentieth century.

—G. RUNCIMAN, *Two Approaches to Sociology*

2.   Daniel Shays was a captain of the militia during our Revolution against the British. Later, during the period of the Confederation and in a time of financial depression, Shays led an armed insurrection against the Massachusetts government. The insurrectionists were made up substantially of farmers. They protested that the salaries of public officials were too high. In addition they petitioned against the imposition of high taxes. Shays' petitions, protestations, general dissensions, and finally his insurrection are believed to have hastened the ratification of the Federal Constitution by Massachusetts.

[ʒ] (zh) As in *Azure, Treasure, Rouge,* and *Decision*

The sound [ʒ] is a voiced, post-alveolar fricative. It is produced like the [ʃ] with accompanying vocal fold vibration.

[ʒ] occurs medially or finally in English words. The most frequent spellings for this sound are the *z* as in *seizure*, *s* as in *treasure*, *si* as in *vision* and *ge* as in *rouge*.

Practice Materials

Medial

azure	intrusion	vision	persuasion
casual	measure	regime	incision

confusion	pleasure	glazier	derision
contusion	seizure	delusion	precision
decision	treasure	explosion	exposure
explosion	usual	erosion	illusion
conclusion	version	lesion	occasion

Final

| beige | corsage | garage | persiflage |
| camouflage | entourage | menage | rouge |

Sentences

1. The Eurasian found nothing more pleasurable than an azure sky.

2. The collision was a result of one driver's poor vision and another's poor decision.

3. The physician had to make an incision to cut through the adhesion.

4. A mirage is a visual delusion causing mental confusion.

5. Because he was given to persiflage, his decisions always seemed casual.

6. The invasion by an infantry division was preceded by an explosion of the camouflaged airfield.

7. The glazier won prestige by the precision of his work.

8. Confusion resulted in numerous contusions among members of the treasure-hunting entourage.

9. The intrusion of the police prevented the seizure of the gold.

10. Persuasion brought about legislation to prevent soil erosion.

Selections

1. He weaves, and is clothed with derision;
      Sows, and he shall not reap;
   His life is a watch or a vision
      Between a sleep and a sleep.
                    —ALGERNON CHARLES SWINBURNE, *Atalanta in Calydon*

2. Rich the treasure,
   Sweet the pleasure,
   Sweet is pleasure after pain.
                    —JOHN DRYDEN, *Alexander's Feast*

3. Frazier, an expert glazier, was given to visual illusions and to occasional delusions. Unfortunately, he also acted in the light of

these visionary aberrations. Frazier's demise was a result of this inclination. On the final and fatal occasion, Frazier was confronted with an escaped tiger which had hidden in his garage. Because of a visual illusion, Frazier insisted that the tiger was a house cat. In the light of this decision, he began to pat the animal. The beast, not sharing the illusion and having no delusions about himself as a domestic treasure, attacked and devoured Frazier. The job was done with dispatch and precision. Thus poor Frazier was consumed, a victim of a visual illusion and of delusionary behavior. Frazier was no measure for a real tiger.

4.   When a man's busy, why, leisure
     Strikes him as wonderful pleasure:
     'Faith, and at leisure once is he?
     Straightway he wants to be busy.

—ROBERT BROWNING, *The Glove*

[tʃ] (ch) As in *Chest, Orchard*, and *Match*

The sound [tʃ] (ch) is a blend or compound of [t] followed immediately by [ʃ]. It may occur initially, medially, or finally. The blend, a combination of a stop-plosive and a voiceless fricative sound, is classified phonetically as an *affricate*. This voiceless affricate is regularly represented by the letters *ch* in spelling.

The sound may be troublesome for speakers for whom English is not a first language and in whose native language the [tʃ] does not occur. For example, it may be troublesome to native French speakers because it does not occur in French. For such persons, the most frequent tendency is to substitute the second element [ʃ] for the blend [tʃ].

Practice Materials

The exercises that follow should be of help in differentiating between [tʃ] and [ʃ].

cheer	sheer	hatch	hash
cheat	sheet	latch	lash
choose	shoes	march	marsh
chairs	shares	match	mash
chin	shin	much	mush
catch	cash	witch	wish

crutch	crush	watching	washing
ditch	dish	catching	cashing

Sentences

1. The sailors had to chip the paint from the ship.
2. Fido liked to chew on an old shoe.
3. The sheik had a scar on his cheek.
4. It may be pleasant to share a chair.
5. Tom bruised his chin and his shin.
6. Charles insisted that one spoonful of mush is much to much.
7. The marines went on a march through the marsh.
8. Macbeth hoped that the witch would help him realize his wish.
9. After a tennis match, Tom enjoyed a dish of hash.
10. The fishermen had a good fish catch which they sold for spot cash.

Initial

cheese	chance	churn	chore
chief	chant	chug	change
chill	chewed	chum	Charles
chimp	choose	chunk	chirp
chain	choke	chowder	choice
chafe	chose	chide	chat
check	chalk	China	chicken
chess	chuck	chive	chin
channel	chop	chime	Chester
champ	char	child	chap

Medial

reaching	brooches	marching	bachelor
beeches	broaching	urchin	batches
pitcher	coached	birches	paunches
kitchen	encroaching	lurching	parched
exchange	orchard	searching	righteous
hatchet	launched	bunched	preaching

Final

each	match	staunch	couch
teach	dispatch	porch	slouch
speech	blotch	scorch	pouch

Final (Cont.)

ditch	watch	torch	touch
witch	pooch	lurch	clutch
fetch	encroach	birch	such
wrench	coach	bunch	research
detach	reproach	hunch	squelch

Sentences

1. Charles was taught by those he coached to observe the difference between teaching and preaching.
2. After searching in the orchard, Chester found the chart under the beech-tree.
3. Chuck liked cheese and chives.
4. The church supper featured chicken and chowder.
5. The child was chided for chewing his chalk.
6. The farmer had a hunch that the peaches in his orchard needed watching.
7. In a close match, the Chilean champion won the chess contest.
8. Some choose to eat their steak charred.
9. Birches are a climbing challenge for many children.
10. Chilton was partial to chowder.

Selections

1. When I was a child, I spake as a child, I understood as a child, I thought as a child; but when I became a man, I put away childish things.

I Corinthians 13:11

2. Choice word and measured phrase, above the reach of ordinary men.

—WILLIAM WORDSWORTH, *Resolution and Independence*

3. I'm not a chicken, I have seen
   Full many a chill September.

—OLIVER WENDELL HOLMES, *The September Gale*

[dʒ] (dzh) As in *Age, Adjust,* and *Budge*

[dʒ] is the voiced counterpart of [tʃ]. This voiced sound blend may occur either initially, medially, or finally. In *judge* and *George* it occurs both *initially* and *finally*. In agent and engine the affricate [dʒ] occurs medially. The most frequent spellings for [dʒ] are *g, j,* and *dg* as in *wage, jam* and *ridge*.

Many American and English speakers tend to unvoice [dʒ] when the blend occurs in final positions. French, Spanish, and German speakers may have difficulty with the voiced affricate because the sound does not occur in their native languages.

Speakers who have difficulty in deciding whether a given word calls for [dʒ] or [tʃ] should be helped by the relative frequency of the *ch* spelling for the unvoiced sound and the inclusion of the letter *j* or *g* for the voiced affricate.

Practice Materials

The first set of exercise materials is for the purpose of establishing the distinction between the two affricates.

gin	chin	jigger	chigger
jar	char	jug	chug
jeer	cheer	bridges	breeches
jest	chest	badge	batch
jump	chump	ridge	rich
jeep	cheap	surge	search
joke	choke	liege	leech

Initial

jeans	jewel	germ	junior
jib	June	jar	jury
giraffe	judicial	journey	just
gipsy	joke	jowl	jute
jig	jovial	jug	jade
jail	Jonah	jump	jilt
jay	jaunt	giant	general
jet	jaw	jibe	germane
gem	job	joint	genius
jack	jog	join	gentle

Medial

besieged	agent	adjust	larger
regent	changed	adjourn	margin
imagine	ranging	surgeon	region

Medial (Cont.)

regenerate	major	urgent	disjoint
hedging	stranger	merger	enjoin
wedged	ajar	legion	lounging
ledger	rajah	soldier	gouging
badger	plunged	budget	rejoin

Final

liege	huge	nudge	sponge
siege	sledge	grudge	bilge
ridge	forge	oblige	discharge
bridge	engorge	gouge	dirge
rage	barge	singe	grange
stage	large	fringe	strange
edge	urge	surge	derange
wedge	merge	emerge	average
carriage	bulge	orange	peerage
marriage	fudge	revenge	steerage

Sentences

1. Judge Jones urged the jury to be judicious.
2. A legion of soldiers was landed by giant jet planes.
3. Dr. James, a surgeon, adjusted Joe's disarranged jaw.
4. Jonah had a strange journey in a giant whale.
5. The gentleman now of the peerage once traveled by steerage.
6. Justice cannot always be determined by jurists.
7. Jargon is a strange form of language usage enjoyed by children.
8. June was in a rage because she was rudely nudged by Julian.
9. Jim's genius was in making germane judgments.
10. Sturgeon is a major Russian item exported in jars.
11. The hedge under the bridge was edged with geraniums.
12. Jade is a semiprecious gem.

The sentences that follow should be practiced with a view to maintaining vocalization for the final [dʒ]. Make certain that vocalization continues so that there is no substitution of [tʃ] for the voiced affricate.

Sentences

1. The judge enjoined George and Marge from marriage.
2. Madge would not budge from her strange position.
3. John stood at the edge of the ridge but did not jump.
4. Jones yielded to his urge and ate a large orange.
5. At two years of age the average child can speak his language.
6. A large suspension bridge was built over the huge gorge.
7. The grange was the scene of a battle of revenge.
8. The stage was set for a strange play.

In the following sentences make certain that you distinguish between the [dʒ] and the [ʒ]. The first italicized word will include the blend [dʒ]; the second will have the voiced fricative [ʒ].

Sentences

1. A *general* commands a *division*.
2. Charles *pledged* himself to a life of *pleasure*.
3. A *jury* found Wilson guilty of *usury*.
4. *Agile* Peter climbed a hill to admire the *azure* sky.
5. *Drudgery*, in *measure*, is part of living.
6. Ben *rejected* attempts at *collusion*.
7. *Judge Johnson* carefully announced his *decision*.
8. Charles liked to *imagine* finding rich *treasure*.

Selections for [dʒ]

1. Casey Jones was a railroad engineer and a figure legendary for his courage. Casey had a predecessor, an engineer named Jimmie Jones, for whom the following verses were written:

> On a Sunday mornin' it began to rain,
> 'Round the curve spied a passenger train,
> On the pilot lay poor Jimmie Jones,
> He's a good old porter, but he's dead and gone.

This verse for Casey Jones varies somewhat:

> On a Sunday morning it begins to rain,
> 'Round the curve spied a passenger train,
> Under the cab lay poor Casey Jones,
> He's a good engineer, but he's dead and gone—

Casey, born John Luther Jones, for all the legend built about him, was a real engineer who worked for the Illinois Central Railroad. When he had his fatal collision, Jones headed engine Number 638 out of the Memphis yards. The switchmen "knew by the engine's moans that the man at the throttle was Casey Jones." Casey, cannon-balling through the rain, knew that he was about to pile up into a freight train on the siding. He ordered his fireman to jump, and Casey himself died an engineer's death, one hand on the brakes and the other on the whistle cord.

—JOHN A. and ALAN LOMAX (eds.). Adapted from "The Legend of Casey Jones," *American Ballads and Folk Songs*

2. And what's a life?—a weary pilgrimage,
    Whose glory in one day doth fill the stage
    With childhood, manhood, and decrepit age.

—FRANCES QUARLES, *What Is Life?*

3. George Jenson generalized that judgments are generally made most judiciously when the judger does not jump too hastily to con-clusions. This generalization, Jenson acknowledged, was a subjective judgment, but one about which he could feel objective because it germinated slowly after genuine and judicious study.

THE LINGUA–ALVEOLAR NASAL

[n] As in *No*, *Any*, and *Again*

[n] is a voiced, nasal, tongue tip to upper gum ridge sound. In common with the other nasal consonants, [n] requires nasal rein-forcement and is emitted nasally. [n] is a continuant sound.

To produce the [n], the tongue should be elevated and the entire tongue tip should be in contact with the upper gum or alveolar ridge. The soft palate is relaxed (see Figure 17–4).

In spelling, [n] is represented by the letter *n*. In some words a silent letter precedes the *n* as in *know, gnat,* and *pneumatic.*

The sound [n] presents little difficulty except that it may be slurred or replaced by a nasalized vowel in medial positions, espe-cially in unstressed syllables as in *contact, infer,* and *inform.* The [n] is likely to be treated with greater articulatory respect in initial and

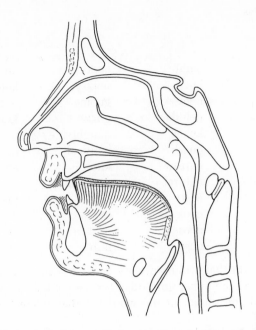

FIGURE 17–4. Articulatory adjustments for [n]. Note relaxed (lowered) soft palate.

final positions. Because of the high frequency of occurrence of the sound in American-English speech, careful articulation of the [n] is strongly recommended.

Practice Materials

[m], we recall, is produced with the lips in gentle contact and, like [n], with the soft palate lowered. For [m] the tongue usually lies relaxed at the floor of the mouth. You may increase your awareness of the difference between the [n] and [m] by practice with the word pairs that follow.

knit	mitt	nock	mock
knee	me	knob	mob
need	mead	note	mote
nude	mood	neat	meat
nail	mail	night	might
net	met	nice	mice
name	main	Norse	Morse

Initial

knee	natal	node	nut
niece	knell	notary	knuckle
neat	neck	gnome	number
kneel	nebula	gnaw	knife
near	knack	naughty	nice
knit	gnash	nautical	noise
nip	narrow	knob	now
nimble	natural	nocturn	notch
nape	nasty	nurse	pneumonia
name	nook	nerve	knew
nail	noose	nurture	knoll
nasal	nose	nub	knowledge

Make certain that an articulatory contact is made between your tongue tip and the upper gum ridge for the medial [n]. Prolong the contact, and the sound, in the word list that follows.

Medial

anneal	grinning	plaintive	fender
menial	spinet	fainting	rented
screening	sinful	feigned	banded
dinner	hinted	fence	handed
sinner	tainted	fend	landing
thinner	saintly	defence	standing
blandish	demanded	intoned	spondee
vanish	cannibal	morning	respond
candy	stoned	dawning	despondent
dandy	telephoned	bonfire	fonder
bundle	bind	joining	pinch
trundle	kindly	connect	bench
cunning	miner	intact	branch
hunted	finer	instead	launch
gunner	ground	confer	munch
burning	hound	consume	lynch
turned	pound	confess	binge
furnace	frowning	definite	strange
burnish	lounge	inflect	lounge
furnish	coined	infest	sponge

Final

bean	amen	cone	spurn
lean	main	hone	stern
scene	lane	drone	burn
dean	grain	moan	run
mean	can	roan	done
sin	fan	brawn	stun
win	plan	faun	fine
tin	began	scorn	dine
hen	span	barn	down
ten	spoon	darn	frown
again	loon	gone	crown
when	dune	turn	brown

The consonant [n], like [m], can sometimes have syllable value without the "help" of a vowel. [n] is or may be pronounced as a syllabic sound when it occurs in a final unstressed position. This is the case in the words that follow.

button	kitten	mutton	seven
cotton	leaden	open	sudden
deaden	maiden	oven	token
heaven	mitten	rotten	leaven

Additional Practice Materials

main avenue	mutton dinner
strange scene	cunning hunter
dine at seven	fine and dandy
eleven turns	morning news
again and again	tin horn
barn dance	change of plan
munch lunch	cotten mittens
ground sirloin	pound of beans

Sentences

1. Amanda and Dan were fond of meandering in the garden.
2. Nathaniel wondered why his friend Dan, the owner of a ninety-foot launch, could ever find reason to frown.
3. The missionary endeavored to teach the cannibal the differ-

ence between having a friend for dinner and having dinner with a friend.

4.   Nona, as a sign of affection for her husband, began baking in her oven at seven in the morning.

5.   Frances looked stunning in her ten-pointed crown.

6.   Minton confessed that he was inclined to strange hunches.

7.   Nine sloops were anchored at Blanding's Landing.

8.   Nettleton insisted that today's apparently insane notions may be the next day's brilliant insights.

9.   Spencer and his son used a bundle of branches for their bonfire.

10.   Every morning Ben intoned nine plaintive tunes.

11.   A neologism is a new, or invented, word.

12.   The new highway connected nine old towns.

13.   The maiden was smitten by the antics of the kitten.

14.   Cotton was inserted between the partitions to deaden the sound.

15.   Nell knitted mittens for her friend Newton.

Selections

1.   The true test of civilization is not the census, nor the size of cities, nor the crops—no, but the kind of man the country turns out.

—RALPH WALDO EMERSON, *Society and Solitude*

2.   John Henry, Cardinal Newman, in his *Idea of a University* considered that "it is almost a definition of a gentleman to say he is one who never inflicts pain."

3.   There were gentlemen and there were seamen in the navy of Charles II. But the seamen were not gentlemen, and the gentlemen were not seamen.

—THOMAS BABINGTON MACAULAY, *History of England*

4.   Experience informs us that the first defence of weak minds is to recriminate.

—SAMUEL TAYLOR COLERIDGE, *Biographia Literia*

5.   Know then thyself, presume not God to scan;
     The proper study of mankind is man.

—ALEXANDER POPE, *Essay on Man*

6. A nap, my friend, is a brief period of sleep which overtakes superannuated persons when they endeavor to entertain unwelcome visitors or to listen to scientific lectures.

—GEORGE BERNARD SHAW, *Back to Methuselah*

7. I have met with women who I really think would like to be married to a Poem and to be given away by a Novel.

—JOHN KEATS, *Letters to Fanny Braun*

8. Yet half the beast is the great god Pan,
      To laugh as he sits by the river,
    Making a poet out of a man:
    The true gods sigh for the cost and pain—
    For the reed which grows nevermore again
      As a reed with the reeds of the river.

—ELIZABETH BARRETT BROWNING, *A Musical Instrument*

9. When Nan was young and had no sense
    She bought a horn for eighteen pence,
    But the only tune that Nan could learn
    Was "High on a Hill and Around a Turn."

—Adapted from an old English ballad

10. Sicilian tyrants never invented a greater torment than envy.

—HORACE, *Epistles, Book I*

THE LINGUA–ALVEOLAR LATERAL

[l] As in *Late, Alone,* and *Bell*

[l] is a lingua-alveolar, voiced, lateral sound. This vowel-like consonant may occur initially, medially, or finally. As may be noted from the spellings of several of the words in the first two sentences of this paragraph, [l] is represented in spelling by the letter *l* or the letters *ll*.

[l], like [t] and [d], is produced with the tongue tip in contact with the upper gum ridge. Unlike the plosives [t] and [d], the [l] has a continuant and vowel-like quality. To achieve this quality, the blade of the tongue (the portion just behind the tongue tip) is lowered to permit vocalized breath to escape over the sides. The soft palate is raised to prevent nasal emission of sound. Vocal-fold vibration regularly accompanies the articulatory action for the [l].

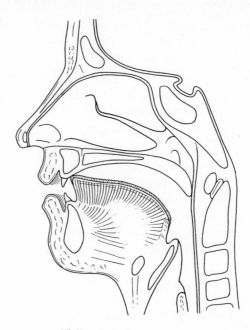

FIGURE 17–5. **FIGURE 17–5.** Articulatory adjustments for [l].

Practice Materials

In producing the sound [l] make certain that the *tip* and *not the blade* of your tongue is in contact with the gum ridge. Avoid contact between the tongue tip and teeth.

Initial

leap	lute	learn	lake
lip	loom	lug	lower
late	load	lie	lapse
let	lawn	like	lane
lack	lot	low	linger
laugh	lost	lout	loin

In some contexts, before consonants and in final positons, a variant of the [l] sound may be produced with a quality referred to as "dark." This results from a slight elevation of the back of the tongue. It may be heard in many of the words that follow.

Medial

heels	pooled	alike	allow
hills	pulse	align	pallid
hailed	cold	sleep	palace
held	stalled	ballad	tailor
gals	gold	elope	tilt
bells	enfold	alter	build

Final

keel	tool	earl	gale
till	full	gull	ball
pale	foal	foil	guile
fell	hall	tile	eel
pal	doll	cowl	pearl
dale	roll	broil	hurl

Initial and Medial

lively	listless	lifelong
lonely	lullaby	likely
lowly	Lillian	leaflet
lately	lilting	liability

Initial and Final

legal	lawful	Lionel
labile	lentil	loll

Phrases

light laughter	tile floor
lie low	cold lair
learn a lot	clanging bells
linger longer	build a wall
let live	gold and pearls
lovely lullaby	hill and dale
sleep well	mail a letter
dull tool	lower the load
held Hal	dill pickles

[l] Preceded by [p] or [b]

Some persons produce an "infantile" sound in contexts in which the [l] is immediately preceded by a [p] or [b]. This effect is frequently a result of failure to make the tongue tip to gum ridge contact for [l]. A [w]-like sound is produced as a carry-over of the lip movement of the [p] or [b].

Practice Materials

For the following practice materials, avoid lip movement for the [l]. Make certain that there is a definite tongue tip to gum ridge contact for the sound.

please	plume	bleed	blue
Pliocene	pluck	blame	blood
pleasant	plausible	blink	bloat
play	plot	blend	bluff
plan	plunder	bland	blot
pledge	plight	black	blind

The following word pairs should help to establish a clear distinction between [l] and [w].

weep	leap	wade	laid
wack	lack	wit	lit
wag	lag	way	lay
wax	lacks	wear	lair
went	lent	wet	let
wick	lick	wane	lane

Additional Practice Materials

lean	loom	glide	claw
lip	law	glaze	clue
lace	lock	glower	club
left	log	glimpse	cloy
lance	learn	glue	clan
glance	lunch	glutton	climb
loot	lion	clean	clutter
lose	glow	class	cluster

Sentences

1. Lola rarely listened to her lover's lilting lyrics.
2. The melodramatic play had an implausible plot.
3. Lila dreamed of a knight with a plume and a lance.
4. Lyman hoped to lead Linda to the altar.
5. William built a pool in the middle of his lawn.
6. The gulls flew over Great Salt Lake.
7. Hal and Lou were childhood pals.
8. The politician was long on verbiage but short of lucid explanations.
9. Light laughter may be eloquent if well timed.
10. Gold was found in the hills of California.
11. Dale planned to pilot his own plane.
12. The ballad related an unlikely tale.
13. Lillian was scolded for falling asleep in her Latin class.
14. A gold locket was lost on the lawn near the lodge.
15. Wilson was slow at leaping—especially to misleading conclusions.

Selections

1. In his *Popular Fallacies,* Charles Lamb held, "A pun is a pistol let off at the ear; not a feather to tickle the intellect."

2. The cruellest lies are often told in silence.

    —ROBERT LOUIS STEVENSON, *Virginibus Puerisque*

3. Old and young, we are all on our last journey.

    —ROBERT LOUIS STEVENSON, *Crabbed Age and Youth*

4. Glory be to God for dappled things—
    For skies as couple-colored as a brindled cow;
    For rose-moles all in stipple upon trout that swim.

    —GERALD MANLEY HOPKINS, *Pied Beauty*

5. I do not love thee, Doctor Fell,
    The reason why I cannot tell,
    But this alone I know full well;
    I do not love thee, Doctor Fell.

    —THOMAS BROWN (Paraphrase of Martial)

6. The so-called British public schools, which are comparable to the private schools in the United States, are training establish-

ments to provide Britain with many members of Parliament, with the upper clergy, with judges, generals, civil servants, and diplomats. The public schools enable the students to get considerably more than a formal education. These schools are places for special vocational training for the exercise of responsibility as well as authority in a gentlemanly, firm, but not wholly inflexible way.

7. A late development hailed as an aeronautical milestone is the "slit wing" plane with a revolutionary inhalation system. The system is called Laminar Flow Control or LFC. This plane requires less fuel than older jet aircraft and can carry 50 per cent more load or fly 50 per cent longer than older models of jets. The LFC was designed so that pull or "friction drag" is significantly reduced. Laminar Air Flow Control eliminates turbulence resulting from friction drag or pull. In the LFC planes the turbulent air particles that "lie" over the plane's wings are removed by "inhalation" through hundreds of almost invisible slits cut lengthwise into the upper and lower surfaces of the plane's wings. The inhaled air travels between slits and is pumped through channels of precisely calculated sizes and shapes. The result is a long-range plane that may travel for two days or more without refueling.

8.   Charles Hussey, an untitled English editorial writer, in 1960 estimated that the adult population in England might well be classified along the following lines: Twenty-five million might be included in the so-called working class, six and a half million in the lower middle class, five million in the plain and unmodified middle class, and something like a half million in the "top-level" or the upper middle class and aristocratic elite.

The "love of a lord" is helping to preserve the rights of the class structure. The class that includes the nobility preserves a good deal of power by its ability to dispense and influence the disposal of patronage. Titles and honors, still the final reward for social and political service, give strength and also help to increase the potential power of the aristocracy. In tradition-bound England, Clement Atlee, the former Socialist Prime Minister, is concluding his career as Earl Atlee; Herbert Morrison, the son of a policeman and a parlormaid, became the Baron Morrison of Lambeth.

These well-earned titles and rewards help to maintain class distinction. The new peers bask in the reflected glory of the old nobility, while the old nobility acquires new luster by having men of accomplishment added to this elite and proportionately small class. So, while rapid changes are continually taking place in British society, the changes are able to take place within the established structure of the class system.

—Adapted from an article by Charles Hussey,
New York Times Magazine, (January 17, 1960)

9. Lionel marveled, as he reviewed his readings of historic military encounters, at why the enemy regularly *retreated in rout* in contrast to one's own soldiers, who *retired to previously prepared locations.* When was it *rout* and where were the *previously prepared locations?* Lionel also puzzled about the difference in total score when a home ball team *overwhelmed the visitors* compared with the result when the visiting athletes *barely won* over the local ballplayers. Scores, at least numerical ones, certainly shed little light on these crucial differentials. Lionel never really solved these problems, except that after long deliberation he concluded philosophically that some problems have no reliable solutions.

10. *B. Franklin: Printer:* Americans know Benjamin Franklin as a man with varied and practical abilities. We may know Franklin as an inventor and may even be fortunate to have had the opportunity to be warmed by a Franklin stove. We of course recognize him as a writer and a philosopher, even if we are reminded only of *Poor Richard's Almanac.* Perhaps his picture on a half-cent Franklin stamp may recall to us Franklin the frugal man, the best respected if not the original penny pincher. Some of us seldom hear a clap of thunder without some awareness of Franklin as an electrical engineer. Early in the history of our country, Franklin was sent abroad because in European countries he could serve our country well because of the warmth his personality radiated as well as for his far-seeing statesmanship. The practical Franklin also improved street lighting and figured out how streets may be better cleaned. He also organized the first fire brigade. He founded the first public library and the first learned society in America. With all of these varied and highly respected abilities, we may wonder how did Franklin weigh his own attributes. A hint may be gained from his own epitaph. Franklin had it inscribed B. Franklin, Printer.

—Adapted from "Benjamin Franklin's 'Bold and Arduous Project,'"
by Katherine Dunford, ETC. (October, 1962)

CHAPTER 18

The Vowel-like Sound [r]

There is considerable variation in the production and pronunciation of [r] according to context and regional practice. In regard to the latter, as we indicated earlier, some persons in the areas of eastern New England, eastern Canada, New York City, and the southern coastal states pronounce [r] only when it is immediately followed by a vowel as in *reach, rise, grows, boring,* and *Marion* and omit [r] in other contexts. Most Americans, however, pronounce an [r] sound whenever the letter *r* appears in the spelling of a word regardless of whether the immediate next sound is a vowel or a consonant. The general tendency for most Americans is to produce an [r] in words such as *cart, bargain,* and *turn* as well as for contexts such as *around, through,* and *pour it.*

We will consider three varieties of [r]. Two of these call for the production of the *r* as a semivowel or vowel-like consonant. The third is a fricative, more characteristically consonant sound.

[r] As in *Rise, Rose,* and *Around*

We shall consider two ways of producing the [r] when the sound is immediately followed by a vowel in a stressed syllable. The first

313

method is to raise the tongue tip toward the roof of the mouth. The tongue tip may be brought close to the gum ridge, but actual contact with the gum ridge should be avoided. The tongue tip may also be flexed slightly toward the back of the mouth. Compare Figure 18–1 demonstrating production of this type of [r] with Figure 14–1 illustrating the [t], [d], and [l] sounds.

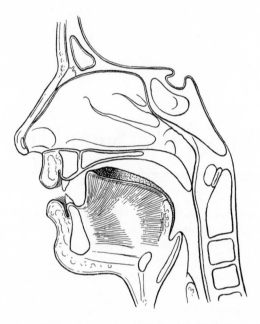

FIGURE 18–1.   Articulatory adjustments for retroflex [r].

The second method of articulating an [r] before a vowel in a stressed syllable more nearly approximates the production of a vowel sound. The tip of the tongue is lowered and the central portion of the tongue is raised toward the roof of the mouth about where the hard palate ends and the soft palate begins. This is illustrated in Figure 18–2. For both of these varieties of [r], the sound is produced with accompanying vocal-fold vibration.

If you have no difficulty with either variety of [r], there is no need for concern or consistency as to manner of production. If you have difficulty with the sound, however, and tend to produce the [r] so that the effect is much like a [w], then you should analyze

your efforts for tongue-tip and central [r] and try to produce consistently your best [r] sound. Experience suggests that persons who
tend to confuse [w] and [r] usually improve by establishing and
regularly using a tongue-tip [r]. Persons who tend to confuse [l]
and [r] are likely to do better by establishing and consistently pro

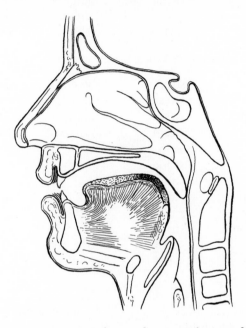

FIGURE 18–2.   Articulatory adjustments for central [r].

ducing a central position [r]. Whichever variety you produce, do
not prolong the sound excessively and do not convert the [r] into a
distorted vowel.

Practice Materials

Initial

read	rail	room	roll
reach	rage	rude	rope
ream	red	rule	raw
rid	rest	rook	wrought
rim	rack	roof	rock

Initial (Cont.)

rate	rap	rote	rod
rug	rice	royal	wren
rough	rise	roam	wreck
run	rhyme	roost	roast
rout	ripe	raucous	wrangle
round	real	road	wrestle

Medial (Followed by a Vowel)

dream	street	three	trait
drip	stream	threat	try
drench	stress	thrash	trail
drank	strain	through	trump
dry	strip	thrust	trust
drug	stride	thrush	treasure
draw	straight	treat	truth
drown	street	trip	marry
freeze	straw	tryst	peril
freedom	struggle	tramp	arrange
merit	stirrup	trigger	erode
morose	syrup	tripe	awry

Phrases

green grass	orange drink
grim bride	merry marriage
grinning bridegroom	gross grub
red rose	grubby drag
riffraff and rubble	brandy grog
raw rope	enraged parent
royal road	rhythmic run
raucous wrangle	rain rinse
rough rider	rudely raging
rote memory	really rugged
wrought iron	rim of brine
roam forests	run around
rice bread	wretched aroma
rise proudly	wrecked lorry
ripe berries	arose in peril

For the medial [r] followed by a consonant check your practice and pronunciation with what is current in your community. Do you include or omit the [r]?

Medial (Followed by a Consonant)

pierce	art	smart	mourn
fierce	part	dart	dormitory
beard	warm	swarm	wired
seared	warn	forlorn	tired
chart	farm	orphan	hired
charm	unharmed	scarf	Martha
storm	absorb	dwarf	Marvin
alarm	fork	north	York
harm	pork	forth	inform
ark	hard	ward	torn

Phrases

partly warm	pierce the pork
tired and forlorn	inform the partner
orphan of the storm	harmful warts
absorbing art	charming in parts
bearded dwarf	chart the course
fierce farmer	alarmed York

For the final [r], is your practice for the omission or inclusion of the final [r] consistent with that for medial [r] followed by a consonant? It is, for most speakers.

Final

dear	are	four	bother
hear	bar	more	mother
fear	car	lore	ignore
near	far	core	father
care	mar	soar	sister
dare	star	ire	tower
fair	boor	dire	shower
mare	moor	sire	paper
their	cure	sour	plumber
lair	tour	flower	summer

Phrases

hear sister	ignore brother
near the bar	tour the moor
their paper	lair for the bear
dire cure	summer flower
dear mother	four to a car

For special medial [r] words review the discussion of the [ɜ] and [ɝ] vowels (see pages 205–206).

Special Medial Words

birth	burn	turf	curl
mirth	stern	shirt	curtain
terse	girl	girth	certain
first	whirl	nerve	lurch
nurse	heard	serve	churl
purse	hurl	spurn	yearn

Phrases

terse girl	burned earth
earn the purse	heard in church
lurch and whirl	burst with mirth
serve the nurse	uncertain person
first spurned	hurled to the turf

Distinction Between [r] and [w]

Persons who tend to produce [r] so that it resembles [w] should work to establish a clear acoustic difference between these sounds. The [r] should be produced without lip activity and, preferably, with the tongue-tip raised toward the gum ridge. The [w] should be produced with lip movement and without front of the tongue activity.

Practice Materials

The following materials should help to establish the distinction. Use a mirror to see what you do, and listen carefully to hear what happens with and without lip movement.

Distinguish between [r] and [w]:

reap	weep	roof	woof
read	weed	run	won
reek	week	ring	wing
red	wed	rue	woo
wren	wen	room	womb
rest	west	row	woe
rag	wag	ride	wide
rage	wage	rise	wise
rate	wait	rare	wear
rain	wane	rile	wile

Difficult [r] Combinations

Words beginning with [p] and [b] followed by [r], as in *prize* and *breeze*, may be troublesome because of the lip activity required for the first sounds. The fault is similar to the one discussed earlier in our discussion of the [l] preceded by [p] or [b].

Practice Materials

Avoid lip movement for the [r] as you practice with the materials that follow.

preach	praise	prude	sprawl
preen	press	prove	proud
prince	precious	probe	prow
print	prank	prone	pride
pray	prattle	prawn	price
pretty	prudent	spry	spring
breech	braise	brood	brought
breeze	breast	brew	broad
brick	break	broke	brow
bring	brain	broth	bride
bray	brash	brawn	brine
brass	abrasion	brief	upbringing

Sentences

1. Van Wyck Brooks averred that a great writer is a great man writing.

2.   Kurt Lewin presented psychologists with the provocative assertion that there is nothing as practical as a really good theory.

3.   It was frequently difficult to determine whether Brown was erudite or broadly abstruse.

4.   Preston's behavior seemed to be crisp and abrupt, but his friends protested that it was probably pretense.

5.   Pritchard's manners made it apparent that his abruptness was nurtured by underlying rudeness.

6.   Frequently cries of outrage may be avoided when competitors are made aware of the ground rules.

7.   Many laboratories for testing hearing have specially treated rooms for audiometric evaluations.

8.   Brenda's bright laughter brought warmth to mornings which would otherwise have been gray and dreary.

9.   The bridge crumbled under the burden of the overloaded truck.

10.   The soprano virtuoso performed brilliantly in a program of original lyrics.

Some persons find the combinations [gr] and [kr], as in *green* and *cream*, somewhat difficult. If you are one of those who do, we suggest that you establish a central tongue [r], the second of the [r] sounds described, for the [gr] and [kr] combinations.

Practice Materials

The following materials should be of help.

cream	crest	crew	crock
creek	crept	crude	crowd
crib	cram	crow	crown
crayon	crash	croak	crime
cradle	craft	crawl	scribe
green	grew	grind	grist
greet	group	grape	grief
grin	grope	grime	grace
grit	grow	groom	grade
grate	gross	gruel	grant
grain	groan	groove	graze
grenadine	grog	grand	growl
grass	grotto	grunt	grudge
grapple	grub	grasp	gruff

Phrases

green grass	grand grin
grind grain	prone to prattle
grunt and groan	pride in upbringing
greet Grace	crash the craft
ground grain	Cripple Creek
craved a crumb	grew grapes
green grub	greasy crock

Sentences

1. Grace ground the grain for bread.
2. Great pride may bring greater grief.
3. The gray horse was well groomed.
4. The green car crashed into the gray cart.
5. Grayson, a practical man, came to grips with his problem.
6. More than grain may be grist for a mill.
7. Brian poured the grog out of the cracked crock.
8. The wrestlers grunted and groaned as if they carried a mutual grudge.
9. The proud groom grinned at his prudent bride.

Another combination that causes some difficulty is [r] preceded by [f]. Practice with the following words.

free	freckle	fruit	from
freeze	fresh	frugal	frock
frigid	friend	fro	front
frail	fragile	froze	fry
freight	frank	frog	fraught

Sentences

1. Ice cream and frozen fruit make a good frappé!
2. Frank and his freckled friend like frogs' legs.
3. Freda, though frugal, bought herself a French frock.
4. Frank enjoyed fried fruit.
5. Freedom cannot survive unless it is shared by those who are free.

[r] As in *True, Through,* and *Dry*

A third variety of [r] approximates a fricative sound in manner of production. It is articulated by placing the tip of the tongue close to but not quite touching the gum ridge. When air is forced over the tongue tip, a fricative [r] is produced (see Figure 18–3). When this variety of [r] occurs in the initial position, the sound is vocalized. When it occurs after a voiceless sound, as in *three* and *tree,* the [r] may be completely or partly unvoiced. This [r] is not

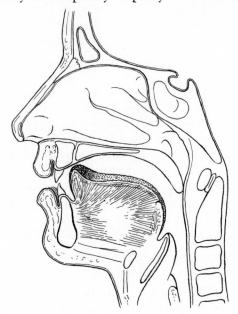

FIGURE 18–3.   Tongue position for fricative [r].

as frequently produced by American speakers as the other varieties earlier considered.

This variety of [r] is described as a postdental fricative. It is most likely to be produced after tongue-tip consonants such as [t], [d], and [θ] (th).

Practice Materials

Practice with the material that follows:

treat	tread	true	trot
tree	track	troop	trouble
trip	trap	truce	trunk

trigger	trash	trout	tripe
train	tram	trophy	try
trade	transit	tropic	trowel
three	thrash	throttle	throng
thrift	through	thrush	Thrace
thrill	throne	thrall	threaten
thresh	throw	thrive	throat
thread	throb	thrombus	thrust

Sentences

1. The weary troops arranged a morning truce.
2. Trenton enjoyed his train trips.
3. The fast-running stream was noted for its trout.
4. The triple-threat athlete won several trophies.
5. Dumas observed that truth is great because fire cannot burn nor can water drown it.
6. For many persons tripe is a nourishing if not a thrilling food.
7. The throng cheered as the trotters raced around the track.
8. Throttle in hand, the engineer sped the train through the night.
9. A thrush built a nest in the branch of the tree.
10. Trash should not be thrown from moving trams.

Linking [r] and Intrusive [r]

Earlier, we discussed the regional tendencies in producing and pronouncing words in which the letter *r* is final in the spelling. The [r] in contexts such as *far away, near us, for it, for old,* and *bear it* is usually heard as a linking sound between vowels. If you listen closely to the production of the linking [r], you will note that it is produced with less vigor and is of shorter duration than the initial [r] or the medial [r] in stressed positions. Acoustically, the sound is much like the [r] in unstressed syllables, as in the words *berry, marry, carry,* and *ferry.*

Occasionally, an [r] sound is intruded where the spelling of the word does not include the letter *r.* It is most likely to be intruded in combinations such as *law and order, idea of, America is,* and *vanilla ice.* It is apparently easier to maintain speech fluency by inserting an [r] between words when one ends and the next begins with a vowel than to produce two vowels in succession. The intrusive [r] is generally considered substandard and its use is therefore not recommended.

Practice Materials

Practice the following sentences. Read each slowly and avoid the intrusive [r].

Sentences

1. North America and South America are in the Western Hemisphere.
2. I saw Ed order a vanilla ice cream soda.
3. Peterson liked his job as a law officer.
4. Barbara is fond of sliced banana in her breakfast cereal.
5. The idea of an essay should be apparent to an intelligent reader.
6. Grandma almost always enjoyed reading stories to her grandchildren.
7. We saw a three-act drama at the Astor Theater.

[l] and [r] Contrast

Some speakers for whom English is a second language seem to have difficulty in making clear distinctions between [l] and [r]. The phoneme [l] is not present in some Asiatic languages and the phoneme [r] is absent in others. The following pairs of contrast words and the phrases should help to establish the distinction between the phonemes.

leap	reap	look	rook
leaf	reef	law	raw
lend	rend	load	road
lid	rid	lock	rock
lip	rip	lot	rot
laid	raid	low	row
lap	rap	lie	rye
lack	rack	lies	rise
lug	rug	light	right

Phrases

lot of rot	look for the rook
right sheds light	a load on the road
lie in the rye	a lack of a rack
a leaf of the reef	a wrap for the lap

The material following should provide practice for [r] in various positions.

Sentences

1. Brown showed no gratitude for the state's providing him with free room and board for four years and broke out of the brig.
2. O'Brien took every possible opportunity to proclaim his Irish breeding and his proud name.
3. Random thoughts are the products of free reveries.
4. The mixture contained approximately four parts of nitrogen to one part of oxygen.
5. The timorous groom was afraid to carry his bride across the threshold into their new and very own three-room apartment.
6. Crisp and crackly leaves inform us of summer's end.
7. Contemporary weather forecasters are much more accurate than were their predecessors a generation ago.
8. Rabies are transmitted by animals that have contracted hydrophobia.
9. Vandenburg Air Force Base has rocket-firing apparatus.
10. Thoreau for long periods lived as a recluse.
11. The crafty real estate broker appropriated the poor widow's property when she could not meet the mortgage requirements.
12. Theories should be supported by relevant data and proven by experience.
13. In *Prue and I*, George Curtis remarks: "The pride of ancestry increases in the ratio of distance."
14. Three officers of the law arrested the disturbers of the peace.
15. The right to freedom of expression is part of the American heritage.

Selections

1. How was the Devil dressed?
   O, he was in his Sunday's best;

His coat was red, and his breeches were blue,
And there was a hole where his tail
    Came through.

—ROBERT SOUTHEY, *The Devil's Walk*

2.   Dear mother, how pretty
         The moon looks tonight!
She was never so cunning before:
         Her two little horns
         Are so sharp and so bright,
I hope she'll not grow any more.

—ELIZA FOLLER, *The New Moon*

3.   Before the beginning of years
         There came to the making of man
    Time with a gift of tears,
         Grief with a glass that ran.

—ALGERNON CHARLES SWINBURNE, *The Year of the Rose*

4.   Richard Rumbold's last words, according to the historian
Macaulay, were "I never could believe that Providence had sent a
few men into the world, ready booted and spurred to ride, and
millions ready saddled and bridled to be ridden."

—THOMAS BABINGTON MACAULAY, *History of England*

5.   Come all you fair and tender ladies,·
    Be careful how you court young men,
    They're like a star of summer's morning,
    They'll first appear and then they're gone.

    They'll tell to you some loving story,
    They'll declare to you their love is true;
    Straightway they'll go and court some other,
    And that's the love they have for you.

    I wish I was some little sparrow,
    That I had wings, could fly so high;
    I'd fly away to my false lover,
    And when he's talkin' I'd be by.

    But I am not a little sparrow,
    And neither have I wings to fly!
    I'll sit down here in grief and sorrow
    To weep and pass my troubles by.

If I'd a-known before I courted,
I never would have courted none;
I'd have locked my heart in a box of golden,
And pinned it up with a silver pin.

—*Come All You Fair and Tender Ladies,* American Ballad

6.   To most English-speaking persons who know of Richard III, this king who reigned briefly from 1483 to 1485 is reputed to be a villain. Shakespeare is probably responsible for Richard's characterization. In his melodramatic historical play about the allegedly arch-Machiavellian monarch, Shakespeare has Richard utter the following:

I, that am curtail'd of this fair proportion,
Cheated of feature by dissembling nature,
Deform'd, unfinish'd, sent before my time
Into this breathing world, scarce half made up,
And that so lamely and unfashionable
That dogs bark at me as I halt by them . . .

A more kindly and generous characterization of this English king is presented by Paul Murray Kendall in his biography *Richard the Third.* Kendall holds that Richard tried to enforce laws that were proper and just; that his brief reign is remarkable for enlightened legislation that safeguarded the rights of individuals against abuse. Richard tried to be a just and humane sovereign. Unfortunately, he alienated some of the nobility by curtailing their rights to abuse others, and in doing so, lost their military support.

7.   I go for all sharing the privileges of the government who assist in bearing its burdens.

—ABRAHAM LINCOLN, Letter to an Editor

CHAPTER 19

The Velar and Palatal Sounds and the Laryngeal Fricative

THE VELAR PALATAL SOUNDS [k] AND [g]

[k] As in *Key, Because,* and *Luck*

[k] is a voiceless, velar, plosive sound. It is produced by raising the back of the tongue to the elevated soft palate so that a firm contact is made between these articulators (see Figure 19–1). In contexts in which the [k] is followed immediately by a vowel, air is impounded at the place of contact and suddenly and completely released when the contact is broken. The sound is then said to be aspirated.

The sound of [k] has several representations in spelling. The most frequent include *k* as in *key, c* as in *cat, ch* as in *chasm, qu* as in *quick,* and one element of the sound blend of *x* as in *fix* and *six.*

The [k] sound must be produced with energetic action of the articulators. Persons with normal control of their articulatory organs should find the [k] sound an easy one to make, whether in initial, medial, or final position.

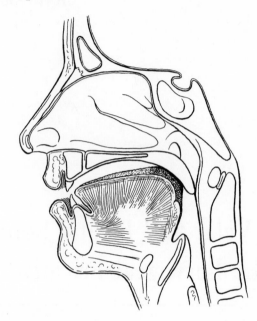

FIGURE 19–1.   Articulatory adjustments for [k] and [g].

Practice Materials

Initial

keep	could	came	cough
key	coach	cap	cod
queen	cope	calf	chord
chemical	chorus	character	quash
ken	caught	cool	curb
kit	call	coop	curt

Medial

beacon	because	blacken	Manx
weaken	recourse	cracker	thanks
bicker	require	booked	attacking
wicked	requite	looking	blocked
checker	enquire	turkey	boxed

Final

beak	stork	lake	forsook
meek	talk	take	mistook
sick	Turk	back	stock
tick	spike	rack	dike
fake	amuck	hook	like

Initial and Final

kick	quack	kirk	coke
kink	cook	quirk	comic
quick	cosmic	konk	cork

Phrases

keep calm	honking turkey
keen kitten	basket of biscuits
camp cook	murky liquid
calm cow	mocked uncle
queer cat	quick kick
quaint chorus	cock crow
quiz kid	sick calf
call Kate	cook book
sick knocks	thank Carl
wrecked car	checkered career
critical crowd	clean cloth
crusty crown	clumsy clown
crude crystal	clatter and clash
crossed crop	cloistered clergy
Kris Kringle	clever clue
crackle and crunch	clippety clop
creep and crawl	cluttered closet

[k] Blends

clean	class	clot	climb
cleat	clue	clergy	cloud
click	close	clerk	clown
clip	claw	club	cloister
cleanse	clod	clump	Klondike
clash	clog	clutch	clause

[k] *Blends* (*Cont.*)

cream	credit	crew	crust
crease	credulous	crude	crouch
creed	crest	crow	crowd
creek	crane	crawl	crown
crib	crag	crop	crime
crisp	crack	cross	cry

Sentences

1. Kent kept his collie in a kennel.
2. Kate was calmed by the ticktock of the clock.
3. The drunkard was lachrymose because his crock contained no alcohol.
4. Quartz is a common mineral that occurs in crystals and is a frequent component of many rocks.
5. Carl found it calming to bask in the sun.
6. The schooner carried a cargo of crackers, cookies, and kindred cakes for tykes.
7. Connie liked percolated coffee and scones for breakfast.
8. The choir sang quaint songs in the Scottish kirk.
9. Kitson was the captain of the cruiser that carried a cargo of Turkish goods to the Congo.
10. The blackhearted crook was caught in the crowd.

Selections

1. Themistocles, being asked whether he would rather be Achilles or Homer, said, "Which would you rather be—a conqueror in the Olympic Games, or the crier that proclaims who are conquerors?"

—PLUTARCH, *Themistocles*

2. Nor all that heralds rake from coffin'd clay,
Nor florid prose, nor honied lies of rhyme,
Can blazon evil deeds, or consecrate a crime.

—LORD BYRON, *Childe Harold*

3. By the pricking of my thumbs,
Something wicked this way comes.
Open, locks,
Whoever knocks!

—WILLIAM SHAKESPEARE, *Macbeth*

4. The whole difference between construction and creation is exactly this: that a thing constructed can only be loved after it is constructed; but a thing created is loved before it exists.

—G. K. CHESTERTON, Preface to Dickens' *Pickwick Papers*

5. Nice customs curtsy to great kings.

—WILLIAM SHAKESPEARE, *Henry V*

[g] As in *Go, Forget, Aghast, Egg,* and *Rogue*

[g], the voiced counterpart of [k], is a velar, stop sound. It is produced like the [k], except that a less vigorous contact is required for the [g].

[g] is usually represented by the letter *g* in spelling; less frequently it is represented by *gh*. The sound is also part of the consonant blend represented by the letter *x* in words such as *examine* and *exact*. The sound may occur initially, medially, or finally.

Practice Materials

Initial

gear	gale	good	gird
geese	gape	goat	girth
gift	gaff	gall	gull
give	gap	gauze	goiter
guilt	ghoul	got	gown
guest	goose	guard	guide

Medial

meager	vaguely	embargo	beguile
begin	began	regard	disguise
digging	aghast	engulf	misguided
signal	again	laggard	tiger
forget	lagoon	beggar	bogus
regale	regulate	haggard	dugout

Final

league	Hague	rogue	bug
fatigue	plague	morgue	snug
intrigue	vague	hog	shrug

Final (Cont.)

dig	hag	log	dug
rig	snag	iceberg	flog
egg	fugue	erg	vogue

[g] *Blends:* [gl] *and* [gr]

glean	glad	glob	mingle
glib	gland	glum	single
glisten	glass	glut	haggle
glitter	gloom	glide	tingle
glaze	gloat	glower	tangle
glen	globe	eagle	struggle
greed	grand	grope	grind
green	grass	groan	gripe
grid	grew	grow	egress
grip	groom	gross	angry
grade	group	growl	engrave
grain	groove	ground	ingrate

Phrases

grin grimly	growl and gripe
glitter and glisten	grind grain
angry ingrate	glum glower
glad groom	global struggle
green grass	engrossed group

Contrasting [k] and [g]

There are two elements of contrast for the [k] and [g]. The first is the readily apparent element of voice which is present for the [g] and absent for the [k]. The second is the less obvious aspect of vigor of articulation which characterizes the [k] more than the [g].

Practice Materials

cam	gam	pick	pig
cat	gat	rack	rag
kill	gill	hack	hag

coat	goat	tack	tag
coast	ghost	sack	sag
cool	ghoul	buck	bug
cull	gull	tuck	tug
cut	gut	chuck	chug

Sentences

1. Chuck liked to hear the chug-chug of locomotives.
2. The half-empty sack was inclined to sag.
3. An old ghost haunted the Gold Coast.
4. Goatskin makes a crude but warm coat.
5. A tack was used to hang the rag tag on the rack.
6. A gull can cull food along a seacoast.
7. When Buck was tucked into his sleeping bag, he felt as snug as the proverbial bug in the rug.

Additional Practice Materials

Sentences

1. Margo, a good cook, gained a reputation for her baked goose.
2. Morgan, a gourmand, was glad to be married to Margo.
3. An embargo was placed on the cargo of sugar.
4. Greta was aghast when, in an unguarded moment, she forgot to stop for a traffic signal.
5. Gordon's luggage had an engraved name tag.
6. Despite his name, Goodfellow was a rogue whose beguiling smile ensnared the misguided.
7. Despite his hunger, the beggar would eat nothing but frogs' legs.
8. The fog lingered on and grounded the planes in Gander.
9. Peg, like most girls, was eager for a bargain.
10. The gargoyle appeared to have a vague grin.

Selections

1. "Ay," quoth my uncle Gloucester,
   "Small herbs have grace, great weeds do grow apace";
   And since, methinks, I would not grow so fast,
   Because sweet flowers are slow, and weeds make haste.
   —WILLIAM SHAKESPEARE, *Richard III*

2.   The Gods
Grow angry with your patience, 'tis their care,
And must be yours, that guilty men escape not:
As crimes do grow, justice should rouse itself.

—BEN JONSON, *Catiline*

3.   The gift, to be true, must be the flowing of the giver unto
me, correspondent to my flowing unto him.

—RALPH WALDO EMERSON, *Of Gifts*

4.   Great is the art of beginning, but greater the art is of ending.

—HENRY WADSWORTH LONGFELLOW, *Elegiac Verse*

5.   Oh, Brignall banks are wild and fair,
        And Greta woods are green,
    And you may gather garlands there
        Would grace a summer's queen.

—SIR WALTER SCOTT, *The Bridal of Triermain*

THE VELAR NASAL [ŋ]

[ŋ] (ng) As in *Wing* and *Singer*

[ŋ] is a velar nasal sound. It is produced, as indicated in Figure
19–2, by raising the back of the tongue so that it is in contact with
the lowered soft palate while the vocal folds are in vibration. [ŋ]
is a continuant sound that is reinforced and emitted nasally. In
American-English speech the [ŋ] occurs either medially or finally,
but never initially.

The [ŋ] is represented by the letter *n* or the letters *ng*. The sound
occurs usually in words in which the letter *n* is followed by either a
k or a *g* in the same syllable. [ŋ] is generally not heard in standard
speech in combinations where the *n* and the *g* which follows are in
different syllables, as in *ingrate, congratulate,* and *engross.*

Except for possible confusion between the [n] and the [ŋ], there
is seldom any difficulty in the actual articulation of the velar nasal
sound. There is some tendency, however, for some speakers to add
either a [g] or a [k] following the [ŋ] so that all words containing
the velar nasal sound are pronounced either [ŋg] or [ŋk]. This
tendency may frequently be traced to the influence of a foreign dialect. A second influence may be attributed to the speaker's failure

to remember the pronunciation of the particular word relative to the omission or inclusion of the [g] or [k]. A third influence is a direct result of the manner of articulating the [ŋ]. If the soft palate is raised before the contact between the tongue and palate is broken, a [k] or [g] sound is produced. To avoid adding either of these sounds when only the velar nasal is required, the speaker must watch his

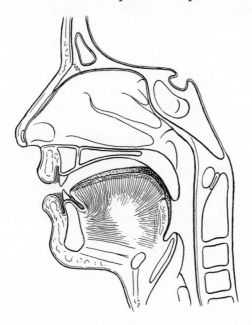

F I G U R E 19–2. Articulatory adjustments for [ŋ]. Note relaxed (lowered) soft palate.

articulatory timing. Specifically, he must make certain that the back of his tongue is moved away from his soft palate before he raises his soft palate to block off the entrance to the nasal passage.

To know how to produce an [ŋ] is not enough. We must also know whether the velar nasal is to be followed by a velar stop [k] or [g], or by some other sound. There is, of course, only one reliable way to learn the pronunciation of a word with velar nasal consonants. The reliable way is to study each word individually, using an up-to-date large dictionary as a pronunciation guide. A second approach of general help is to learn the so-called rules for the use of the velar consonants in English speech.

1. When a word ends with the letters *ng* or *ngue*, the pronunciation calls for the [ŋ]. Examples include *wing, rang, tongue,* and *meringue.*

2. Usually, when a suffix is added to a root word that is pronounced with the [ŋ], the pronunciation calls for the [ŋ]. Examples include *swings, rings, singer, longing,* and *stinging.* The exceptions to this general tendency include the comparative and superlative forms of the adjectives *long, young,* and *strong*—e.g., *longer, longest; younger, youngest; stronger, strongest.* These have the [ŋ] followed by [g].

3. Where the letters *ng* are medial in a root word, as in *finger, tingle, hunger, angle, extinguish,* and *single,* standard pronunciation calls for the use of [ŋg]. An exception is the pronunciation of *gingham* as [giŋəm].

4. In combinations in which the letter *n* is immediately followed by *k, c,* or *x* in the same syllable, the [ŋk] is used. Examples include *link, hank, distinct, anxious,* and *larynx.*

Note that not all words which include the letters *ng* in their spelling call for [ŋ] in their pronunciation. For example, words such as *range, singe,* and *longevity* are pronounced with the combination [ndʒ] rather than with either the [ŋ] or the [ŋg].

Apply these rules to the list of words that follow.

[ŋ]	[ŋg]	[ŋk]
wing	single	link
rang	spangle	anchor
young	younger	wink
harangue	elongate	sank
evening	anger	bunk
ringing	bungalow	trinket
longing	longest	sphynx
swings	tingle	length[1]
strong	stronger	strength[1]
singing	longest	larynx

Practice to Establish a Final [ŋ]

Speakers who tend to add a [g] or [k] to words that should properly end with the [ŋ] should be helped by contrasting the plosives

---

[1]The words *strength* and *length* are acceptably pronounced with or without a [k] before the final sound.

[g] and [k] with the nasal continuant [ŋ]. The plosive sounds call for an abrupt stopping of the breath and the emission of a puff of air. The [ŋ] should be produced so that the nasally emitted sound dies away gradually. At the outset, exaggerate the length of the sound so that it is prolonged to two or three times the length of what it might be in normal conversational speech.

Practice Materials

In your practice with the material that follows, establish your timing and control. Prolong the [ŋ] and continue, without stopping, to complete the phrase.

hang on	reaching it
young once	during an evening
giving up	baking apples
swing it	exciting acts
going on	being able
teaching all	altering everything
cooking oil	telling a truth
trying on	tongue exercise
staying away	exciting events
running on	cutting up
standing up	cruising around
doing all	taking a break

Sentences

1. Browning and his family lived on Long Island.
2. Browning's able wife was fond of cooking anchovies.
3. Blanding explained his actions by reminding all that one can be young only once.
4. The time for growing up is also the period for cutting up.
5. To bring up parents properly may be as trying and as exciting as for parents to bring up their children.
6. Long ago young Albert learned that telling a truth solved more problems than running away.
7. Ewing always longed for things that might have been.
8. A throng assembled at the Long Island train station.
9. Long ago is a fond and indefinite time for recalling old dreams.
10. Young Arthur, the future king, did not know the source of his strength for pulling out the sword from the stone.

Final [ŋ]

Practice the following final [ŋ] words and then incorporate them into phrases in which each word is followed by one beginning with a vowel—e.g., *among us.*

among	morning	asking	rang
bang	owning	boring	swing
bring	pacing	chanting	tong
doing	putting	fading	yearning
everything	sing	gasping	zooming
fling	sting	handing	daring
hang	throng	humming	darling
king	wrong	landing	fang
long	young	moaning	amazing
mining	looming	nothing	being

Medial [ŋ]

The words that follow conform to rule 2; a suffix is added to a word ending in the letters *ng.*

bearings	longs	borings	clanged
beings	mornings	fangs	endings
bringing	paintings	gaspings	firings
darlings	pronged	hanged	gangster
evenings	questionings	longing	drawings
flinging	songbird	throngs	strongly
hangmen	tracings	twangy	tongueless
kingly	wrongly	youngster	winged

Sentences for Medial and Final [ŋ].

1. Damocles' sword, hanging by a single hair over him, was constantly threatening to him.

2. The young man banged on the door because there was no response to his ringing.

3. The Swiss youngsters longed to become bellringers.

4. The mockingbird is an imitating songbird.

5. The king asked his minstrel to sing a song of exciting events.

6. Billing complained that his wife was ever altering the furnishings in their dwelling.

7. As a youngster, Sterling learned that telling the truth was more than a tongue exercise.

8. Topping specialized in raising longhorn cattle.

9. Corning enjoyed teaching all he knew to his young students.

10. Mrs. Channing thought her children to be darlings whenever they listened to her singing.

[ŋg]

When the letters *ng* occur within the root of a word, the pronunciation includes [ŋg] as in *angle*.

Practice Materials

anger	fungus	languish	tangle
Anglican	ganglion	languor	tingle
anguish	gangly	mangle	wrangle
Bangor	hunger	mingle	distinguish
bungle	ingot	Mongol	Rangoon
Congo	jangle	mongrel	sanguine
dangle	jingle	penguin	singular
dungaree	jungle	shingle	triangle
England	kangaroo	single	linger
finger	language	spangle	elongate

The following suffix words are pronounced [ŋg] and are exceptions to the *ng* rule.

longer	stronger	younger	prolongate
longest	strongest	youngest	diphthongal

[ŋk]

The following words are pronounced with [ŋ] followed by [k]:

anchor	dank	Manx	slink
ankle	drink	mink	spunk
banker	dunk	monk	tank
bankrupt	flunk	monkey	trunk
blank	frank	pink	twinkle
brink	hanker	plank	uncle

[ŋk] (*Cont.*)

Bronx	ink	rank	lynx
bunker	jinx	rink	larynx
clink	junk	sank	pharynx
crank	lanky	sink	conquer

Practice Materials for [ŋg] *and* [ŋk]

English language	Uncle Frank
singular Anglican	trunk of junk
anger and anguish	ranking banker
elongated wrangle	dunk in tank
hungry mongrel	blink and wink
single spangle	Bronx conqueror
Congo jungle	pink mink
linger longer	larynx and pharynx
dangling dungarees	lanky Yank
mangled ganglion	slinking lynx

Although rules have been suggested for determining the pronunciation of words spelled with *ng* and *nk*, there are many words that do not conform to the rules and have current pronunciations that are a result of assimilative influences or of the influences of analogy. Thus, a word such as *hangar* is now likely to be pronounced no differently from the word *hanger* (influence of analogy); *income* is likely to be pronounced with a velar adjustment [ŋ] rather than the alveolar [n] (influence of assimilation). In the final analysis, if the speaker is not certain of the pronunciation of an *ng* or *nk* word, he must check the pronunciations either by listening to other respected speakers or by consulting an "authoritative" current dictionary. It is suggested that the student check the following words if he is at all uncertain about the pronunciations.

banquet	fishmonger	rancor
Binghamton	gingham	tranquil
congress	inquest	wrangler

Sentences for [ŋg] *and* [ŋk]

1. The older sibling was stronger than his younger brother.
2. Frank often irritated his larynx by making angry noises.

3.   Despite their natural carrying cases it seems unlikely that kangaroos will replace donkeys for bearing our burdens.

4.   Fielding wanted to become a distinguished linguist.

5.   If vowels are elongated, they tend to become diphthongized.

6.   The New York Yankees have their ball park in the Bronx.

7.   Uncle Sam's nephews speak with some distinctive differences from their English cousins.

8.   Corning's wife could not decide whether lynx or mink was her favorite fur.

9.   Waring enjoyed eating languidly at banquets.

10.   The bronchi divide into bronchioles in the lungs.

Additional Practice Materials for [ŋ]

1.   The youngsters enjoyed singing "The Daring Young Man on the Flying Trapeze."

2.   Movements of the tongue modify breath from the lungs in creating articulate speech.

3.   Wilding learned that listening for longer periods than speaking was earning him a reputation for conversing.

4.   After long years of waiting and striving, Browning's yearnings were rewarded.

5.   Planes flying at ever-increasing speeds are making small ponds of our oceans.

6.   The angry waves pounded the New England shore.

7.   The word *wrangler* has distinctly different meanings in England and in the United States.

8.   Loring was no stranger to angling in swift-running waters.

9.   Though she was dressed in gingham, the maid from Birmingham caught the eye of the young king.

10.   The bellringer needed all his strength to keep the bells clanging.

11.   Many banquets are spoiled by long harangues.

12.   Bob enjoyed filling his lungs with the fresh morning air before undertaking the day's chores.

Selections

1.   The cataract strong
     Then plunges along,
     Striking and raging

As if a war waging
Its caverns and rocks among;
Rising and leaping,
Sinking and creeping,
Swelling and sweeping,
Showering and springing,
Flying and flinging.
Writhing and ringing,
Eddying and whisking,
Spouting and frisking,
Turning and twisting,
Around and around
With endless rebound;
Smiting and fighting,
A sight to delight in,
Confounding, astounding,
Dizzying and deafening the ear with its sound;

—ROBERT SOUTHEY, *The Cataract of Lodore*

2. O strong winged soul with prophetic
        Lips hot with the bloodbeats of song,
    With tremor of heartstrings magnetic,
        With thoughts as thunders in throng.

—ALGERNON CHARLES SWINBURNE, *To Walt Whitman in America*

3. On deck beneath the awning,
    I dozing lay and yawning;
    It was the grey of dawning,
        Ere yet the sun arose;
    And above the funnel's roaring,
    And the fitful wind's deploring,
    I heard the cabin snoring
        With universal noise.

—WILLIAM MAKEPEACE THACKERAY, *The White Squall*

4. Deep in that darkness peering, long
        I stood there, wondering, fearing,
    Doubting, dreaming dreams no mortal
        Ever dared to dream before.

—EDGAR ALLAN POE, *The Raven*

5. As I went out one morning to breathe the morning air
   I heard a dear old mother saying, "O my daughter fair,
   You better go wash them dishes and hush that flattering
       tongue,
   You know you want to marry and that you are too young."
   —Adapted from *Lolly-Too-Dum*, American Ballad

6. A little learning is a dangerous thing;
   Drink deep, or taste not the Pierian spring.
   —ALEXANDER POPE, *An Essay on Criticism*

7. A very merry, dancing, drinking,
   Laughing, quaffing, and unthinking time.
   —JOHN DRYDEN, *Alexander's Feast*

8. Day in the melting purple dying,
   Blossoms all around me sighing,
   Fragrance from the lilies straying,
   Zephyr with my ringlets playing,
   Ye but waken my distress:
   I am sick of loneliness.
   —MARIA G. BROOKS, *Song of Egla*

9. From grief, that is but passion;
   From mirth, that is but feigning;
   From tears, that bring no healing;
   From wild and weak complaining;
   Thine old strength revealing;
       Save, oh, save.
   —MATTHEW ARNOLD, *Stagirius*

10. It's every Monday morning
    When the blue birds begin to sing,
    You can hear those hammers a mile or more,
    You can hear John Henry's hammer ring,
    O Lord! John Henry's hammer ring.

    John Henry was hammering on the mountain
    And his hammer was striking fire,
    He drove so hard he broke his poor heart
    And he put down his hammer and he died,
    Lord, Lord, he stopped his hammering and he died.

They took John Henry to the graveyard
And they buried him in the sand
And every locomotive comes roaring by,
Says, "There lays a steel driving man,"
Lord, Lord, says, "There lays a steel driving man."

—*John Henry*, American Ballad

THE PALATAL GLIDE

[j] (y) as in *Year, Unite,* and *Loyal*

[j] is a vocalized, palatal glide sound. In acoustic effect, because it is an unobstructed and continuant sound, it is vowel-like in quality. [j] gliders or moves from the initial position of the vowel [i] to a final position determined by the sound that immediately follows it. The initial articulatory position calls for the tongue to be arched toward the front of the hard palate and for the lips to be parted and retracted as though for a smile. The soft palate is raised and the vocal folds are in vibration throughout the production of the sound.

When the [j] sound is represented by a single letter in spelling it is by the letter *y*. In medial positions [j] may be represented in spelling by the letters *io, ie,* and *ia*. Frequently, however, in both initial and medial positions, there is no spelling representation for the [j]. The sound often becomes part of vowel blends as in *unite* and *unify*.

Practice Materials

Initial

yield	yak	yoho	Europe
yeast	Yankee	yacht	young
yearly	you	yonder	yowl
yes	youth	yard	yucca
yen	York	yule	yesterday
yet	yawn	yearn	usual
yellow	yawl	use	usurp
yank	yoke	unit	eulogy

Medial

Daniel	companion	accuse	volume
genial	familiar	refuse	collier
genius	billiard	confuse	review
senior	canyon	amuse	stallion
vineyard	million	onion	argue
lanyard	abuse	bunion	opinion

[j] Preceded by an Initial Consonant

The inclusion of a [j] after an initial consonant varies according to context and regional practice. It is optional in words such as *Tuesday, tune,* and *new* and in many other words that begin with the sounds [t], [d], or [n]. If there are no special influences to direct your choice, regional usage should be followed.

Practice Materials

[j] is regularly included after the first consonant in the word list that immediately follows. It is optional for the second word list.

pure	fuel	cute	music
pupil	few	future	futile
beauty	feud	huge	fusion
muse	humane	view	mule
mute	humorous	cupid	puny
Tuesday	due	knew	nuisance
new	tube	nuclear	nude
tune	numerous	duke	Nubian
tuba	duty	tumult	newt
constitute	reduce	institute	gratuity
destitute	annuity	plume	restitute
induce	platitude	acumen	enduring

Sentences

1. The feud began on Tuesday over a puny gratuity.
2. Daniel's attitude indicated that he had no use for platitudes.
3. The dude took a dim view of his own future.

4. A united Europe has not yet been achieved.
5. The youth yearned for baked yams.
6. Cupid sometimes seems amused by those he seems to confuse.
7. The pack mule carried a huge load through the canyon.
8. William, a Yale student, enjoyed yesteryear's music.
9. Newton, a Yankee, enjoyed sailing his yawl.
10. Eugene, a Yorkshire millionaire, was fond of billiards.

THE LARYNGEAL FRICATIVE

[h] As in *He* and *Who*

The sound [h] lacks fixed or distinctive articulatory position. The sound which immediately follows the [h] determines the position assumed by the lips and tongue for this voiceless fricative.

[h] consists of a stream or puff of breath made discernible by the degree of contraction and vocal-fold vibration in the larynx.

Few persons are likely to have difficulty in the actual production of the [h]. The most likely basis for difficulty is that of determining whether, despite or because of the spelling of the word, an [h] is to be produced or omitted in the pronunciation. It may be of help to know that in American-English speech the [h] is appropriately included chiefly before vowels in stressed syllables as *he, hot,* and *hate.* Some speakers also include the sound in words that begin with a *wh* as in *which* and *whale.* [h] is usually not pronounced in medial, unstressed syllables.

Practice Materials

Initial

he	help	hoof	harm
heed	ham	home	harsh
hit	hatch	hope	her
hilt	hoot	haughty	hurl
haste	who	halt	hurt
hate	whom	hog	heard
head	hood	hot	heart
hull	height	house	humid[2]

hump	hide	howl	huge²
hungry	hoyden	human²	humor²

Medial (Note Its Position in Stressed Syllables Before Vowels)

unheeded	behind	unharmed	coherent
reheat³	behold	unheard	dehydrate
inhabit	inhuman	rehearse	inherit
inhale	overhaul	uphold	upheaval
behave³	rehash	rehouse	prehistoric
behead³	cohort	somehow	enhance

Sentences

1. Henry paid little heed to heights.
2. Harry was so hungry that he enjoyed Hazel's reheated ham.
3. Horton enjoyed living in high mountain areas that had low humidity.
4. The hen was heard to cackle after she hatched her egg.
5. Hate can be inherited if it is not inhibited.
6. The hog who had a habit of entering the new house was cured as a ham.
7. Hiram's heart and his sense of humor were humane.
8. The hyena held up his head and howled to the heavens.
9. Harriet's uninhibited behavior won her a reputation as a hoyden.
10. The rehearsals for *Hamlet* were held in a house held to be haunted.
11. Schopenhauer held that hatred comes from the heart and contempt from the head.
12. Hildred happily announced that Hope found a home in her new house.

²In words such as *human, humid, huge,* and *humor,* some speakers blend or merge the initial [h] with the immediately following [j] so that a "new" and distinctive voiceless palatal fricative sound is produced which may be represented by the symbol [ç]. If the blending is not complete, the result may be represented by the symbols [hj] as in [hjudʒ] for *huge.* We shall accept C. K. Thomas' suggestion that "Since . . . no change in meaning is effected by the shift from [hj] to [ç], most students will prefer not to bother with the extra symbol [ç]." See his *An Introduction to the Phonetics of American English* (2nd ed.; New York: Ronald Press, 1958), p. 138.

³In words in which the [h] occurs between vowels, as in *reheat, behave,* and *behead,* the [h] may be produced with voice. The IPA representative is [ɦ].

CHAPTER 20

Epilogue

Books, even those dealing with voice and diction, should have a proper closing. This one will be closed with quotations that, in retrospect and prospect, should help us to feel that the efforts spent in the study and practice of the preceding chapters were worthwhile. So, to begin our ending, we are reminded:

> Mend your speech a little
> Lest you may mar your fortunes.
>
> —WILLIAM SHAKESPEARE, *King Lear*

While, from the Bible, we may learn that:

> Speech finely framed delighteth the ears.
>
> —2 Maccabees 15:39

From Shakespeare, again, we may accept advice on how to frame our speech:

> Speak the speech, I pray you, as I pronounced it to you, trippingly on the tongue; but if you mouth it, as many of your players do, I had as lief the town-crier spoke my lines. . . . Suit the action to the word, the word to the action; with this special observance, that you o'erstep not the modesty of nature.
>
> —WILLIAM SHAKESPEARE, *Hamlet*

351

We can also accept Emerson's advice as to one desirable result of good speaking:

> The music that can deepest reach,
> And cure an ill, is cordial speech.
>
> —RALPH WALDO EMERSON, *Merlin's Song*

Finally, we close with an ancient observation:

> Speech is the mirror of the soul: as a man speaks, so is he.
>
> —PUBILIUS SYRUS, *Maxim 1073*
> (Translated by Darius Lyman)

APPENDIXES

Glossary of Terms

Affricate—The blend of a plosive and fricative sound; the phonemes [tʃ] (ch) and [dʒ] (dzh) are affricates.

Allophones—Members or varieties of sounds within a phoneme. The sounds which are classified as belonging to a phoneme in a given linguistic system (see *Phoneme*).

Articulation—The modification of the breath stream by the organs of the mouth (the lips, tongue, and palate) and the laryngeal mechanism to produce identifiable speech sounds (phonemes).

Arytenoid cartilage—A pyramidal-shaped cartilage situated in the posterior portion of the larynx. There are two arytenoid cartilages in the larynx to which the vocal bands are attached. The movements of the arytenoids influence the position and state of tension of the vocal bands.

Aspirate quality—Breathiness that accompanies vocalization or articulation.

Assimilation—The phonetic changes that take place in connected speech when one speech sound is modified as the result of a neighboring sound or sounds.

Back vowels—The vowel sounds produced as a result of the action (position) of the back of the tongue.

355

Bilabial consonants—The consonants that are produced as a result of lip-closing action that stops or diverts the flow of breath.

Abdominal breathing—Breathing characterized by controlled action of the abdominal muscles.

Breathiness—An excess of breath that may accompany vocalization.

Buccal cavity—The oral or mouth cavity.

Clavicular breathing—Breathing characterized by action of the upper part of the rib cage and the shoulders.

Cavity reinforcement—The building up of selected vocal tones resulting from the size and shape of the individual cavity. Cavity resonance.

Cerebellum—The "little brain," a part of the Central Nervous System, situated posteriorly and under the cerebrum. The cerebellum is importantly involved in the coordination of motor activity needed for speech production.

Cerebral cortex—The gray outer covering of the cerebrum. The cortex contains billions of nerve cells. Some portions of the cortex have special functions significant for the understanding and production of speech.

Central Nervous System (CNS)—The parts of the nervous mechanism that include the cerebrum, cerebellum, medulla, and spinal cord. The CNS is responsible for the coordination, control, and regulation of responses to stimuli and so for the establishment of patterns of behavior.

Central vowels—Vowel sounds produced as a result of the action (position) of the central or mid-portion of the tongue.

Consonants—Speech sounds produced as a result of either a partial or complete (temporary) obstruction or modification of the breath stream by the organs of articulation.

Continuant consonant—A consonant sound having duration and produced with the articulator in a fixed position, such as [s] and [l], in contrast to *stop* consonants which are short and result from the interruption of the breath, such as [p] and [g].

Cricoid cartilage—The ring-shaped cartilage in the lower and back portion of the larynx. The posterior part of the cricoid serves as a base for the arytenoid cartilages.

Diacritical symbols (marks)—A system of alphabet letters and a number of markings used by dictionaries to indicate phonetic values.

Diaphragm—The double, dome-shaped muscle of respiration situated between the chest and abdominal cavities.

Diction—The production of speech sounds for a given linguistic code; also the selection and arrangement of words within a linguistic system.

Diphthongs—Vocalic glides of two vowels uttered in a single breath impulse within one syllable. The phonetic symbols of the diphthong represent the approximate initial and final sounds of the glide.

Front vowels—The vowels produced as a result of the action (position) of the front, or blade, of the tongue.

Fundamental pitch—The pitch resulting from the frequency of vibration of the body as a whole; the lowest tone in a complex tone.

Glide sounds—Sounds produced as a result of the continuous movement of the articulators. The initial position of the articulators in the production of a glide is stable. The final position of the articulators is determined by the sound that immediately follows.

Glottal—Referring to sounds produced as a result of laryngeal tension and action, as by a sudden stoppage and release of breath by the vocal bands.

Glottis—The opening between the vocal bands.

Habitual pitch—The pitch level at which an individual most frequently initiates vocalization.

Inflection—Pitch changes that occur without interruption of phonation during the production of a syllable or word. Inflectional changes may be *downward, upward,* or *circumflex* (downward and upward or upward and downward).

International Phonetic Alphabet (IPA)—A system of representing the distinctive sounds (phonemes) of a linguistic code through special visual symbols.

Labiodental sounds—Consonants produced as a result of activity of the lip (lower) and teeth (upper); lip-teeth sounds.

Laryngeal fricative—The sound [h] made discernible as a result of laryngeal tension and vocal-fold activity.

Laryngopharynx—The portion of the pharynx nearest to the larynx.

Larynx—The uppermost part of the trachea; the structure that includes the vocal bands; the voice box.

Lateral consonant—The sound [l] produced as a result of the emission of vocalized breath at both sides of the tongue with the tongue tip at the gum ridge.

Lingua-alveolar consonants—The consonants produced as a result of contact between the tongue tip and the gum (alveolar) ridge.

Mid-vowels—See Central vowels.

Nasality—The quality of voice resulting from reinforcement in the nasal cavities.

Nasal cavaties—The cavities in the head directly above the roof of the mouth.

Nasal consonants—The speech sounds produced with nasal reinforcement. In American English these are [m], [n], and [ŋ].

Nasopharynx—The portion of the pharynx nearest the entrance to the nasal cavities; the uppermost portion of the pharynx.

Optimum pitch—The pitch level at which one can usually achieve the best vocal quality and the necessary loudness with the least expenditure of energy; the pitch level at which one can initiate voice with greatest ease and effectiveness.

Oral cavity—The cavity of the mouth; the buccal cavity.

Oral resonance—The reinforcement of vocal tones by the oral cavity.

Oropharynx—That portion of the pharynx nearest the oral cavity; the middle portion of the pharynx.

Palatal sounds—The sounds produced as a result of activity of the mid-tongue or back of the tongue and the palate.

Pharynx—The cavity between the esophagus and the entrance to the nasal cavity; the throat.

Phoneme—The basic unit or sound family within a linguistic system; a group or family of closely related sounds which share distinctive acoustic characteristics; the distinctive phonetic or sound "elements" of a word. Phonemic differences permit us to distinguish between spoken words.

Phonetic alphabet—See International Phonetic Alphabet.

Pitch—The attribute of sound resulting from the frequency of vibration of the vibrating body; the attribute of auditory sensation in terms of which sounds may be ordered on a scale from high to low; our subjective reaction to frequency changes or differences.

Plosive or stop sounds—Those produced with a complete closing of the breath channel.

Plosive sounds—The consonants produced by a stoppage and release of the breath stream.

Postdental sounds—The consonants produced as a result of contact between an anterior portion of the tongue and the area of the mouth behind the dental ridge.

Pronunciation—The articulation of meaningful units of speech; the combining of phonemes in meaningful contextual utterance; the utterance of appropriate sounds and the placement of stress in the production of contextual speech.

Resonance—The strengthening or building up of sound either through cavity reinforcement or through sympathetic vibration of a body in close proximity to the source of sound (the vibrating body); the vibratory response of a body or a cavity to a sound frequency imposed on it.

Resonators—Structures so shaped that they can reinforce selected pitch ranges of sound; the principal human resonators are the cavities of the mouth, throat, nose, and larynx.

Thoracic cavity—The chest or thorax.

Thyroid cartilage—The large, shield-like fused cartilage of the larynx.

Trachea—The cartilaginous tube-like structure between the pharynx and the bronchi; the windpipe.

Velar sounds—Sounds produced as a result of articulatory activity between the soft palate and the back of the tongue.

Vocal attributes—The characteristics by which we distinguish vocal efforts—pitch, loudness, duration, and quality.

Vocal bands—Two small, tough bands, or folds, of connective, or ligamentous, tissue situated in the larynx. The vocal bands are continuous with folds of muscle tissue and are connected to cartilages in the larynx. Pulsations of the vocal bands give rise to *voice*.

Vocal cords—See Vocal bands.

Vocal folds—See Vocal bands.

Voice box—See Larynx.

Vowels—Sounds produced as a result of articulatory action without obstruction or interference of breath; unobstructed sounds produced by changes in the size and shape of the oral cavity and by difference in the elevation of portions of the tongue.

Windpipe—See Trachea.

Voice Improvement Check List

Breathing

1. Is amount of air intake adequate for speech effort? _____
2. Is breathing controlled and synchronized with speech effort? _____
3. Is flow of breath sustained for proper phrasing? _____
4. Is breath expelled between phrases? _____
5. Is muscular action basically abdominal-thoracic? _____ Clavicular? _____
6. Is there any evidence of tension in the larynx or throat? _____

Pitch

1. Is range narrow? _____ Wide? _____ Patterned (monotonous)? _____
2. Are changes consonant with meanings? _____ Feelings? _____
3. Is habitual pitch the same or close to optimum pitch? _____
4. Does the major part of the speech effort occur within the optimal range? _____

5. Are individual inflectional changes appropriate to meanings and feelings intended to be communicated? _____
6. Is overall intonation suggestive of a foreign pattern? _____

Loudness

1. Is the loudness of your voice adequate for the size of your group of listeners? _____
2. Do any of them have to strain to hear you? _____
3. May your voice be characterized as full? _____ Thin or weak? _____ Overloud? _____ Sufficiently varied and appropriate for meanings? _____
4. Are changes independent of variations in pitch? _____

Quality

1. Is your voice hypernasal? _____ Denasal? _____ Breathy? _____ Husky? _____ Guttural? _____ Hard or metallic? _____
2. Is your voice reinforced only at part of pitch range? _____
3. Is your voice varied according to nature of content? _____

Pronunciation and Articulation Check List

Pronunciation

1. In your overall pronunciations are you aware of any individual variations of vowels or diphthongs from those current in your community? _____

2. Are these variations ones you wish to maintain or modify? _____

3. Do you follow regional practices with regard to [r]? _____

Articulation

1. What sounds or sound blends need improvement:
   a. Consonants? _____
   b. Vowels? _____
   c. Diphthongs? _____
2. Is there any tendency to slur or to overassimilate? _____
3. Are medial nasal consonants given full value? _____

4. Do you tend to give excessive nasal "coloring" to vowels or diphthongs in close proximity to nasal consonants? _____

5. Do you tend to unvoice final sounds such as [z], [ʒ], and [dʒ]? _____

Index